Developments in
Cognitive Psychotherapy

Developments in
Cognitive Psychotherapy

edited by Windy Dryden and Peter Trower

SAGE Publications
London · Newbury Park · Beverly Hills · New Delhi

First published 1988

SAGE Publications Ltd
28 Banner Street
London EC1Y 8QE

SAGE Publications Inc
2111 West Hillcrest Street
Newbury Park, California 91320

SAGE Publications India Pvt Ltd
C–236 Defence Colony
New Delhi 110 024

SAGE Publications Inc
275 South Beverly Drive
Beverly Hills, California 90212

British Library Cataloguing in Publication Data

Developments in cognitive psychotherapy.
   1. Medicine. Cognitive therapy
   I. Dryden, Windy II. Trower, Peter, 1938–
616.89'14

ISBN 0-8039-8134-1

Library of Congress catalog card number 88-060349

Typeset by System 4 Associates, Farnham Common, Buckinghamshire
Printed in Great Britain by J. W. Arrowsmith Ltd, Bristol

Contents

Preface

The term 'cognitive psychotherapy' is a generic one which we use to refer to the various cognitively orientated and cognitive-behavioural approaches to psychotherapy. While the roots of this therapeutic genre can be traced back to the work of early Roman and Greek philosophers, the mid-1950s saw the first discernible trend in this field of development. Pioneers such as Albert Ellis, George Kelly, Julian Rotter and E. Lakin Phillips published independently texts which delineated clear cognitively orientated approaches to psychotherapy. The 1960s saw (a) the growth of Aaron Beck's contribution to a cognitive theory of depression and a treatment approach based firmly on cognitive principles, and (b) the early attempts of behaviour therapists to include cognitive factors as a focus for clinical intervention. The 1970s was marked by a hastening of the cognitive revolution in behaviour therapy with the contributions of Arnold Lazarus, Donald Meichenbaum, Marvin Goldfried and Michael Mahoney, and others at the forefront of this movement. Texts with the phrase 'cognitive-behaviour' began to appear and are now quite common. In the 1980s the trend has been a widening of interest in the scope of cognitive psychotherapy. Here, with the growth of work done on information-processing and constructivistic paradigms (for example, the work of Guidano and Liotti), explorations concerning the relationship between the fields of social, cognitive and clinical psychology are particularly noteworthy. At the same time the field of psychotherapy has become preoccupied with the issues of eclecticism and integration, and leading figures who have made a contribution to cognitive psychotherapy are now seeking to place this approach within a wider clinical framework.

The purpose of this book is to present a sample of recent developments in cognitive psychotherapy which represent the breadth of work being carried out in this field. The book is divided into two parts: the first on principles and the second on applications. In Part One, Cheryl Carmin and Tom Dowd set the scene by discussing the various paradigms that can be discerned in the field of cognitive psychotherapy. In Chapter 2 Richard Wessler considers the place of affect and nonconscious processes in cognitive psychotherapy, related issues which have received much recent attention. Wessler places his discussion within the context of his pioneering work on cognitive appraisal therapy. In Chapter 3 Paul Gilbert develops his much-acclaimed work on depression and brain state, and applies this to other emotional disorders within a psychosocial evolutionary context. In Chapter 4 Russell Grieger presents his contextual model of rational–emotive therapy (RET), which is then discussed by both Windy Dryden and Albert Ellis, the founder of RET. To round off Part One, Mark Glover explores the theoretical relevance and practical application of the term 'responsibility' from a cognitive perspective, but in such a way that its existential roots are preserved.

In Part Two we present a sample of work in the applied arena of cognitive psychotherapy. In Chapter 6 Kevin Howells presents an up-to-date review of the literature on the cognitive-behavioural view of angry aggression, and discusses the treatment approach developed from the pioneering work of Novaco in this area. In Chapter 7 Moira Hamlin describes her work on an integrated approach to helping people to withdraw from tranquillizers that is firmly based on a state-of-the-art overview of the literature on this subject and on a cognitive-behavioural foundation. In Chapter 8 Jan Scott describes her approach to using Beck's cognitive therapy within an in-patient hospital setting, and stresses the importance of all team members adhering to a common approach to treatment – a sentiment echoed by the work of Carlo Perris in Umeå, Sweden. In Chapter 9 we move from the clinical context to the field of occupational psychology. Here, Diana Richman shows how cognitive psychotherapists can intervene at important points in the career cycle to help workers achieve and maintain career satisfaction. Finally, in Chapter 10, Elin Evans and Elspeth McAdam describe their cognitive-behavioural approach to effective parenting, showing how cognitive psychotherapy can be used as a powerful preventative intervention.

Most texts in cognitive psychotherapy feature North American work. In this volume, however, we have sought to include work from both sides of the Atlantic, but feature, in particular, British work that is not otherwise very accessible. But no matter where the developments originate, we hope that readers will gain a sense of the growth of cognitive psychotherapy from these chapters.

Windy Dryden, *London*
Peter Trower, *Birmingham*

Notes on the Editors and Contributors

Windy Dryden is Senior Lecturer in the Department of Psychology at Goldsmiths' College, University of London. He has written or edited eleven books on counselling and psychotherapy and is co-editor of the *Journal of Cognitive Psychotherapy*.

Peter Trower is clinical psychologist at Solihull Health Authority, where he is Co-ordinator of rehabilitation in mental health and mental handicap. He has written or edited six books in the areas of social skills training and cognitive psychotherapy.

Cheryl N. Carmin is an Assistant Professor at Kent State University, Kent, Ohio. Her interests and publications include research on mentoring, the interface of personality and social psychology theory and counselling, and measurement and assessment.

E. Thomas Dowd is Professor and Director of Counselling Psychology Training at Kent State University, Kent, Ohio. He is co-editor of the *Journal of Cognitive Psychotherapy* and serves as a reviewer for numerous professional publications. His scholarly interests lie in cognitive-behaviour therapy and paradoxical interventions.

Albert Ellis is Executive Director of the Institute for Rational–Emotive Therapy, New York City. He is co-author (with Windy Dryden) of *The practice of rational–emotive therapy* (1987) and author of *How to stubbornly refuse to make yourself miserable about anything – yes, anything!* (1988).

Elin H. Evans is a Senior Clinical Psychologist at the Child and Family Centre, Bethel Hospital, Norwich. She is co-author (with Elspeth McAdam) of articles on parent effectiveness groups and on day care programmes for families.

Paul Gilbert is a Principal Psychologist in southern Derbyshire. He is author of *Depression: from psychology to brain state* (1984) and *Human nature and suffering* (in press).

Mark Glover is Senior Clinical Psychologist with the Adult Mental Health Service of Brighton Health Authority and a Visiting Research Fellow at the University of Sussex. He is Co-ordinator of benzodiazepine and smoking withdrawal projects in Brighton and is author of *Sleep and sleeplessness* (in press).

Russell M. Grieger is a clinical psychologist in private practice in Charlottesville, Virginia and an Adjunct Associate Professor at the University of Virginia. He is co-editor of the *Journal of Rational–Emotive and Cognitive-Behavior Therapy*, co-author (with John Boyd) of *RET: a skills-based approach* and co-editor (with Albert Ellis) of the two-volume *Handbook of RET*.

Moira Hamlin is Head of the Community Centre for Addiction, Slade Road, Birmingham. She is author of the Open University course book, *Tranquilliser withdrawal: current concerns and treatment practices* (1987).

Kevin Howells is Senior Lecturer in Clinical Psychology and Head of the Clinical Psychology Training Course at the University of Birmingham. He is co-editor of *Adult sexual interest in children* (1981), editor of *The psychology of sexual diversity* (1984) and co-author of *Psychology and you* (1987).

Elspeth McAdam is a Consultant Child and Family Psychiatrist at Bethel Hospital, Norwich. She has published articles on cognitive-behaviour therapy with adolescents, and parent effectiveness groups.

Jan Scott is a Senior Lecturer and Consultant in the Department of Psychiatry, University of Newcastle-upon-Tyne. She has published articles on chronic depressive disorders and their treatment, is Assistant Editor of the *British Journal of Clinical and Social Psychiatry* and co-editor (with J. Mark G. Williams and Aaron T. Beck) of *Cognitive therapy in clinical practice* (1988).

Diana R. Richman is a Senior Supervisor at the Institute for Rational–Emotive Therapy, New York City, and Adjunct Assistant Professor at St John's University, Jamaica, New York. She has published articles on a skills programme for job finding for the unemployed, and career counselling for women.

Richard L. Wessler is Professor of Psychology and Chairman of the Psychology Department at Pace University, Westchester, New York. He practises cognitive appraisal therapy in New York City at Cognitive Psychotherapy Associates. He is co-author of two books and many articles on individual and group therapy, and is on the editorial board of the *Journal of Cognitive Psychotherapy*.

PART ONE PRINCIPLES

1

Paradigms in Cognitive Psychotherapy

Cheryl N. Carmin and E. Thomas Dowd

Eifert (1984) has claimed that the cognitive-behaviour therapies (CBT) represent neither one identifiable therapy, technique, or treatment package, nor do they have a single unifying theory. Rather, he states that CBT provides a conceptual orientation toward defining problems in a particular way. Likewise, Mahoney and Arnkoff (1978) note that CBT has yet to move beyond being a diversified amalgam of principles and procedures which can be used to guide intervention strategies. While evaluating the process and outcome of these therapies is a formidable first step, therapy cannot exist in isolation from some theoretical overarching infrastructure. It is to this end that theoretical systems, conceptual models, and utilitarian paradigms can eventually form a hierarchy to guide research and practice in cognitive psychotherapy.

It is the purpose of this chapter to discuss those metatheoretical paradigms or overarching principles which function to unify and organize the cognitive psychotherapies into a coherent framework. In doing so, we will also trace the evolution of the field in its relatively short history.

An examination of the influence of cognitions on human behaviour is not as recent a phenomenon as we are often led to believe. Wessler (1986) aptly points out that if cognitions are broadly defined as any mental (that is, conscious or unconscious) activity, then even such notable figures as Sigmund Freud and Joseph Wolpe could be considered cognitive theorists/therapists. While this statement may be a cause for discussion in some circles, it does put the role of cognitions as intervening variables into a broader perspective.

The early learning theorists and behaviourists took issue with the mentalistic nature of such internal events as conscious and unconscious processes. Instead, they chose to view behaviour only in terms of discrete, observable, measurable events. This position created some problems when applied to the complexities of human behaviour. The principles that guided conditioning and reinforcement had to be extended and altered to include much human functioning. Wessler (1986) notes that verbal behaviour came to be viewed as conditioned stimuli and were taken to be a part of a second signalling system. This extension of traditional behaviourism laid the groundwork for a model of covert conditioning whereby thoughts were regarded as covert stimuli and responses. Needless to say, a position supporting the existence of covert behavioural mediators represented a break with the radical behaviourists who continued to decry the return to mentalistic notions that cognitions represented (for example, Skinner, 1986).

As cognitive concepts became increasingly used in psychotherapy, the role of expectancy in behaviour change was re-examined. The concept of expectancy had been originally used by Rotter (1954) in constructing his social learning theory and was further developed by Bandura and Walters (1963) in their later social learning theory. The role of expectancy furthered the transition from behavioural models which endorsed uni-directional environmental determinism and the importance of external events, to models which endorsed the more reciprocal nature of deterministic events and in doing so emphasized the interaction between internal and external events. External events clearly played an important role, but the human organism was no longer regarded as a passive recipient of environmental influence. Rather, people were regarded as taking an active part in their own developmental process (Mahoney and Arnkoff, 1978).

The transition continued. Researchers such as Mahoney (1974) and Meichenbaum (1974, 1977) presented explanations of behaviour change which resulted from the cognitive control of both behaviour and affect. Similarly, Lazarus (1981) broke from the traditional approach to systematic desensitization and presented an approach which stressed the importance of mental activities. Goldfried (1971) reconceptualized systematic desensitization from an automatic process to an active, coping-skills model.

Most recently, two additional approaches to CBT have been discussed in the literature. The first is a metacognitive perspective which is concerned with how individuals think about what they are thinking. It is an epistemic view, which is concerned with theories pertaining to the content and structure of knowledge systems (Kruglanski, 1981). The second is grounded in the writings of such notables as George Kelly and Alfred Adler and represents a constructivist approach. Constructivists argue that individuals create their own reality rather than simply incorporating and responding to an existing reality. These new approaches differ in that the metacognitive perspective is fundamentally an information-processing model in which external reality is viewed as a constant, whereas the constructivist approach views reality as ultimately relative. Mahoney and Gabriel (1987) suggest that the cognitive metatheoretical and constructivist positions represent a challenge to what they label as the 'realistic and rationalistic' approaches in terms of how these approaches view the focus of interventions, the way problems are conceptualized, the role of insight, the therapeutic relationship and, finally, how these approaches view relapse and regression. Rationalistic approaches, they state, assume that the world is given and the task is to perceive it. Constructivistic approaches assume that each person constructs his or her own unique perception of reality.

Clearly, CBT has undergone a metamorphosis. The paradigms which will be discussed in this chapter reflect this evolution from a perspective which focused solely on principles derived from operant or classical conditioning, through those which involve social systems and metacognitions, to those which view the nature of reality in fundamentally different ways. The cognitive psychotherapies have shifted their focus from a unidirectional environmentally deterministic paradigm to paradigms which encompass elements of reciprocal determinism and beliefs and expectancies as determinants of human behaviour (Dowd, 1981). Specifically, we are defining paradigms as those elements which serve to unify or provide coherence to the variety of theoretical and applied approaches that are considered to be the cognitive psychotherapies. As such, the paradigms we are proposing include (1) behavioural control, (2) covert control, (3) reciprocal determinism, (4) molecular approaches, (5) metacognitive approaches, and (6) constructivist approaches.

Behavioural Self-Control

The first CBT paradigm is also the most atomistic, traditional, and reactive with respect to the influence of discrete environmental events. It is presented here because it was originally used to explain the role of self-regulation in human activity. Self-regulation itself implies a cognitive activity. In Mahoney and Gabriel's (1987) view, this S–R approach is termed 'functionalism' (that is, behaviour is viewed as a function of the environment). The paradigm employs a traditional behavioural model to account for the role of self-regulatory mechanisms in modifying the input–output relationships inherent in the S–R model (Kanfer, 1971). In clinical application, these procedures usually combine S–R approaches with other components (such as self-punishment or praise) of self-regulation or distal external reinforcement (Kanfer, 1980). While this paradigm does not represent a purely cognitive approach, it is the forerunner of the more cognitive paradigms.

Behavioural control of self-reinforcement, then, represents a special type of self-initiating behaviour that permits an individual to maintain or change his/her behaviour with relatively little dependence on the environment. It does, however, presumably require that the individual evaluate a previously established contingency and only then deliver an appropriate consequence to him/herself (Kanfer, 1980). What this mechanism for reinforcing one's own behaviour suggests, then, is that consciously attending to one's own behaviour, or self-monitoring a cognitive activity, is necessary in order to establish whether or not the conditions for reinforcement can be met (Kanfer, 1971). In self-reinforcement, a freely available material reward which exists in the subject's environment is replaced by a contingent verbal symbolic reward (for example, self-praise for a successfully completed task). Alternatively, the individual may deliver to him/herself a material reinforcement contingent on the desired behaviour. Similarly, a self-administered negative self-consequence may be enjoined (such as self-criticism or self-blame). The important distinction is that in self-praise the individual cognitively chooses to deliver a self-reinforcement, whereas in refraining from delivering a negative consequence the individual cognitively chooses not to administer the consequence.

Kanfer (1980) indicated that positive self-reinforcement may take two forms. An individual may make a new or previously unavailable reward accessible (for example, one self-administers a 'treat'). The second type of reward involves initially denying oneself a pleasant experience and then later self-administering the experience as a contingent reinforcer of a desired behaviour. In the latter case, a temporal variable is introduced – reinforcement is delayed until the goal is achieved.

Both of the noted self-reinforcement categories rely upon self-reinforcing behaviours independent of extraneous environmental influences. Jones, Nelson and Kazdin (1977) point out that self-reinforcement is seldom consistently independent of the environment. Thoresen and Mahoney (1974) note that the act of self-monitoring itself can significantly alter the frequency of occurrence of the behaviour – though the behaviour generally soon returns to the base rate. Further, Kanfer (1971) notes the necessity for the subject to make self-evaluative discriminations in order to provide an outcome upon which further self-reinforcing operations will be contingent. Both Jones, Nelson and Kazdin's (1977) and Kanfer's (1971) observations stress the need for an appropriate means for self-evaluation, particularly when there are unexpected environmental events which disrupt the behaviour control process.

The behavioural control paradigm was only a first step towards fully cognitive models of human change and is not an important part of any current cognitive psychotherapies. It was an attempt to apply operant and classical conditioning models to the self-regulation of behaviour, and to that extent implied a reciprocal behaviour control that was to be developed more fully by Bandura (1978). In addition, its tacit assumption that humans are at least partly in control of their own destiny was a repudiation of an important principle of behavioural psychology and in that sense this assumption can be said to underly all cognitive psychotherapies. It led, however, to no therapeutic techniques that were not already part of the behavioural armamentarium; it simply applied them to a different target. In addition, the research it fostered, while sound, also led to no new behavioural laws. It simply showed that the application of operant and classical conditioning principles when applied to humans did not always lead to the same constant and predicted results that they did when applied to animals. There seemed to be greater variability when these principles were applied to humans.

Covert Control

Mahoney and Gabriel (1987) note how concerns over behavioural self-control progressed from conceptualizations regarding external and environmental influences toward a framework that involved more symbolic/cognitive influences. These techniques were first described as covert conditioning or coverants by Homme (1965) and marked a movement away from the radical behaviourists' not-so-benign neglect of private events (Mahoney and Arnkoff, 1978).

Homme (1965) argued that thoughts or private events could be analysed and modified simply by extrapolating from the then-extant principles of behaviourism and behaviour change. Homme observed that internal events, such as cognitions, could not be considered as wholly unobservable if the individual originating these thoughts is considered capable of making his/her own observations of these events (Mahoney and Arnkoff, 1978).

Cautela's (1966, 1967) research, specifically in the area of covert sensitization, did much to solidify the link between cognitive and behavioural approaches. The covert conditioning paradigm postulates that covert operants, or coverants, can be treated like operant responses even though such responses are not directly observable. The technique uses client imagery either as a stimulus, response, or reinforcing event. While this paradigm bears a resemblance to operant conditioning, it is distinguished from it in that covert processes may include verbal, symbolic, or imaginal representations (Kanfer, 1971).

The area of covert control which has received the greatest attention is covert sensitization (Kanfer, 1980). In covert sensitization, the client is asked to imagine, vividly and in great detail, engaging in the undesired behaviour and then to imagine an aversive stimulus, such as vomiting, occurring immediately after. The client is then asked to imagine ceasing the undesired behaviour and immediately feeling much better. This supposedly sensitizes the client to subsequent performance of the undesired behaviour. The therapist and/or the client offers positive reinforcement for ceasing the undesired behaviour (Kanfer, 1980).

Covert modelling has been used to increase the probability of a desired behaviour (Cautela, 1985) and can be considered an adaptation of overt modelling. The client is asked to vividly imagine in detail someone like themselves engaging in that behaviour. Cautela has stated that covert modelling is particularly suitable for young children.

Another once-commonly used covert control technique is thought-stopping. The individual is instructed to terminate the occurrence of intrusive thoughts by such devices as shouting 'stop' (preferably to oneself!) or by snapping one's wrist with a rubber-band. The intention is that through the use of such strategies the frequency of occurrence of these thoughts will decline.

Covert techniques have been used with reinforcement, extinction, and modelling (Kanfer, 1980). Mahoney and Arnkoff (1978) aptly point out that proponents of systematic desensitization, while eschewing the role of cognitive processes, have argued for the use of intervention strategies which use imagery to build desensitization hierarchies. Similarly, counter-conditioning models of behaviour change have relied on the use of covert events for over two decades.

A word of caution is advised, however. Mahoney (1974) and Scott and Rosenstiel (1975) observe that there is limited empirical support for the use of covert methods. Kanfer (1980), while noting the usefulness of covert sensitization in chemical dependency counselling, indicates that methodological problems make the evaluation of this technique difficult. He observes that covert stimuli and behaviours, by their very nature, are inaccessible to direct observation and measurement by others. Psychotherapists tailor the process to the individual needs of their clients so that treatments are differentially, rather than identically, administered. Lastly, Kanfer (1980) notes that the essential component of the covert sensitization process is the disruption of the imagined sequence of events. Foreyt and Hagan (1973) point out that the interruption of a natural chain of events by imagining a more satisfying event, rather than an aversive one, may accomplish the same goal. Mahoney and Gabriel (1987) have recently commented that the use of covert techniques is now infrequent in CBT.

The noted limitations notwithstanding, the use of a covert control paradigm marked a major conceptual shift away from the total reliance on external events to strategies which use imagery and visualization techniques as a means of changing behaviour. Currently, interventions employing imagery may not be explicitly referred to as covert conditioning, but they may be used more frequently than Mahoney and Gabriel (1987) have come to believe. The use of imagery and visualization in stress reduction (for math anxiety or in sports psychology, for example) is widely accepted in clinical practice despite lack of strong empirical support. In addition, imagery strategies have been increasingly incorporated into modern hypnotherapeutic approaches (Golden, Dowd and Friedberg, 1987). However, the efficacy of these techniques is no longer explained using covert conditioning principles. Thus, there have been significant changes in the way in which systematic desensitization has been conceptualized. While the original theoretical explanation for its effectiveness has fallen into disrepute, the techniques generated from the theory are still used.

Covert conditioning and behavioural self-control have much in common, both historically and conceptually. Both represented attempts to explain some aspects of cognitive processes using behavioural principles. Whereas behavioural self-control dealt largely with the self-regulation of overt behaviour and used cognitive processes primarily in self-monitoring activities, covert conditioning involved the direct regulation and utilization of private events. Although both represented early attempts at scientifically investigating the role of cognitive processes in human change, several of the covert conditioning techniques have become part of the repertoire of many cognitive psychotherapists, while the techniques derived from the behavioural self-control model have largely fallen into disuse. In neither case, however, are the explanatory constructs of either paradigm seriously employed by cognitive psychotherapists today. These constructs simply lack the sophistication and comprehensive quality necessary to explain adequately the complexity of human behaviour.

Molecular Approaches

The paradigms discussed thus far retain a substantial number of behaviouristic elements in that they focus on principles of conditioning and on external events. The molecular paradigm represents a considerable advance on these, both in terms of complexity and sophistication on one hand and a focus on purely cognitive phenomena on the other. It is so named from its focus on what Marzillier (1980) and Meichenbaum and Gilmore (1984) term 'cognitive events' as opposed to cognitive processes and cognitive structures. They define cognitive events as 'conscious identifiable thoughts and images' (p. 274). These are discrete self-statements that were once overt, conscious self-instructions that have gradually become covert and automatic. Although they are now automatic, these thoughts or self-statements can be recovered by a deliberate cognitive self-monitoring process, either alone or with the assistance of a therapist. However, as Meichenbaum and Gilmore note, this recovery process may be biased, in that recall may be influenced by *post hoc* rationalizations, present mood, or demand characteristics.

These covert self-instructions are called by a variety of names, depending on the system of cognitive psychotherapy from which they originate. Beck (1976; Beck et al., 1979) has referred to them as 'automatic thoughts'; Ellis (1962) has called them 'irrational thoughts'. Meichenbaum (1977) used the terms 'self-statements' or 'self-instructions' and stated that they form the basis of the 'internal dialogue'. The self-help group, Neurotics Anonymous, calls them examples of 'Stinkin' thinkin''. Whatever the term, however, they share some common elements. They are discrete, molecular units of thoughts that are subject (within limits) to recall and can be modified by engaging in more adaptive self-statements. They can be modified not only by purely cognitive interventions, such as rational disputation (Ellis, 1962) and reality testing of automatic thoughts (Beck et al., 1979), but also by behaviourally based interventions, such as mastery and pleasure exercises (Beck et al., 1979) and shame-attacking exercises

(Dryden and Ellis, 1986). All involve some sort of cognitive restructuring, cognitive or behavioural rehearsal, and homework (Golden and Dryden, 1986). In addition, these cognitive events can consist of images, symbols, and affect, as well as verbal cognitions.

Different cognitive psychotherapies differ in their treatment of molecular events. Meichenbaum's (1977) Cognitive-Behaviour Modification stresses behavioural procedures more than the others. Ellis (1962) postulates generalized irrational beliefs common to most or all individuals (which have been colloquially referred to as the 'Dirty Dozen'), whereas Beck (1976; Beck et al., 1979) advocates a more idiosyncratic approach that attempts to uncover a particular client's cognitive distortions. A cogent and insightful analysis of the similarities and differences between Beck's Cognitive Therapy and Ellis's Rational-Emotive Therapy has recently been presented by Dryden (1984).

Cognitive conceptualizations of the change process which derive from the molecular paradigm have both strengths and weaknesses. On one hand, they represent a cognitive approach which takes full account of the mediational ability of discrete cognitive units. They thus transcend the limits of an S–R model which attempts to ignore cognitive mediation or treats cognitions simply as dependent variables (private behaviours) in a nonmediational manner. The molecular paradigm, by contrast, treats cognitions as independent and mediational variables in their own right. Over time, the molecular approach has become increasingly sophisticated and complex as specific self-statements have been grouped and categorized into beliefs and belief structures. Certainly, the research attesting to the efficacy of the techniques which are part of the cognitive psychotherapies representing the molecular paradigm has been quite encouraging. The popularity of these approaches has been immense, and CBT now is a leading contender for the system with the largest following among psychotherapists in North America (Smith, 1982).

At the same time, the molecular approaches are also afflicted with weaknesses which are becoming increasingly apparent. They tend to be ahistorical and to pay little or no attention to developmental issues. Thus, they can appear as one-dimensional descriptors of human behaviour. Mahoney and Gabriel (1987) have noted that much of the research on the efficacy of the techniques derived from these approaches is methodologically limited and tells us less about basic change processes than originally hoped. Meichenbaum (1977) has warned against 'technical eclecticism', in which several psychotherapeutic techniques are compared to each other in a variety of combinations. Such dismantling studies without an undergirding theory are of little use, he says, in the search for more efficacious therapies, since they do not result in theory development. The molecular approaches seem particularly to lend themselves to this type of atheoretical 'technicism'. These approaches do not appear to be as theoretically comprehensive as was once thought. They have difficulty accounting for complex phenomena such as themes in an individual's life over time or for secondary gain. Finally, they are also afflicted with the same defect that pervades most systems of psychotherapies – they assume a unidirectional causation. An implicit assumption of the molecular approaches is that the direction of influence is from environment or therapist to client, and they do not explicitly take into account the ability of humans to control their own environment and to construct their own reality.

Reciprocal Determinism

The problems inherent in unidirectional causation are partially resolved in the reciprocal determinism paradigm. Rottschaefer (1985) describes reciprocal determinism as the interaction between environmental, behavioural, and cognitive factors in affecting behaviour. He further notes that successful and unsuccessful task performance, including the regulation of thoughts and feelings, is explained by including in addition to natural, social environmental, and generically cognitive causes of behaviour a set of cognitive processes which are self-referential (Rottschaefer, 1985: 226). As such, reciprocal determinism involves the mutual influence of person and environment on each other.

Research in the domain of behavioural self-control provided the foundation for Bandura's work on reciprocal determinism (for example, Bandura, 1978) and his recent work in the area of self-efficacy (for example, Bandura, 1977, 1982). This paradigm emphasizes the complex, causal, and reciprocal interaction between an organism and its environment as compared with the unidirectional environmental determinism proposed by the traditional behaviourists (Mahoney and Arnkoff, 1978).

Bandura (1978) observed that the proponents of environmental determinism both study and theorize about how the organism's behaviour is controlled by situational influences. Those supporting a psychodynamic philosophy seek to explain human behaviour in terms of such dispositional elements as instincts, drives, traits, and similar motivational forces that are located within the individual. The interactionists advocate a middle ground which would accommodate both situational and dispositional factors. Unfortunately, this stance still retains an essentially unidirectional perspective of behaviour processes.

Bandura broke with such unidirectional outlooks. His social learning approach emphasizes reciprocal determinism. Behaviour, internal states such as cognitions, and environmental influences all act as determinants of each other. Each one thus causes all the others in an interlocking fashion (Bandura, 1978). As such, reciprocal determinism does not define cause and effect relationships in a traditional way. Bandura stresses that an event may function as a stimulus, a response, or as an environmental reinforcer. How the event is viewed depends on where in the sequence the analysis begins.

What, then, is the role of cognitions? Bandura states:

> Most external influences affect behaviour through intermediary cognitive processes. Cognitive factors partly determine which external events will be observed, how they will be perceived, whether they have any lasting effects, what valence and efficacy they have, and how the information they convey will be organized for future use. (1978: 345)

Cognitions provide the individual with a mechanism for both exerting an influence over the environment and for providing oneself with the conditional incentives necessary for influencing behaviour. Bandura not only sees behaviour as being responsive to the environment but acknowledges that the individual has an active role in shaping his/her social milieu.

In part, then, cognitions serve a regulatory function. However, this process is not governed solely by the influence of antecedent and consequent events; a cognitive appraisal in the form of a probabilistic evaluation of a sequence of events also takes place. This process takes into consideration beliefs regarding action–outcome contingencies, meanings attributed to outcomes, and expectations regarding the effect an action will have on people's reinforcement practices (Bandura, 1978). Cognitions, then, represent both controlling and controllable influences. Behaviour becomes mediated by self-evaluations and self-directed actions (such as self-rewards) that are geared toward change.

In his more recent research, Bandura (1982) also notes the importance of the individual's perceptions or cognitions (self-percepts) regarding judgements of how well one can master courses of action required to deal with prospective situations. The nature of such probabilistic evaluations regarding one's self-efficacy or self-perceived competency are believed to influence choice of action as well as environmental setting, effort, expenditure, persistence at a task, and thought patterns and emotional reactions during anticipatory and actual transactions with the environment (Bandura, 1982). The thread representing the dynamic exchange between the individual and his/her environment remains a key feature of Bandura's work.

Research pertaining to reciprocal determinism requires methodologies different from the standard factorial analysis of persons, situations, and their interactions. Bandura (1978) calls for sequential analyses of triadic, interdependent factors which occur in interlocking systems. Studies which examine the reciprocal effect of cognitions on behaviour, and on the sequential analysis of social and environmental influences and their mutual determinism on behaviour, are needed. As Bandura notes, 'self-generated influences cannot be excised from among the determinants of human behaviour without sacrificing considerable explanatory and predictive power' (1978: 351).

Bandura's reciprocal determinism model goes a long way towards overcoming the problems inherent in a linear, unidirectional model of human change. Because of its circular bidirectional assumption of causality, it is able to explain self-regulation and goal-oriented behaviour more powerfully and parsimoniously than previous models. The model has a strong future-orientation in that expectancy is a significant construct and in that sense it is a teleological paradigm (Mahoney and Gabriel, 1987). The ability of a reinforcer to modify behaviour, a hallmark of traditional behaviourism, is challenged. Behaviour, according to Bandura (1977), is governed more by a perceived reinforcer than by an actual reinforcer. Thus, cognition is viewed as a powerful independent and mediational variable in its own right. Developmental processes are accorded some importance, since early and ongoing social interaction with others is thought to be of primary importance in human change processes.

At the same time, however, reciprocal determinism has some significant limitations. Its very circularity makes it difficult to study using standard research methodology which assumes linear causation. In addition, it is basically an information-processing rationalist model, in which reality is assumed to be invariant and is to be apprehended by the knowing individual (Mahoney and Gabriel, 1987). Despite its emphasis on the interaction of person and environment, it lacks certain important systems-based concepts, such as secondary gain. In addition, it lacks strong developmental constructs, which deficit it shares with other cognitive psychotherapies discussed under the molecular paradigm. There is no doubt, however, that the reciprocal determinism model has exercised a powerful influence on cognitive psychotherapy.

Metacognitive Approaches

One of the more recent developments in cognitive psychotherapy and the next paradigm to be discussed is a focus on metacognitions in cognitive structures. Metacognition can be defined as a self-reflexive examination of one's own thinking processes and structures, or what might be called thinking about thinking. Metacognitive development represents the knowledge and examination of the development over time of one's cognitive processes and structures. Metacognition has been defined by Meichenbaum and Gilmore (1984) as a focus on cognitive structures and cognitive processes rather than on cognitive events. Cognitive structures, also referred to as schemata, are relatively enduring aspects of cognitive organization. Cognitive processes refer to the principles and rules by which we organize and encode data. The individual, then, has an awareness of or becomes aware of his/her own cognitive machinery and its method of operation. Flavell describes this process as referring 'among other things, to the active monitoring and consequent regulation and orchestration of those procedures in relation to the cognitive objects or data on which they bear, usually in service of some concrete goal or objective' (1976: 232).

Flavell (1979) also notes how the acquisition of metacognitive skills is a developmental process. He provided an example whereby pre-school children thought they better understood a set of directions than they actually did as compared with elementary-school-aged children. Jaremko (1986) seems to view rule-governed behaviour similarly in that a child acquires knowledge at an incremental level and then this knowledge is eventually generalized to novel situations. In this regard, the 'rules' about how the world works become internalized, and based on this understanding the individual is able to generate subsequent assumptions about similar situations. Leva (1984), in applying Piagetian theory to cognitive behaviour therapy, describes the gradual growth in the rules and structures governing knowledge acquisition over time. Central to Piaget's theory are the concepts of assimilation, accommodation, and equilibration. Assimilation refers to the process of incorporating new internal or external data into an already existing cognitive structure. Accommodation refers to changes in that cognitive structure as a result of the incorporation of new data. Equilibration refers to a balance between the forces of accommodation and assimilation and its function is to maintain a homeostasis that compensates for disturbances. Developmental change, in Piaget's view, proceeds by a sort of ratcheting effect much like a fixed-interval reinforcement schedule, and represents a balance between the force for stasis provided by assimilation and the force for change provided by accommodation. Individuals seek therapy when the balance between these opposing forces has temporarily broken down. An important point for the present discussion is that cognitive development implies progressive changes over time in an individual's cognitive processes and structures.

Metacognitive activity, then, provides us with self-communication regarding our behaviour before, during, and after performing a task (Meichenbaum and Genest, 1980). It also provides more general information in regarding people as cognitive creatures with their diverse cognitive tasks, goals, actions, and experiences (Flavell, 1979).

Safran et al. have recently described a similar concept. They distinguish core from peripheral cognitive processes in the following manner:

> (1) Core cognitive processes are related to the definition and experience of the self in some fundamental way, (2) peripheral cognitive processes are subsumed by, or derive out of, core cognitive processes, (3) core cognitive processes can be distinguished by their ability to predict an individual's emotional and behavioral responses to a wide range of situations, and (4) an attempt to modify core cognitive processes is likely to evoke more anxiety than the modification of peripheral cognitive processes. (1986: 512)

It can be seen that core cognitive processes are similar conceptually to metacognitive structures since they arise from peripheral cognitive processes and involve response consistency across time and situations. Meichenbaum and Gilmore (1984) refer to these core cognitive processes as 'core organizing principles'.

Greenberg and Safran (1980, 1981) suggest that two related processes contribute to the acquisition of metacognitions-encoding and the formation of schemata. They state that production rules or generalized psychological stimulus–response rules are employed to transform information within the thinking process. Encoding is that transformational process which engages certain cognitive strategies while information is being processed (Greenberg and Safran, 1980). Encoding may represent how we acquire and organize knowledge.

The above authors also note that individuals construct their reality based on those elements of themselves and their environment that they attend to. This focus of attention, with respect to what is perceived and eventually encoded, channels causal attributions. Certain information is automatically attended to and processed. Greenberg and Safran (1981) describe a cognitive schema as the template or filter for that information which is eventually acquired. Likewise, Mahoney and Arnkoff (1978) suggest that schemata or knowledge structures may vary in their general themes depending on processes such as selective attention, magnification, and/or arbitrary inference.

Metacognitive approaches have as their eventual goal the acquisition of cognitive strategies which are generalizable to other situations. They are concerned with cognitive structures rather than cognitive events. As such, they can be contrasted with the learning of concrete, task-specific, self-statements (Meichenbaum and Genest, 1980). The metacognitive paradigm thus stresses the relationship of a present problem to past events or future consequences (Platt, Prout and Metzger, 1986).

Mahoney and Nezworski (1985) extrapolate the metacognitive approach from principles of basic biological adaptation. They note that 'Most theories of adaptation are themselves embedded in a tacit epistemology – a theory of how we know and learn' (p. 470). This approach emphasizes the viability of cognitive representations and acknowledges the dynamic interaction between organism and environment (Mahoney and Gabriel, 1987). In this respect they are close to the reciprocal determinism model.

Kruglanski (1981) discusses this epistemic approach to cognitive psychotherapy at some length and describes the epistemic process as a form of hypothesis testing. Kruglanski assumes that knowledge has two fundamental aspects – its content and the subjective confidence one has in that knowledge. The content is acquired through hypothesis generation and confidence in the hypothesis is gained through an internal, subjective evaluation process. He describes the goal of the change process as the client's executing a belief-shift (Kruglanski, 1981).

Within this metacognitive paradigm, the goal of therapy would be to facilitate a change in a client's world view, belief system, or set of rules for organizing incoming data. Rather than focusing on self-statements or contingent behaviour, the goal is a reworking of cognitive style, structure, or schema. The framework which governs the manner by which knowledge is acquired and processed is what will be altered. To use Kruglanski's (1981) language, it is the basic dysfunctional hypothesis generating constructs which will be replaced by more functional hypotheses.

The metacognitive paradigm represents a considerable advance over the molecular paradigm discussed earlier. Rather than focusing on cognitive events as does the latter, it focuses on the way that these events are organized over time (cognitive structures) and the rules by which these events are processed and organized (cognitive processes). There is thus a strong developmental flavour to the metacognitive paradigm that is not possessed by the other paradigms to nearly the same extent. In addition, by its focus on the ways in which individuals organize and categorize cognitive events, it takes advantage of the unique self-reflexive ability of humans to think about their own thinking. The emphasis on changing basic cognitive structures should lead to greater generalization and maintenance of psychological change, as opposed to the focus on changing cognitive events. Only in so far as changes in cognitive events (for example, self-statements) lead to changes in cognitive processes and structures over time should cognitive change be expected to maintain itself. That this does indeed happen with therapeutic repetition has been commonly observed by many clinicians. While there is not an overt consideration of person–environment interaction, as provided for by the reciprocal determinism paradigm, there is an implicit acknowledgement of the importance of this interaction. There is also an emerging awareness, especially by Piaget, of the part played by individuals in constructing their own reality.

It should be noted that the cognitive psychotherapies discussed earlier under the molecular paradigm can also be discussed under the meta-cognitive paradigm as well. Thus, the 'irrational beliefs', proposed by Ellis, while sharing some features of cognitive events, can be seen as cognitive structures as well. Likewise, Beck's (1976; Beck et al., 1979) cognitive distortions can be seen as cognitive processes. However, Safran et al. have argued that Ellis's approach may not involve a modification of core cognitive principles since 'it does not involve an exploration of the higher level constructs in terms that are idiosyncratic for each patient' (1986: 514). Likewise, they state that Meichenbaum's (1977) assumption that negative automatic thoughts can simply be replaced with more adaptive self-statements may be ill-founded. They advocate the assessment of fundamental core beliefs on the basis of the peripheral manifestations of these beliefs, and the subsequent modification of core beliefs by examining the peripheral statements which express them. These peripheral cognitions are then examined and tied back to the client's core beliefs by the therapist.

An evolution has recently been occurring from a focus on peripheral cognitions to an examination of core beliefs and self-statements. Ellis (1985), in a paper outlining his position on reciprocal determinism, has recently expanded RET to include the interaction among individuals within a system or between individuals and their environment. Meichenbaum has moved from an almost total reliance on cognitive events to a strong consideration of cognitive processes and structures. Indeed, there seems to have been a significant evolution of most of the cognitive psychotherapies from the molecular perspective to the metacognitive. In this regard, it is instructive to compare Meichenbaum and Cameron (1974) with Meichenbaum and Gilmore (1984), or Ellis (1985) with his earlier writings.

The major weakness of this paradigm is perhaps its lack of an explicit consideration of the reciprocal nature of the person–environmental interaction. While many of its characteristics are drawn from the information-processing model, it contains some elements of constructivistic thought. It is somewhat suspect in certain quarters since many of its constructs appear to be very similar to constructs that are part of psychodynamic approaches in general and psychoanalysis in particular. For example, the emphasis on cognitive themes and schemata are conceptually similar to unconscious patterns of meaning in psychodynamic thought, though without the motivational aspect. Likewise the developmental flavour of much of the metacognitive paradigm is similar to the developmental flavour that pervades psychodynamic thought. The paradigm's very complexity makes it difficult to research using classical group designs. Its theoretical postulates have tremendous heuristic value for clinicians, however, and we expect it to increase in influence in the future.

The Constructivistic Paradigm

All the cognitive paradigms discussed to this point have several assumptions in common. First, they are associationistic in nature. By that we mean that they derive their explanatory power from the principle of association – when one experience is recalled, other experiences which have been associated with this experience in certain ways also tend to be recalled. The three primary methods of association are similarity, contrast and contiguity. Although this is basically a description of what we know as classical conditioning, the operant conditioning model is associationistic in nature as well, the associationist principle in this case being consequence-oriented. Second, their basic mechanism for modifying an organism's behaviour is feedback. Feedback refers to the process by which the behavioural output of the organism is fed back into the input, thus modifying the latter and resulting in turn in a subsequently modified output. Third, their epistemologies are perceptual in nature. They view the task of the organism as collecting sensory data which is subsequently used to create the cognitive rules and assumptions which organize and regulate behaviour. The results of this behaviour then provide the necessary sensory input to modify subsequent behaviour, if necessary or desired. Fourth, they assume that reality is more or less invariant and exists independently of the knowing subject. The task of the subject is to more accurately perceive that reality and act accordingly. The fundamental assumption is that the therapist perceives correct reality more accurately than the client and attempts, by a variety of means, to transmit that reality to the client. Fifth, their psychology is linear causal in nature, in that events have causes which in turn cause subsequent events. Although the causality may be interactional and reciprocal in nature and therefore bidirectional, it is still linear. The notion of every event being at once a cause of every other event and simultaneously being caused by every other event is foreign to the previous paradigms.

Constructivism represents a radical break with these systems of thought and operates from an entirely different set of assumptions. While a detailed description of its major premises is beyond the scope of this chapter, its major postulates will be outlined here. For more detailed expositions of constructivistic approaches to psychotherapy, the reader is referred to Guidano (1984), Guidano and Liotti (1983, 1985), and Joyce-Moniz (1985).

Constructivism takes as its starting assumption that knowing individuals are active creators of their own reality. Although people do indeed gather sensory information and cognitively process it, they are far from passive elements in this process. Rather, they are active constructors of a pro-gressively differentiated hierarchical model of reality, which is increasingly elaborated over time. This model of reality finds expression in an organized system of beliefs, expectations, hypotheses, and tacit assumptions. Further-more, this constructivist process is circular in nature, rather than linear. It assumes that models of reality which people construct for themselves in turn determine the ways in which they subsequently perceive reality. Therefore, these models of reality contribute to experience itself rather than simply reflect experience. This is more than reciprocal interaction, in which each element in the system – self and environment – has an impact on the other. Constructivist psychotherapists argue that in the act of perceiving environmental reality the individual creates that reality, which further determines how reality can subsequently be perceived. Thus, the linear causality model is replaced by a circular self-reflexive arc in which two or more elements simultaneously create each other.

As sensory input is brought into the cognitive system, the individual attempts to organize it into already-existing schemata and assumptions. Relatively consistent information can be fitted into pre-existing cognitive categories without much difficulty. It is discrepant information that presents difficulties, and often forces a radical revision of the person's basic assumptions and beliefs. This revised cognitive structure in turn attempts to incorporate incoming data in a consistent manner. Thus, human cognitive development occurs by a sort of ratcheting effect, in which change via discrepancy oscillates with maintenance via consistency. The process by which incoming information is processed according to the individual's cognitive structure has been termed a 'feedforward' mechanism (Mahoney, 1985).

It follows from the above discussion that reality, from a constructivist perspective, is not invariant but is uniquely created by the perceiving and knowing individual. It is therefore senseless to speak of and work towards a standard outcome for all clients, even those with similar problems. Constructivism tends to be teleonomic as opposed to teleological (Mahoney and Gabriel, 1987). 'Teleological' refers to a purposeful direction towards a final and explicit destination or final cause; 'teleonomic' refers to a direction without an explicit destination. Likewise, it is incorrect to assume that the therapist has a better view of reality than the client, though it might be a more useful one. However, one need not slip into solipsism, which teaches that nothing exists beyond the mind of the perceiving subject because the individual cannot directly experience anything beyond itself. Rather, constructivism assumes that there are a number of more or less equally valid realities, not that there is no reality at all. Constructivism is therefore opposed to those cognitive psychotherapies which view reality as something to be discovered and apprehended. Reality is seen as continuously created out of the individual's repeated interaction with the environment.

As Dowd and Pace (in press) have noted, certain elements of the existing cognitive psychotherapies are not completely incompatible with the constructivistic perspective. Beck et al's (1979) cognitive therapy of depression, for example, assists clients in constructing new models of the world by challenging their current model in such techniques as constructive alternativism. However, although these therapies may incorporate certain constructivistic elements, they do not take constructivistic assumptions as their starting point.

There are both advantages and disadvantages to the constructivistic approach. One important advantage is that it is capable of explaining the obvious fact that there have been, are, and probably will be in the future, a large number of different approaches to psychotherapy. What they all have in common, like religions (with which they share many similarities), is a belief that they alone teach the truth. A constructivist would argue that psychotherapists create therapeutic systems (that is, systems of meaning) out of their experiences with the world. Constructivism, as Dowd and Pace (in press) have noted, is also able to account for such phenomena as 'Functional Autonomy' (Allport, 1937) in which beliefs and behaviours perseverate long after the reinforcing stimulus has been removed or even after they have ceased to have any apparent function whatever. Functional autonomy can be viewed as an example of the search for consistency (Guidano, 1984), in which incoming information is shaped and moulded to fit already-existing cognitive structures. Constructivism tends to be developmental in nature (Joyce-Moniz, 1985) and stresses the progressive accumulation of data in the building of an individual's cognitive framework. Constructivism is also able to explain the efficacy of such second- or higher-order change-producing mechanisms as paradoxical interventions (Dowd and Pace, in press) which seem to defy explanation by both behavioural and cognitive psychology. Paradoxical strategies can be viewed as powerful discrepancy-producing techniques that challenge clients to examine their model of reality by undercutting current models and by decontextualizing the symptoms.

The constructivistic paradigm also has severe limitations as a model of cognitive change, however. These are basically related to the self-reflexive nature of constructivistic thinking. Because its basic process is circular in nature rather than linear, there is a fundamental inability either to postulate a first cause or to arrive at final meaning. Constructivistic thought processes bend back upon themselves in a self-reflexive arc that starts nowhere and ends nowhere but where they began (which was nowhere). Such thinking is extremely unsettling to the human mind and, indeed, it is debatable whether anyone can sustain a purely constructivistic frame of reference for long. To many (Watzlawick, 1984), constructivism is nihilistic in nature and demands that life be lived without hope of ultimate meaning. Few of us are prepared to cope with this possibility with equanimity.

Watzlawick (1984) has argued that a truly constructivistic thinker need not feel threatened by the above and has set down several criteria which might characterize a constructivist's world. While his reasoning is persuasive, in the final analysis this world is a construction of its own, neither more nor less true than any other. This, incidentally, illustrates the circular trap of constructivism: that its own construction is itself a construction. Watzlawick states that a constructivist would be tolerant since, if we see our world as a construction, we would apply this logic to the worlds of others as well. Second, this individual would, he says, feel responsible for self and would be less likely to blame others. This responsibility would mean total freedom to create whatever reality one wanted. While all of this may be true, by the same logic, it is likely that a constructivist would also find it difficult to believe in anything or to be committed to much. For what is the point of committing oneself to a deeply held belief that in the final analysis is simply a construction of one's own mind, neither better nor worse than anyone else's constructions? In other words, a constructivist could have no sense of transcendence, no feeling that anything mattered beyond the self. Such a person may indeed be tolerant, but it would probably be the tolerance of unconcern and uncaring. For all of us find it easy to be tolerant regarding matters about which we do not care. We question, however, whether a desirable end state for humanity is an aloof detachment and unconcern.

Future Directions

Paradigms exist in part to be challenged. Future research and clinical practice will, no doubt, prove the merits of some of these paradigms as they eventually are incorporated into theories of cognitive psychology or are excluded. New paradigms will likewise evolve as our knowledge base expands, and they will replace or build upon pre-existing research. In surveying the literature, we have found a number of possible future directions.

As we direct our attention to the future, Sarason (1979) reminds us not to lose sight of the past. He points out that the cognitive therapies have been primarily concerned with how to change cognitions and consequent behaviour and affect, rather than why those faulty or maladaptive cognitions occurred in the first place. Sarason stresses the need to identify antecedent conditions and the process by which personal and social problems develop. He also argues that one lacuna in the cognitive therapies is the lack of attention to insight. Mahoney and Gabriel (1987) see insight as a form of metacognition. The notion that a cognition has some personal historical basis would fit with those paradigms which share an organism–environment interaction or a constructivistic perspective. Recent research in the area of child development, particularly with respect to how developmental events are interpreted, may prove to be an influential area for continued research (Sarason, 1979).

Mahoney and Gabriel (1987) persuasively argue the need for a more systematic approach to cognitive psychotherapy. Adhering to a linear, or unidirectional, model of causality is the hallmark of the behaviourists. Cognitive psychotherapy appears to be gaining a deepening appreciation for the dynamic interaction between the individual and his/her environment as a means of affecting behaviour. Mahoney and Gabriel advocate more developmentally oriented approaches which could take the dynamic equilibrations of change throughout the lifespan into account, and which would direct cognitive psychotherapy away from reductionistic linear models of causality. Bandura (1978) has provided a cornerstone for such a perspective with his research and theorizing concerning reciprocal determinism. A logical extension of Bandura's linear model would be the more circular and contextual thinking that systems theory, as applied to cognitive psychotherapy, could potentially represent. While this approach would be developmental in nature, it would also involve systemic thinking as well. Cognitive psychotherapy, as well as behaviour therapy, has historically been intrapsychic in nature and has paid relatively little attention to the social network of significant others in which our clients exist, or to such interactional and systemic concepts as secondary gain. Perhaps some of the insights of the systems theorists can be applied to cognitive psychotherapy.

In expanding to encompass many of the theories and procedures of other systems of psychotherapy, cognitive psychotherapy has also expanded into the realm of philosophy as well. In its attempt to explain the procedures by which maladaptive responses can be replaced with more adaptive responses, cognitive psychotherapy should not lose sight of the need for transcendental meaning which transcends a particular individual at a particular time and situation. Frankl (1963) has written eloquently about this issue. Meaning can be found in a variety of places by a variety of ways. In the final analysis, however, systems of psychotherapy are systems for the construction of personal meaning; for ourselves as well as for our clients. We should not forget this.

References

Allport, G. W. (1937) *Personality: a psychological interpretation*. New York: Henry Holt.

Bandura, A. (1977) Self-efficacy: toward a unifying theory of behavior change. *Psychological Review*, 84: 191–215.

Bandura, A. (1978) The self-system in reciprocal determinism. *American Psychologist*, 33: 344–58.

Bandura, A. (1982) Self-efficacy mechanisms in human agency. *American Psychologist*, 37: 122–47.

Bandura, A. and Walters, R. E. (1963) *Social learning theory and personality development*. New York: Holt, Rinehart & Winston.

Beck, A. T. (1976) *Cognitive therapy and the emotional disorders*. New York: International Universities Press.

Beck, A. T., Rush, A. J., Shaw, B. F. and Emery, G. (1979) *Cognitive therapy of depression*. New York: Guilford.

Cautela, J. R. (1966) Treatment of compulsive behavior by covert sensitization. *Psychological Record*, 16: 33–41.

Cautela, J. R. (1967) Covert sensitization. *Psychological Record*, 20: 459–68.

Cautela, J. R. (1985) Covert modeling. In A. S. Bellack and M. Hersen (eds), *Dictionary of behavior therapy techniques*. New York: Pergamon.

Dowd, E. T. (1981) Cognitive behavior therapy: dangers and new directions. *Academic Psychology Bulletin*, 3: 387–93.

Dowd, E. T. and Pace, T. (in press) The relativity of reality: second order change in psychotherapy. In A. Freeman, K. S. Simon, H. Arkowitz and L. E. Beutler (eds), *Handbook of cognitive therapy*. New York: Plenum.

Dryden, W. (1984) Rational-emotive therapy and cognitive therapy: a critical comparison. In M. A. Reda and M. J. Mahoney (eds), *Cognitive psychotherapies: recent developments in theory, research and practice*. Cambridge, Mass.: Ballinger.

Dryden, W. and Ellis, A. (1986) Rational-emotive therapy (RET). In W. Dryden and W. L. Golden (eds), *Cognitive-behavioural approaches to psychotherapy*. London: Harper & Row.

Eifert, G. H. (1984) Cognitive behavior therapy: a critical evaluation of its theoretical and empirical bases and therapeutic efficacy. *Australian Psychologist*, 19: 179–91.

Ellis, A. (1962) *Reason and emotion in psychotherapy*. Secaucus, NJ: Lyle Stuart.

Ellis, A. (1985) Expanding the ABC's of rational-emotive therapy. In M. J. Mahoney and A. Freeman (eds), *Cognition and psychotherapy*. New York: Plenum.

Flavell, J. (1976) Metacognitive aspects of problem-solving. In L. Resnick (ed.), *The nature of intelligence*. Hillsdale, NJ: Lawrence Erlbaum.

Flavell, J. H. (1979) Metacognition and cognitive monitoring: a new area of cognitive-developmental inquiry. *American Psychologist*, 34: 906–11.

Foreyt, J. P. and Hagan, R. L. (1973) Covert sensitization: conditioning or suggestion? *Journal of Abnormal Psychology*, 82: 17–23.

Frankl, V. (1963) *Man's search for meaning* (rev edn). New York: Washington Square Press.

Golden, W. L., Dowd, E. T. and Friedberg, F. (1987) *Hypnotherapy: a modern approach*. New York: Pergamon.

Golden, W. L. and Dryden, W. (1986) Cognitive behavioural therapies: commonalities, divergencies, and future development. In W. Dryden and W. L. Golden (eds), *Cognitive-behavioural approaches to psychotherapy*. London: Harper & Row.

Goldfried, M. R. (1971) Systematic desensitization as training in self-control. *Journal of Consulting and Clinical Psychology*, 37: 228–34.

Greenberg, L. S. and Safran, J. D. (1980) Encoding, information processing, and the cognitive-behavioral therapies. *Canadian Psychology*, 21 (2): 59–66.

Greenberg, L. S. and Safran, J. D. (1981) Encoding and cognitive therapy: changing what clients attend to. *Psychotherapy: Theory, Research, and Practice*, 18: 165–9.

Guidano, V. F. (1984) A constructivistic outline of cognitive processes. In M. A. Reda and M. J. Mahoney (eds), *Cognitive psychotherapies: recent developments in theory, research and practice*. Cambridge, Mass.: Ballinger.

Guidano, V. F. and Liotti, G. (1983) *Cognitive processes and emotional disorders*. New York: Guilford.

Guidano, V. F. and Liotti, G. (1985) A constructivistic foundation for cognitive therapy. In M. J. Mahoney and A. Freeman (eds), *Cognition and psychotherapy*. New York: Plenum.

Homme, L. E. (1965) Perspectives in psychology: XXIV. Control of coverants, operants of the mind. *Psychological Record*, 15: 501–11.

Jaremko, M. E. (1986) Cognitive-behaviour modification: the shaping of rule-governed behaviour. In W. Dryden and W. L. Golden (eds), *Cognitive-behavioural approaches to psychotherapy*. London: Harper & Row.

Jones, R. T., Nelson, R. E. and Kazdin, A. E. (1977) The role of external variables in self-reinforcement: a review. *Behavior Modification*, 1: 147–78.

Joyce-Moniz, L. (1985) Epistemological therapy and constructivism. In M. J. Mahoney and A. Freeman (eds), *Cognition and psychotherapy*. New York: Plenum.

Kanfer, F. H. (1971) The maintenance of behavior by self-generated stimuli and reinforcement. In A. Jacobs and L. B. Sachs (eds), *The psychology of private events*. New York: Academic Press.

Kanfer, F. H. (1980) Self-management methods. In F. H. Kanfer and A. P. Goldstein (eds), *Helping people change* (2nd edn). New York: Pergamon.

Kruglanski, A. W. (1981) The epistemic approach in cognitive therapy. *International Journal of Psychology*, 16: 275–9.

Lazarus, A. A. (1981) *The practice of multimodal therapy*. New York: McGraw-Hill.

Leva, I. M. (1984) Cognitive behavioral therapy in the light of Piagetian theory. In M. A. Reda and M. J. Mahoney (eds), *Cognitive psychotherapies: recent developments in theory, research, and practice*. Cambridge, Mass.: Ballinger.

Mahoney, M. J. (1974) *Cognition and behavior modification*. Cambridge, Mass.: Ballinger.

Mahoney, M. J. (1985) Psychotherapy and human change processes. In M. J. Mahoney and A. Freeman (eds), *Cognition and psychotherapy*. New York: Plenum.

Mahoney, M. J. and Arnkoff, D. (1978) Cognitive and self-control therapies. In S. L. Garfield and A. E. Bergin (eds), *Handbook of psychotherapy and behavior change: an empirical analysis* (2nd edn). New York: Wiley.

Mahoney, M. J. and Gabriel, T. J. (1987) Psychotherapy and the cognitive sciences: an evolving alliance. *Journal of Cognitive Psychotherapy,* 1: 39–59.

Mahoney, M. J. and Nezworski, M. T. (1985) Cognitive-behavioral approaches to children's problems. *Journal of Abnormal Child Psychology,* 13: 467–76.

Marzillier, J. S. (1980) Cognitive therapy and behavioural practice. *Behaviour Research and Therapy,* 18: 249–58.

Meichenbaum, D. (1974) *Cognitive behavior modification.* Morristown, NJ: General Learning Press.

Meichenbaum, D. (1977) *Cognitive behavior modification.* New York: Plenum.

Meichenbaum, D. and Cameron, R. (1974) The clinical potential of modifying what clients say to themselves. In M. J. Mahoney and C. E. Thoresen (eds), *Self-control: power to the person.* Monterey, Calif.: Brooks-Cole.

Meichenbaum, D. and Genest, M. (1980) Cognitive behaviour modification: an integration of cognitive and behavioral methods. In F. H. Kanfer and A. P. Goldstein (eds), *Helping people change* (2nd edn). New York: Pergamon Press.

Meichenbaum, D. and Gilmore J. B. (1984) The nature of unconscious processes: a cognitive-behavioral approach. In K. S. Bowers and D. Meichenbaum (eds), *The unconscious revisited.* New York: Wiley.

Platt, J. J., Prout, M. F. and Metzger, D. S. (1986) Interpersonal cognitive problem-solving therapy (ICPS). In W. Dryden and W. L. Golden (eds), *Cognitive-behavioural approaches to psychotherapy.* London: Harper & Row.

Rotter, J. B. (1954) *Social learning and clinical psychology.* Englewood Cliffs, NJ: Prentice-Hall.

Rottschaefer, W. A. (1985) Evading conceptual self-annihilation: some implications of Albert Bandura's theory of the self-system for the status of psychology. *New Ideas in Psychology,* 2 (3): 223–30.

Safran, J. D., Vallis, T. M., Segal, Z. V. and Shaw, B. F. (1986) Assessment of core cognitive processes in cognitive therapy. *Cognitive Therapy and Research,* 10: 509–26.

Sarason, I. G. (1979) Three lacunae of cognitive therapy. *Cognitive Therapy and Research,* 3: 223–35.

Scott, D. S. and Rosenstiel, A. K. (1975) Covert positive reinforcement studies: review, critique and guidelines. *Psychotherapy: Theory, Research and Practice,* 12: 374–84.

Skinner, B. F. (1986) *Whatever happened to psychology as a science of behavior?* Presented at the 94th annual convention of the American Psychological Association, Washington, DC.

Smith, D. (1982) Trends in counseling and psychotherapy. *American Psychologist,* 7: 802–9.

Thoresen, C. E. and Mahoney, M. J. (1974) *Behavioral self-control.* New York: Holt, Rinehart & Winston.

Watzlawick, P. (1984) *The invented reality.* New York: W. W. Norton.

Wessler, R. L. (1986) Conceptualizing cognitions in the cognitive-behavioural therapies. In W. Dryden & W. L. Golden (eds), *Cognitive-behavioural approaches to psychotherapy.* London: Harper & Row.

2

Affect and Nonconscious Processes in Cognitive Psychotherapy

Richard L. Wessler

Human kind
Cannot bear very much reality.

T. S. Eliot

This chapter examines certain aspects of affect and nonconscious processes as they relate to cognitive psychotherapy. The main theme is that affect and action are due to automatic (that is, nonconsciously controlled) processes, in addition to consciously controlled processes. The task of cognitive psychotherapy is to discover and describe nonconscious processes, and to modify them when they result in less-than-satisfactory adaptive outcomes.

This chapter consists of a discussion of cognition and affect in two models of cognitive psychotherapy, a closer look at affect and nonconscious processes in view of recent research, and a description of some developments in cognitive psychotherapy that aim beyond the treatment of affective and anxiety disorders.

Models of Cognitive Psychotherapy

Cognitive psychotherapy involves both evaluative cognitions (appraisals) and affect (subjective emotional feelings). In general, the strategy in cognitive psychotherapy is to modify cognitions in order to treat emotional disorders. There are two models of the relationship between cognition and affect that justify interventions into cognitive content when attempting to treat emotions: a cognitive mediational model, and an interactional model.

The cognitive mediation model assumes that affect is the linear result of cognitive appraisal (Lazarus, 1984). Cognitive processing of stimuli, and not the stimuli themselves, produce emotional responses. Many authorities in cognitive psychotherapy have paraphrased the Stoic philosopher Epictetus: people are not disturbed by things and events, but by their opinions about those things and events. Opinion can either mean what one thinks is true (for example, causal attributions: Försterling, 1985, 1986) or how one appraises things and events (cognitive evaluations: Wessler, 1986).

The implication is, that if one changes an opinion one's emotional response to the situation will change, as a result of the causal connection between cognition and affect. In a preface to his compilation of so-called cognitive techniques, McMullin stated this theoretical rationale: 'Therapists begin by helping their clients to find the thoughts, beliefs, or schemata that are *causing* their negative emotions and behaviors' (1986: xv, italics added).

The popularity of this model is probably due to the control – or at least, the potential for control – it ascribes to the person. The person is not a mere passive mechanism that emotes in response to environmental events, but an active participant who can willfully change his/her reactions. The practical problem with the cognitive mediational model is apparent to anyone who has used it either with themselves or with clients: it is difficult to identify what 'opinions' to target for change, and even more difficult to change them. This model is found in highly rationalistic versions of cognitive therapy, for example, 'the therapist helps the clients to change their irrational beliefs from those that are unrealistic and harmful to those that are more rational and useful' (McMullin, 1986: xv).

The interdependent model takes a general systems approach by regarding cognition, affect, and action as components in a mutually dependent co-relationship. A change in one component will produce change in the other components, although none is claimed to be causal to the others. Lazarus and Folkman (1984) offer a nonlinear account of the interdependence of affect, cognition and behaviour. Bower (1981) has proposed a model of the interconnections between mood and memory, and makes the point that people attend to and learn more about events that match their emotional state and recall an event better if, during recall, they experience the same emotion they experienced during learning.

Greenberg and Safran (1984, 1987) have discussed the role of emotion in psychotherapy, and cite studies that support the notion that mood can influence thought as well as thought can influence feeling. Affect is not simply a by-product of cognitive processing of information, but has a separate quality of its own that (1) cannot be understood by seeking its origins in cognition alone, (2) can influence the cognitive processing of information to a significant extent, and (3) has cyclical and reciprocal influence in that cognitions influence affect experiences. Affect is not merely a target for change or an undesirable state to overcome; it is recognized as a modality that can influence other modalities and can be used therapeutically to effect change in action and thought. In practice, this means that a therapist can work in any of several modalities and expect to bring about therapeutic results in the target modality (usually affect or behaviour). This is the approach taken in recent writings in cognitive psychotherapy, such as Beck and Emery (1985), Lazarus (1981), Dryden and Ellis (1986), although one of its earliest statements may be found in Ellis (1962).

Conscious Processes

One view of cognitive psychotherapy emphasizes conscious processes mobilized to control and overcome negative feelings. Nowhere is this more evident than in the adoption of the 'man-as-scientist' metaphor, which holds that humans take a scientific approach to life, construct hypotheses, collect data to test them, and revise and discard unsupported hypotheses (Wessler, 1986). Humans are conceived to be rational in outlook, committed to empiricism and logic, and ready and willing to change their minds when presented with the facts. It is as if psychologists had said: Come, let us create Man after our own likeness. The environment impinges on people not directly but by means of 'symbolic representations' (Mahoney, 1977). Emotion shall be the servant of reason, once the person discovers how to exercise rational, conscious control of his/her information-processing. There is little room for nonconscious processes in this version of human nature that likens man to a computer.

Contemporary cognitive psychology has come to accept a significantly less rational and less conscious version of human functioning. Rather than take nonconscious processes as exceptions to the rational, conscious processes, cognitive psychotherapy must take nonconscious processes as the standard. Bara states that 'evidence from cognitive science and artificial intelligence shows how everything in the cognitive system is unconscious, apart from a small area, still to be understood and explained, which is conscious' (1984: 56).

Cognitive psychotherapy has postulated and worked with nonconscious processes by discovering irrational beliefs, automatic thoughts, and cognitive structures. Ellis (1962), in his early descriptions of irrational beliefs, said that they were what Freudians call preconscious – not deeply buried in the unconscious, somewhat accessible, but definitely not conscious. Beck (1976) characterized the negative thoughts involved in depression as automatic and involuntary, and so habitual that one is not aware of them. Mahoney (1980) forecast an important role for nonconscious thoughts in the cognitive psychotherapy of the future. Meichenbaum and Gilmore (1984), have suggested that this is already happening.

Nonconscious Algorithms

Social information that is not consciously processed is, by definition, nonconscious or automatic (Bargh, 1984). Nonconscious processing is typically limited to the perceptual stage of processing, which furnishes data that conscious processing may operate on. Nonconscious processing is not under the control of the person (Kihlstrom, 1984). It is a stored routine under the control of the environment and activated by relevant stimuli in the situation.

Extensive experimental support for the automatic and nonconscious processing of social information has been furnished by Lewicki, who comments:

> When people learn some cognitive algorithm (e.g., to react in a certain way to certain stimuli) following a consciously controlled process of learning, and then repeat a number of times what they have learned, it often happens that the cognitive algorithm becomes automatic and starts to operate without mediation of conscious awareness. . . . [However,] human information processing involves at its various levels numerous such nonconscious cognitive algorithms: (1) that definitely have never been learned at the level of consciousness, (2) that operate totally beyond one's conscious control, and (3) that are available to a person who follows these algorithms in no other way than by an 'outsider's viewpoint' observation of how they operate. (Lewicki, 1986: 11)

In clinical practice, nonconscious processes can be identified by taking the 'as if' attitude of an outside observer. One can say that the person acts 'as if' he/she were following some nonconscious algorithm. Nonconscious algorithms may be inferred to account for affect generated in specific situations.

In a seminal article Zajonc (1980) raised objections to the then prevailing view in contemporary cognitive psychology that regarded affect as an outcome of prior and extensive processing of information about a stimulus. He took the position that affect, not cognition, is primary in responses to stimuli.

Affective reactions are based on what Zajonc calls preferenda: internal states of an individual that predispose him/her to appraise an object or event as good or bad, personal preferences, or statements of liking and disliking. They are not cognitive inferences or information about stimuli. They are appraisals or evaluations. These appraisals do not occur after cognitive inferences are made, but prior to such cognitive processing. Affect is basic to survival, inescapable, irrevocable, difficult to verbalize, implicated with the self, and not dependent on cognition. An animal would not survive if it had to process information about the environment; it reacts to danger 'long before the completion of even a simple cognitive process' (Zajonc, 1980: 156).

Zajonc distinguished (1) cognitions that consist of information (knowledge) that is accompanied or qualified by affect, (2) instances where affect becomes separated from the original cognitions, and (3) emotional experiences, such as listening to a favourite piece of music. Affective reactions are inescapable, he said: 'When we evaluate an object or event, we are describing not so much what is in the object or event, we are describing something that is in ourselves' (Zajonc, 1980: 157).

This article stirred a great deal of controversy and subsequent research. Much of the controversy focused on exactly where in the sequence of events appraisal takes place. Because both affect and cognitive inference are covert processes, it is difficult to know which came first – indeed, Plutchik (1985) regards it as a 'chicken-and-egg' controversy. Greenberg and Safran (1987) have argued that it is a mistake to assume a one-directional relationship between cognition and emotion; they are 'fused' together, completely inter-dependent, and can be separated only for purposes of analysis.

Affect and Awareness

Feelings have crucial importance in psychotherapy. The person's aware-ness of his/her feelings may fall anywhere on a continuum of fully aware to unaware. Is it proper, within the context of scientifically-based psychotherapy, to say that feelings exist of which the person is not aware?

To qualify as scientific data, phenomena must be observable. Affect of which the person is fully aware but does not overtly display or report marginally qualifies as scientific data. J. B. Watson successfully launched behaviourism in psychology in part because he could attack structuralism's introspective awareness as not objective enough to qualify as scientific observation. One's self-observation cannot be independently verified and, therefore, at best has marginal status as scientific data.

Affect, or subjective emotional feeling, is available to the person by means of self-observation, but it cannot be verified by independent methods. No one knows how the person feels except the person him/herself. It is possible to recall one's own affective experience in recognition of the other person's verbal and nonverbal signals, and match it with the other person's feelings, a sort of verification.

Affect that the person is not aware of cannot be verified by the observer. In fact, the arrangement is exactly the opposite: the person must verify the observer's report about the person's affect. When affect must be pointed out to the person by an observer, phrases such as unconscious feelings, out-of-touch-with-one's feelings, denial of feelings, etc, are used. Such observations seem even more tenuous as scientific data than affect upon which person and observer readily agree.

The problem can be resolved by not accepting either instance of affect as data. Instead, affect can be taken as an inference made by either the person or the observer or both about the person's internal emotional state. Hence, it is permissible for therapists to tell patients/clients what they might be feeling when the client seems unaware of his/her feelings – that is, cannot read his/her own signals.

Theories of psychopathology have often postulated a fundamental emotion that motivates dysfunctional behaviour. Anxiety is the usual name given to the fundamental motivating emotion. Both psychodynamic and behavioural accounts of abnormality share an emphasis on the hedonistic reduction of anxiety as the cause of the development of defence mechanisms and maladaptive behavioural patterns. Although defence mechanisms are unconscious mental operations and avoidance patterns are overtly behavioural, both are said to exist because humans find a high degree of anxiety to be aversive, and are motivated to avoid and reduce it.

However, as Mandler (1984) points out, it is not necessary to postulate a fundamental emotion that motivates neurotic affect and action. One can be motivated to avoid anger, for example, not because it generates anxiety, but because the subjective feeling itself is neither pleasurable nor consistent with one's self-image. Several negative affective states have the power to motivate mental and behavioural operations that serve to diminish negative affect.

Cognitive Appraisal Concepts

Wessler and Hankin-Wessler (1986) have developed a cognitive psycho-therapy approach that utilizes the concept of nonconscious algorithms for processing social information and the motivational principle of re-experiencing certain emotional states. The chief hypothesis of this chapter concerns the role of affect in psychopathology and in psychotherapy. It is that for each person, certain affective states are avoided (defence manoeuvres) and certain affective states sought out (security manoeuvres). Feelings that are avoided or sought cannot be simply classified into negative and positive, respectively. Contrary to the principle of hedonism, certain negative affective states will be sought, generally without the person's awareness, because the motivation to re-experience them is very strong.

These ideas were developed out of clinical experience, and in many respects parallel the work of Guidano and Liotti (1983; Liotti 1986). They especially apply to the psychological treatment of personality disorders. Most cognitive psychotherapy is expressly intended for the short term treatment of anxiety disorders, phobias, and 'neurotic' depres-sion, which are Axis-I disorders in the Diagnostic and Statistical Manual (DSM-III-R). Presently there are no guidelines in cognitive psychotherapy for working with clients who have personality disorders as diagnosed on Axis-II of DSM-III-R. These ideas, then, are not primarily aimed at symptoms of anxiety or depression. They are ways to conceptualize disorders that underlie clients' presenting symptoms for which they sought treatment.

The key concepts of Cognitive Appraisal Therapy are Personal Rules of Living, Defence Manoeuvres, Learned Affective States, Phenomenological Developmental History, Security Manoeuvres, Public image (façade) and Self-image. These concepts are discussed below.

Personal Rules of Living (PRLs) are implicit guides for affective and behavioural responses to situations. Like other algorithms that are nonconscious, PRLs may be detected by noting that the person acts 'as if' he/she were guided by the PRL. People are rule-governed creatures who react more-or-less consistently to similar situations.

PRLs function in three ways. First, they may be conscious mediators of emotional experiences. Second, they are components in an interactive system of cognition, affect, and action. Third, they are preferenda – that is, nonconscious stored programmes for value-based responses.

PRLs can be categorized into two groupings. Natural PRLs are descriptive propositions about how events in the natural and social world are ordered. They may be either correlational or cause-and-effect propositions, and they need not be explicitly expressed by the person in order to infer their presence. At times they are expressed as aphorisms, for example, 'hard work breeds success'.

Moral PRLs are prescriptive propositions about correct behaviour and ethical conduct. Typically, they form the basis for evaluating the actions of oneself and other people, as well as for evaluating oneself and other people as entities. An example is 'I must work hard in order to consider myself a good person'.

The two forms of PRLs may interact. A client once discovered a Natural PRL to the effect that 'good people always suffer', and a Moral PRL that 'I must be a good person'. The result was that this client felt worse at times when most people would feel pleasure. Because pleasure was equated with bad (that is, not good), and because the client also had a Natural PRL that 'bad people get punished', rare moments of pleasure were followed by self-generated periods of punitive unhappiness.

Moral PRLs, which form the basis for appraisals of social phenomena, are involved in the affective process. They function as mediators of certain so-called moral emotions. Sommers presents data which show a relationship between people's emotional range and cognitive complexity, suggesting that 'the more structured the value system, the more emotions the person is likely to experience. Thinking through a moral outlook might well be an essential part of the evaluations that activate emotions' (1981: 559). Such emotions as anger, depression, shame, guilt, remorse and jealousy clearly implicate the self and one's value system.

The person acquires moral rules and these play a part in the processing of information that yields an affective experience. It is not necessary at this point to speculate whether the appraisal based on Moral PRLs occurs prior to extensive cognitive processing or later. It is plausible that either alternative may operate some of the time, depending on how automatic the processing has become.

Defence manoeuvres (DMs) are activated in situations where the person might experience one or more negative affective states, and when the person has a nonconscious information-processing routine for avoiding those affective states that relevant aspects of the situation activate. Defensive avoidance follows certain nonconscious rules which serve to protect the person from experiencing negative feelings. Due to their protective function, defence manoeuvres aid in the person's adaptation to the environment, but not without cost. Actions are seldom purely adaptive or maladaptive; rather, they bring mixed results, and the benefits to the person must be compared with the costs in order to properly evaluate the success of a manoeuvre. When costs exceed benefits, for example, by significantly interfering with the pursuit or attainment of one's personal and social goals, the pattern may be deemed neurotic and a fair target for therapeutic attention.

The *Learned Affective State* (LAS) refers to learned affective experiences that are not mediated by any obvious PRLs. The learning most likely occurs vicariously, as the child uncritically absorbs a large repertoire of customs from parents and other socializing agents. It is useful in this regard to consider the family as a subculture with its own distinctive patterns of knowing, acting and emoting. Just as the child imitates the parental model of acting and thinking, so he/she imitates parental emoting. The imitation of emoting, like the imitation of values and patterns of acting, is acquired mindlessly, and is reinforced within the family subculture.

The LAS, then, is a nonconscious algorithm that determines certain affective responses independently of any conscious processing. Lewicki (1986) cites evidence to support the claim that one is not only unaware of the relevent algorithm activated in a certain situation, but one may even lack awareness of the features of the situation that activate the algorithm. Truly, this is a situation where the environment controls the emotional process without the person's awareness of either the relevant stimuli or the rules for processing the information. The person can correctly say 'you made me angry', or 'that event makes me anxious', for he/she may attend to irrelevant features of the situation rather than the effective stimulus, and be unaware of the evaluative cognitions involved in the emotional episode.

In order to discover a client's LASs, it is necessary to explore his/her past life, particularly the early developmental years. The *Phenomenological Developmental History* (PDH) is the individual's recollection of his/her past life. It is a biased historical and cultural anthropological reconstruction of one's personal story, with emphasis on causal inferences about the effect of certain events on one's development. Further, the PDH is a means to understanding the origins of emotional reactions. For example, a woman reported that she remains frightened of spiders even though she taught biology, fears no insects, and admires the role of spiders in the ecosystem. She recalls that her mother was similarly afraid of spiders and would become panicked when around spiders or objects that might be taken for spiders.

Affect as Motivation

People, on the whole, prefer positive affective states to negative ones. Isen reviews research findings which show that

> people who feel good tend to have positive material more accessible in memory, tend to be more optimistic, tend to judge things to be a little better than usually, and tend to act accordingly.... They are also likely to behave in ways that will help to maintain their positive feeling states. They go about solving problems differently from those not in a positive affective state, using simplifying strategies. (1984: 197)

On the other hand, negative affect does not have the exact opposite effects of positive affect. The influence of negative states is more difficult to predict than that of positive states, and the 'interpretation of the asymmetry between positive and negative affect is that these states may actually be different' (Isen, 1984: 202), and not opposite ends of a single continuum.

At times people tend to prefer negative affective states. Examples of the voluntary seeking of negative affective experiences at cultural and sporting events abound. Some common-sense illustrations that support this proposition include feeling frightened at a horror movie, experiencing vicarious aggressive feelings at a boxing match, feeling anxiety while watching dangerous acts at a circus, and feeling saddened at the tragic death of an operatic hero. Such voluntary quests are based on conscious decisions to re-experience certain affective states which, however negative they might be, are deemed desirable by the individual. Clinical observation indicates that a similar decision-making process operates in a nonconscious fashion and involves the individual not as a spectator but as a participant.

Individuals are motivated to re-experience certain emotional states learned in childhood which, for them, are 'natural'. These are LASs that bring a sense of familiarity and security when they are re-experienced. To understand the motive to re-experience *positive* LASs, one need only apply the hedonistic pleasure–pain principle. However, it is not so easy to understand the motive to re-experience *negative* LASs, since it seems contrary to the pleasure–pain principle. One answer is to view the behaviour as a manoeuvre directed at obtaining feelings of security rather than experiences of pleasure (or pain decrement). Such behaviours are referred to in this chapter as *security manoeuvres* (SMs).

It is postulated that security derives from the experiencing of familiar feeling states. For most people most of the time, these are positive LASs. However, for most people some of the time, and for some people most of the time, security derives from negative feeling states. Preference for any feeling state is learned through repeated exposure (Lewicki, 1986), or as Rachman put it, 'familiarity breeds comfort' (1981: 282).

Feelings of security derived from negative experiences are culturally non-normative, and are pathological. The child may nonconsciously adopt patterns that are adaptive to the non-normative parental situation, but these become maladaptive in later life because the family is not representative of the culture of the larger society. The person, then, is able to adapt to the non-normative family interaction patterns, but is not equipped to function with other people, except perhaps those who are like his/her early family members. To illustrate, the child who grows up with parents who habitually shout at him feels angry but helpless much of the time, and finds security in the feelings generated by the culturally non-normative family practice of shouting. As an adult that person will seek situations to get shouted at, and feel angry, helpless, but strangely secure from an experience the person's conscious mind says should be avoided. Carson (1969) discussed Harry Stack Sullivan's theories, which contain a very similar idea, the idea that people interact in ways that 'pull' predictable responses from others and produce certain familiar feelings in the actor.

The ascendance of negatively-oriented SMs occurs when the individual's self-image is consistent with the negative LASs. As in the previous example, the person behaves as if he/she has a self-image as a person who constantly makes mistakes, which incur other people's anger: 'I am not likeable and I am hard to get along with'. SMs that result in negative LASs are both symptoms of disturbance as well as impediments to therapeutic progress.

SMs encompass a good deal more than merely interpreting events in a negative fashion. Cognitive psychotherapy, thus far in its history, has mainly dealt with negative interpretations of events, especially negative cognitions about the self, the world and the future (the cognitive triad of depressive cognitions: see Beck, 1976). PRLs, both natural and moral, are a means of understanding the interpretative processing that takes place in negative affect (as well as in positive affect, although this point seldom receives much attention, probably due to negative affect being the 'exception' to typical experience). PRLs, irrational beliefs, automatic thoughts, and similar cognitive concepts are intervening variables in emotion (Golden and Dryden, 1986).

SMs include actions that construct reality in such a way that the results can be easily regarded as negative and require little special interpretation to produce negative affect. More simply stated, the person behaves in ways that are very likely to bring negative consequences from his/her environment.

A clinical example may amplify this point: a man had his wallet stolen from his raincoat pocket while walking the streets of a bad neighbourhood. He reported feeling 'angry, victimized', and heaped recriminations upon himself for his carelessness and stupidity in carrying his wallet in such an easily accessible and inappropriate place as a raincoat pocket. A few days later, the replacement wallet he had purchased was stolen under exactly the same circumstances, and he reported experiencing the same negative feelings and self-derogatory thoughts.

Another example illustrates the interaction between behaviour and perception, SMs that once again lead to negative LASs. A woman visited an optician's shop to order new glasses, and asked for a frame identical to the one she already owned. She was informed that her frame was no longer manufactured but that the same company produced an almost identical model. Without looking at the new model, she ordered the glasses. A week later she was horrified as she tried them on, and immediately concluded that they were unflattering and not at all like her old ones. She spent the weekend berating herself for making an impulsive decision, and left herself no recourse other than buying yet another pair of glasses. On Monday she returned to the shop complaining that they did not fit comfortably in the hope that she would be offered a free replacement; she expected to be unsuccessful in her attempt and anticipated feeling humiliated by her failure. The assistant, however, merely showed the woman that the differences between her old and new glasses were almost imperceptible, and she readily concurred when the two were held side by side. Co-workers who saw the two frames agreed that they were nearly identical. Never once during her weekend of self-condemnation and shame did she make this obvious comparison.

The explanation for the behaviour displayed in these two examples rests on an assumption that nonconscious processes are at work to guide and direct the person's actions. The role of nonconscious mental content in cognitive psychotherapy has never been in doubt (Meichenbaum and Gilmore, 1984), but has been confined for the most part to the claim that thoughts are 'automatic' and, hence, not conscious. Nonconscious mental content has been characterized as mediator of affect and action, and not as motivator of complex action patterns. The notion of a Security Manoeuvre is that the behaviour is nonconsciously motivated and functions to recapture familiar feeling states.

The SM explains what might be baffling from a rational standpoint. Rationally, the person may be seen as a scientist who gathers data to test his/her model of reality, and revises the model upon discovery of disconfirming data. Further, the person rationally acts in his/her best interests, promoting the attainment of consciously held goals and pleasurable or satisfying outcomes. Why, then, would a person ever act in ways that thwart the attaining of consciously desired goals and outcomes? The hedonistic explanation is that other pleasurable (or pain-avoiding) goals conflict with the consciously desired goals. For example, one would avoid anxiety-arousing situations even though they might lead to a desirable outcome, as in the instance of a man's avoiding social contacts with women even though his consciously held goal is to have a romantic or marital relationship.

If one assumes that the avoidance of women is not a DM to reduce anxiety, but an SM to experience LASs associated with deprivation, a different hypothesis is permitted, and a different course of treatment required. The man can be said not to fear the humiliation of rejection and failure so much as to fear the shame of undeserved acceptance and success. To make this interpretation it is necessary to know about the person's self-image and his/her Phenomenological Developmental History. The PDH is particularly important in that it reveals any patterns of recurring negative feelings in the person's life that match those recalled as predominant during childhood.

In this example, a conflict exists between explicit goals of enjoyment and fulfilment, and implicit security goals of re-experiencing familiar negative feelings. The incongruence between the explicit and implicit goals is pathologic. A person may seek treatment for dysfunctional aspects of his/her affect and action patterns without realizing that those very patterns serve to satisfy tacit needs. The therapist who does not realize this will fruitlessly treat the person.

The person also and at the same time acts in ways that tend to bring reactions from others that confirm his/her self-image. Far from being an objective scientist who neutrally seeks data to test an hypothesis – in this case, an hypothesis about oneself – the person is a biased stage manager who tacitly arranges events to happen in ways that confirm the hypothesis. The changing of self-hypotheses is not an easy matter, and the person acts as if he/she wished not to be confused with the facts, his/her mind is already made up. The SM not only results in the re-experiencing of familiar feelings, but in addition insures that long-held beliefs and images about oneself will not be threatened by very much reality.

The self-image is not necessarily accurate, and in disturbed persons who seek treatment it is virtually never accurate. However, the self-image is usually consistent with past experience. It is consistent with images developed during childhood that the person adopted from the parental images of him/her, or with the image he/she developed as a result of interaction with the parents. The two are not always the same. The explicit parental message might be 'you are a good and competent child', but the parents then behave toward the child as if he/she were bad and incompetent. A woman recalled that her parents verbally praised her as a child and continued to do so as an adult. However, they made all major decisions for her through her college years, and later she would call on them whenever faced with any but the most trivial problem. She confessed to being baffled by her continued dependence on people she consciously thinks of as less capable than herself, and baffled that her own decisions 'never seem to work out very well'.

Much of the foregoing exposition can be summarized by the following scheme. At the core of our understanding is the self-image. It is not the same as an objective description of the person, and is certainly narrower and more selective than the sum total of objective facts about the person. The self-image involves a great amount of self-deception, usually negative self-deception. The negatively evaluated aspects of the self-image are a source of shame, and become very salient features of the self, often to the exclusion of other features, and may even be generalized as the 'real me'.

The negatively evaluated aspects of the self-image that are the reasons for shame must be kept secret if one has PRLs that require him/her to attain certain levels of goodness. The keeping of the secrets may involve elaborate DMs that handle the anxiety and other negative affect associated with the shame. The shameful secrets must be kept away from other people, and in extreme circumstances from oneself. People perfect and operate behind public images or façades which seek to fool the public, who might possibly see them as competent and confident, and have no idea of the deep levels of negative feeling that underlie these performances.

The particular DMs the person acquires depends on how successfully they are received by other people. The reinforcing consequences of social approval determine the kind of public image the person will project. Indeed, the person may have more than one public image inasmuch as he/she may have more than one public to please and to deceive. His/her actions, emotional expressions, and social interactions will not be 'authentic', because they are based on the public image rather than one's true thoughts and feelings. They are reinforced by social acceptance and lack of criticism, that is, they do not stimulate feelings of shame.

If the self-image includes ideas that oneself is not worthy of acceptance or success, and if shame is an old familiar feeling, one will engage in SMs that, as one client recently said, 'snatch defeat from the jaws of victory'. The person acts as if he/she were seeking negative feelings by failing again and again.

To illustrate: a man recalled during therapy that he had been ignored in early childhood in favour of a younger brother whose birth defect was the focus of parental concern. He felt rejected and resentful, and thought, as children may do, that he was somehow the cause of the lack of parental attention. He was sent to boarding school where, he recalled, he was continually criticized. (Since the PDH is his own account of history, it is not possible to say whether he received worse treatment than others nor is it necessary to confirm the truth of his story; it is a phenomenological account.)

Quite by accident, he discovered that he was good at dangerous sports, particularly mountain climbing. His parents labelled him 'fearless Fred', a name he felt he had to live up to by attempting more and more daring feats in order to win their approval. In fact, he began to experience increasing amounts of fear, but felt very ashamed of having these feelings and therefore consciously concealed them. One day while climbing, he witnessed another climber fall and injure himself badly but far from fatally. He immediately decided never to climb again. He tried to keep both his fear and his decision secret from his parents by pretending first to be injured and later to be too busy to engage in climbing. His parents soon discovered his secrets and years later continued to refer to 'the day you lost your nerve'. He felt miserable, owing to his disappointing them.

In therapy he realized that his decision was an SM which served to confirm his self-image as too fearful to achieve or enjoy lasting success, and which served to reawaken feelings of worthlessness and shame. More importantly, he came to realize that his feelings of shame resulted from severe self-criticism for having 'normal' thoughts and emotions. He came to accept the fact that it is normal to feel fear when in dangerous situations. As his shame eroded and his self-acceptance increased, the need to engage in defence manoeuvres and security manoeuvres likewise decreased.

He further revealed during therapy that he had assumed other defensive poses for other audiences. For his schoolmates, he had appeared witty and charming until a few weeks before he was to leave, when he suddenly reversed himself and began acting boorishly. At university, he was very scholarly, and so unlike his previous poses that 'old acquaintances hardly recognized me'. He embarked on his career with relish, only to find that he resigned from several jobs just at the point of receiving a major promotion. This pattern, as recounted in the PDH, led the therapist to hypothesize about the self-image, public image, SMs, DMs, and PRLs discussed above. However, it is the fact that the client confirmed the therapist's hypotheses, and could use them himself to enhance self-understanding, that established their utility in the therapist's mind.

Conclusions

The views outlined in this chapter hold that certain forms of pathological behaviour are due to the motivation to re-experience certain affective states that have attained importance in one's past development. The theory presented here does not assume a single, fundamental emotion as the primary motivational force. It is neither an anxiety-reduction model of (disturbed) behaviour nor an arousal-of-affect model. Indeed, this model assumes that, under certain circumstances, persons seek to increase anxiety rather than reduce it. Further, the seeking of negative affective states goes beyond anxiety to include other affective states as well.

In order to have emotional experiences, the person may interact with others in such a way as to stimulate affect-provoking actions. For example, a man habitually acted on his consciously held (though not consciously adopted) PRL that 'if I want something I should get it; the world owes it to me'. Not infrequently his actions would get him into interpersonal conflict as others rejected his claim and saw no reason to indulge him as a spoilt child. He used such rejections as grounds for becoming extremely angry with people, and on more than one occasion got into fistfights with them. His spoilt child façade protected his secret shame and worthlessness, and when it resulted in anger and fistfights he re-experienced the predominant feeling he had experienced as a child. Since he basically regarded himself as unworthy, neither getting his own way nor fighting his frustrators brought lasting conscious satisfaction, but did succeed in confirming his self-image and producing negative but familiar feelings associated with it.

The experiencing of affect is a central feature of such approaches as psychoanalysis and gestalt therapy, approaches that are not ordinarily thought of in connection with cognitive psychotherapy. Since much of rationalistic cognitive psychotherapy has been concerned with controlling and/or eliminating negative emotion (McMullin, 1986), there has been little place for the re-experiencing of such feelings or for stimulating affective experiences within therapy sessions.

The viewpoint of this chapter is that affect is not a psychological state to be controlled by cognitive and behavioural means. (There are exceptions to such a generalization. Anger that disrupts interpersonal relations, depression that renders the person useless, and anxiety that immobilizes immediately come to mind.) Rather, the viewpoint of this chapter is that affect must be re-experienced for therapeutic purposes. These purposes are not the same as those identified in dynamic or expressive forms of therapy. The re-experiencing is not intended to produce therapeutic results, but to provide keys for understanding of the person and for self-understanding.

The processes involved in affective experience are not clearly known, but most of the sources cited in this chapter (for example, Isen, 1984; Lewicki, 1986; Bargh, 1984) agree that cognition, affect, and behaviour are interdependent factors or are different aspects of the same process. Cognition does not linearly produce affect, nor is cognition (in the sense of conscious cognition) necessarily primary in a cognition–affect sequence (Lazarus and Folkman, 1984). Indeed, the appraisal may occur early in the process – that is, during the perceptual stage of the process (Greenberg and Safran, 1984). It is also plausible that appraisal may occur at some later point (Isen, 1984; Lazarus, 1984), and probably does at times.

There is ample evidence that affect influences cognition, so that how one thinks (for example, negatively) may be influenced by mood, rather than vice versa. The best description of the process is 'reciprocal': cognition, mood, and action stand in reciprocal relationship. If the reciprocal label applies, then it is necessary to allow affect equal standing with cognition and behaviour.

Just as cognition had to win a place alongside the (at the time) more respectable word 'behaviour', so affect now strives for co-equal status. Such states will not be won by merely adding the word affect to the other two in a hyphenated string that sounds like an American legal firm: cognitive-behavioural-affective psychological therapy. Equality will be achieved by giving affect a central place in the cognitively oriented psychotherapies. Extensive justification for this practice is discussed by Greenberg and Safran (1987), who maintain that emotion is tied into nonconscious processes.

Although nonconscious processes, like affect, have been an important part of psychotherapy since its inception (Kihlstrom, 1984), it seems necessary to re-introduce it to the post-behavioural psychological generation. If it were only meant in a Freudian sense, the term 'nonconscious' would be too narrow and theory-bound (Wessler, 1986). But it has not only a broader meaning but a growing body of research to support claims made on its behalf. As mentioned previously, nonconscious processes have always had a role in cognitive psychotherapy (Ellis, 1962; Beck, 1976), one that behaviourally oriented therapy now includes (Mahoney, 1980; Meichenbaum and Gilmore, 1984). With the current growing emphasis on eclecticism in psychotherapy (Goldfried and Newman, 1986), more rather than less discussion of the role of nonconscious processes can be expected. In this chapter, nonconscious processes were discussed both as motivation and as cognitions of which one is not aware. Thus, Cognitive Appraisal Therapy, an affective version of cognitive psychotherapy, moves closer to more traditional psychodynamic accounts of people and their pathology. If psychoanalysis did not exist, one would have to invent it.

Note

Thanks to Sheenah Hankin-Wessler for suggesting the quotation from T. S. Eliot, *Four Quartets*, 'Burnt Norton, I' and for her contributions to this chapter. The concepts presented as Cognitive Appraisal Therapy were jointly developed.

References

Bara, B. G. (1984) Modification of knowledge and memory processes. In M. Reda and M. J. Mahoney (eds), *Cognitive psychotherapies: recent developments in theory, research, and practice*. Cambridge, Mass.: Ballinger.

Bargh, J. A. (1984) Automatic and conscious processing of social information. In R. S. Wyer, Jr. and T. K. Srull, (eds) *Handbook of social cognition. Vol. 3*. Hillsdale, NJ: Lawrence Erlbaum.

Beck, A. T. (1976) *Cognitive therapy and the emotional disorders*. New York: International Universities Press.

Beck, A. T. and Emery, G. (1985) *Anxiety disorders and phobias: a cognitive perspective*. New York: Basic Books.

Bower, G. H. (1981) Mood and memory. *American Psychologist*, 36: 129–48.

Carson, R. C. (1969) *Interaction concepts of personality*. Chicago: Aldine.

Dryden, W. and Ellis, A. (1986) Rational-emotive therapy (RET). In W. Dryden and W. L. Golden (eds), *Cognitive-behavioural approaches to psychotherapy*. London: Harper & Row.

Ellis, A. (1962) *Reason and emotion in psychotherapy*. New York: Lyle Stuart.

Försterling, F. (1985) Attributional retraining: a review. *Psychological Bulletin*, 98: 495–512.

Försterling, F. (1986) Attributional conceptions in clinical psychology. *American Psychologist*, 41: 275–85.

Golden, W. L. and Dryden, W. (1986) Cognitive-behavioural therapies: commonalities, divergences and future development. In W. Dryden and W. L. Golden (eds), *Cognitive-behavioural approaches to psychotherapy*. London: Harper & Row.

Goldfried, M. R. and Newman, C. (1986) Psychotherapy integration: an historical perspective. In J. C. Norcross (ed.), *Handbook of eclectic psychotherapy*. New York: Brunner/Mazel.

Greenberg, L. S. and Safran, J. D. (1984) Integrating affect and cognition: a perspective on the process of therapeutic change. *Cognitive Therapy and Research*, 8: 559–78.

Greenberg, L. S. and Safran, J. D. (1987) *Emotion in psychotherapy: affect, cognition and the process of change*. New York: Guilford.

Guidano, V. F. and Liotti, G. (1983) *Cognitive processes and the emotional disorders*. New York: Guilford Press.

Isen, A. M. (1984) Toward understanding the role of affect in cognition. In R. S. Wyer, Jr. and T. K. Srull, (eds), *Handbook of social cognition. Vol. 3*. Hillsdale, NJ: Lawrence Erlbaum.

Kihlstrom, J. F. (1984) Conscious, subconscious, unconscious: a cognitive perspective. In K. S. Bowers and D. Meichenbaum (eds), *The unconscious reconsidered*. New York: Wiley.

Lazarus, A. A. (1981) *The practice of multimodal therapy*. New York: McGraw-Hill.

Lazarus, R. S. (1984) On the primacy of cognition. *American Psychologist*, 39: 124–9.

Lazarus, R. S. and Folkman, S. (1984) *Stress, appraisal, and coping*. New York: Springer.

Lewicki, P. (1986) *Nonconscious social information processing*. Orlando, Florida: Academic Press.

Liotti, G. (1986) Structural cognitive therapy. In W. Dryden and W. L. Golden (eds), *Cognitive-behavioural approaches to psychotherapy*. London: Harper & Row.

McMullin, R. E. (1986) *Handbook of cognitive therapy techniques*. New York: Norton.

Mahoney, M. J. (1977) Reflections on the cognitive-learning trend in psychotherapy. *American Psychologist*, 32: 5–13.

Mahoney, M. J. (1980) Psychotherapy and the structure of personal revolutions. In M. J. Mahoney (ed.), *Psychotherapy process*. New York: Plenum.

Mandler, G. (1984) *Mind and body: psychology of emotion and stress*. New York: Norton.

Meichenbaum, D. and Gilmore, J. B. (1984) The nature of unconscious processes: a cognitive-behavioral perspective. In K. S. Bowers and D. Meichenbaum (eds), *The unconscious reconsidered*. New York: Wiley.

Plutchik, R. (1985) On emotion: the chicken-and-egg problem revisited. *Motivation and Emotion*, 9: 197–200.

Rachman, S. (1981) The primacy of affect: some theoretical implications. *Behaviour Research and Therapy*, 19: 279–90.

Sommers, S. (1981) Emotionality reconsidered: the role of cognition in emotional responsiveness. *Journal of Personality and Social Psychology*, 41: 553–61.

Wessler, R. L. (1986) Conceptualizing cognitions in the cognitive-behavioural therapies.
In W. Dryden and W. L. Golden (eds), *Cognitive-behavioural approaches to
psychotherapy*. London: Harper & Row.

Wessler, R. L. and Hankin-Wessler, S. W. R. (1986) Cognitive appraisal therapy (CAT).
in W. Dryden and W. L. Golden (eds), *Cognitive-behavioural approaches to
psychotherapy*. London: Harper & Row.

Zajonc, R. B. (1980) Feeling and thinking: preferences need no inferences. *American
Psychologist*, 35: 151–75.

3

Emotional Disorders, Brain State and Psychosocial Evolution

Paul Gilbert

In this chapter the concept of the prepared nature for emotional disorder is examined. Special interest lies with the capacity for cognitions to evoke, amplify and modify innate psychobiological responses. Biological change in turn further directs processing schema. Our central concern, then, is with the relationship between cognition and biology.

In the study of monosymptomatic phobias there is growing recognition that the eliciting stimuli of certain fear responses are prepared for (Seligman, 1971; Rachman, 1978). Spiders, snakes, various animals and heights are examples of such preparedness. Apart from monosymptomatic phobias most other psychiatric disorders represent particular changes in social relating. Cognitive psychotherapy has made undoubted therapeutic advances in recent years but continues to show reluctance to engage the difficult issue of the innate predisposition to construct social, self–other schema: 'I must be loved by everyone'; 'I must be respected by others'. This is surprising since Ellis has frequently suggested that, for most humans, irrationality is biologically based (for example, Ellis and Grieger, 1977). More recently, Beck, Emery and Greenberg (1985) have proposed a comprehensive model of anxiety disorders which suggest that cognitive processes act on and through an innate biological response system. Beck calls this system the 'fight, flight, freeze and faint response system' which involves various components of sympathetic and parasympathetic arousal.

Beck has begun to articulate a theory of cognitive schemata related to enduring personality characteristics (Beck, 1983; Beck, Emery and Greenberg, 1985). These characteristics relate to dominant incentives of (a) social interpersonal security (sociotropic types), and (b) concerns with autonomy. To understand how cognitive processes activate and produce disturbed physiological patterns of activity, arising from social constructions of the self, it is useful to examine some notion of social preparedness. Such preparedness appears to exist in two major domains: (a) the preparedness to form interpersonal attachments, and (b) the preparedness to form constructs of social status, and autonomy.

Cognitive distortion and information-processing strategies are not enough to distinguish between abnormal and normal responses (Hollon and Kriss, 1984). Rather it is the underlying themes of cognitive processes (such as abandonment and defeat) that provide important clues to emotional disorder (Beck, 1983; Beck, Emery and Greenberg, 1985). The literature has also seen growing interest in the relationship between cognition and emotion (Zajonc, 1980, 1984; Tomkins, 1981; Rachman, 1981, 1984; Lazarus, 1982). There is increasing evidence that affective expression (for example, facial and postural) provides important sources of information for inter-personal communication. Information-processing in these domains is multichannel and, in part, innate.

Running parallel to these debates is a concern with state dependent learning (Reus, Weingarter and Post, 1979; Bower, 1981). Briefly stated, state dependent learning argues that the physiological and emotional state of an individual affects the encoding, storage and retrieval of information such that information processed in one state is more easily retrieved when that state is reactivated (see Gilbert, 1984 for a review). What these various arenas of debate suggest is that emotional disorders can be considered against the background of the evolution of social behaviour. Various social repertoires (for example, for responding to abandonment or defeat) are mediated by psychobiological routines which evolved to enable animals to respond to a variety of social scenarios. To parcel up the psyche into distinct sub-units such as feeling, thinking, behaving and biology is to court confusion, for it loses the essential feature that humans evolved to operate as complete systems in physical and social environments.

Zilboorg and Henry (1941) noted that it was just such an exercise that led to many disorders being labelled by their emotional component, so that today we have disorders which are labelled as depressive disorders, anxiety disorders, anger disorders and so on. This in turn has led some to view these disorders as basically centred on the disregulation of mood or emotion, when in fact they could just as easily be described as cognitive or behavioural disorders (Beck, 1976).

Boyle (1985) has pointed out that there is a tendency to regard emotional disorders in unidimensional terms, with the result that many studies have excluded important sources of information. For example, some depressive disorders are as much marked by changes in the patterns of emotional expression and experience (such as anxiety, jealousy, envy, hostility) as they are by a change in any one particular dimension of mood such as dysphoria. This leads to the notion of there being patterns, or states of psychobiological activity which co-ordinate affective, behavioural and possibly cognitive elements. Examples of such states would be the Alpha state (dominant social animal), the Omega state (lowest, subordinate social animal), and the protest state (suffering loss of attachment object). In each state a different pattern of affective, behavioural and cognitive activity manifests in a state congruent way (see Gardner, in press, for a fascinating discussion of eight possible states of this type).

One way around the problem of artificial dissection of mind and body is to consider the emotional disorders as relating to disturbances in evolved (prepared for) psychobiological routines. That is, emotional disorders represent a pattern of change in multiple systems (cognitive, affective and behavioural), rather than changes in any individual sub-unit (such as disturbances in the pleasure areas).

The brain state approach (Gilbert, 1984) has much in common with state dependent learning but suggests the existence of underlying, evolutionarily derived patterns of brain activity which can be elicited by various appraisals of stress. These patterns of brain activity arise from the evolved pattern-generating processes within the brain which operate to guide attention, learning, memory, feeling and behaving in an interactive fashion. Moreover, the patterns of psychobiological activity relevant to most classes of emotional disorder are those that guide social behaviour and communication (Gardner, in press). Hence, concern here is with the interacting psychological and physiological routines which result in a system change: that is, a change in brain state. Such an emphasis is very much holistic.

This chapter examines this proposition and considers neurophysiological, psychological and clinical data in an effort to understand how brain state disturbances represent the amplification and modification of psychobiological routines which exist by virtue of human evolutionary history. Once particular brain states are turned on, then cognitive and behavioural activity, to some degree, become state specific. For example, once an individual has become highly sexually aroused, the individual is more likely to experience intrusive thoughts and fantasies of a sexual nature. These will only change with a change in brain state. Cognitions, therefore, are in part related to physiological state.

Human evolutionary history is marked by two salient social developments. The first is infant–mother nursing and the evolution of attachment, and the second is the evolution of social dominance hierarchies to facilitate competitiveness in group living mammals.

Historical Aspects

Early psychoanalytic theories started out with various conceptualizations of how the brain works. These conceptualizations were the guiding principles behind many psychoanalytical models. They rested on two concerns. The first concern was to underpin psychoanalysis with biological insight. In 1895, Freud, recently transferred from his neurological studies of cocaine, attempted to formulate a model of neurosis derived from neurophysiological mechanisms. This was outlined in the 'Project for Scientific Psychology'. Although Freud never published it, the Project set the framework for much of the theory that was to follow (Ellenberger, 1970). With the passage of time, many analytically oriented therapists did not involve themselves much with Freud's biological views. Gradually, with the development of existential and ego-analytical theories, together with the humanistic traditions that these gave rise to, there was a distancing from concern with biological issues. In distinction to this tradition are theories which derive their axioms from ethological research.

Attachment theory has been one of the few theories of psychopathology derived from a consideration of the nature of social evolution (Bowlby, 1969, 1973, 1980). In so doing, attachment theory focused on the survival advantages of affectional bonds built through the system of mother–infant nursing. Bowlby suggested that the key determining factors controlling the subsequent emotional life of a child related to internal representations of attachment bonds gained from early experience. Later, we will return to the notion of there being an underlying psychobiological routine, which is activated when separation to the attachment bond occurs. This routine evolved in the context of the evolution of mother–child attachment. However, it may be reactivated by disruption in interpersonal relationships in individuals who rely on significant relationships for sources of self-esteem, security and meaning (sociotropic type). This routine unfolds with the development of separation distress and manifests as protest–despair.

In the domain of competitive behaviour, Price (1972) was amongst the first to note how loss of status (defeat) was often followed by a depressive-like response marked by withdrawal and a loss of reactivity. Gardner (1982) theorized how the mechanisms which evolved for the pursuit of, and loss of, status could underlie bipolar affective illness. Gilbert (in press) has suggested that status related mechanisms are especially prone to activation by autonomous and Type A individuals.

Neurophysiological Response Patterns

As pointed out, concern here is with the psychobiology of evolved response routines: that is, the pattern-generating processes of brain–psychosocial-environment interactions. The idea that animals are born with predetermined and fairly organized response patterns for dealing with various environmental events is not new. Certain new born chicks will automatically crouch in the nest if a hawk-like stimulus passes overhead. The degree of prewiring of response routines aligned with a discriminate stimulus detection system allows for fairly complex behavioural routines to be emitted in otherwise quite simple organisms. The phylogenetic transformation of species allows for greater degrees of elaboration of response routines as provided by experience. That is, individuals can modify, change and adapt what is innate by combining it with experience. Memory becomes important because it provides predictive models of the future. Moreover, memory allows for modification of innate processes to be manifest. Some have discussed this in terms of open and closed programmes relating to an underlying biogrammar (Crook, 1980).

Our concern here is to consider the possible existence of underlying psychobiological routines which could be useful in explaining many of the symptoms which appear to manifest in emotional disorders. It seems that in humans there are patterns of response which tend to manifest, in set order, over time and where the outcome (perceived environmental feedback) to an early phase of responding significantly affects the final sequence of response(s). Selye's (e.g. 1979) famous work on stress, has outlined a pattern or series of biological responses which appear to unfold in sequence over time in stressful situations. This sequence unfolds as: alarm reaction, stage of resistance, stage of exhaustion. Selye outlined the various biological changes that take place with each stage. These include various hormonal changes such as cortisol and other hormones of the hypothalamic pituitary adrenal axis. Importantly, exhaustion states can lead to death. Although criticism has been levelled at the general adaption syndrome (GAS) the idea that there are innately available unfolding sequences of psychobiological activity has proved extremely useful. Many models of psychopathology, especially those concerned with the emotional disorders, now either implicitly or explicitly ascribe to the idea of an unfolding set of psychobiological routines, given relevant provocation.

For the purposes of our discussion we shall focus on a biphasic response sequence although further sequences could be introduced. Biphasic simply means two different response patterns emerging over time in response to a particular stress. For example, in studies of grief the response to a loss has an acute stage which can involve various elements of anxiety, anger and envy together with searching, pining and agitated behaviour. This stage is often followed by a more chronic, withdrawn, passive phase (Hofer, 1984). These different stages have different neurophysiological mediators. Hofer (1984) also makes the fascinating argument that relationships can function as biological regulators. Loss of close relationships invokes many biological changes. Attachment theory suggests that loss of a loved object invokes a state called protest, involving proximity seeking and distress calling. Failure to reunite with the lost object or a substitute leads to despair. This involves behavioural withdrawal, passivity, retardation and various psychobiological changes (Bowlby, 1973). Status conflict models also suggest that during conflict there is invigorated (usually aggressive) activity, but following defeat, especially if the defeated animal loses status, a more passive, retarded, other-avoidant, depressed-like phase sets in (Price, 1972; Gardner, 1982 and in press). MacLean (1985) noted in his study of lizards that death may follow, once this second stage is activated. All these models have concern with specific classes of (social) self–other interactions. In distinction to these social theories are more general process theories. These also subscribe to a biphasic and unfolding pattern of responses to various events.

Incentive disengagement theory is a more general rather than a specifically social model. It suggests that loss of *any* valued incentive or goal first invokes invigorated behaviour (which is designed to remove obstacles to the goal). This is replaced by a disengagement phase as the goal is perceived to be unobtainable. In this disengagement phase, behavioural activity falls below baseline and, depending on the importance of the incentive, may involve considerable degrees of behavioural withdrawal and passivity (Klinger, 1975, 1977). In 1975, Seligman outlined his now famous learned helplessness theory of depression. He argued that in response to trauma, there is first an invigorated behaviour pattern which may loosely be called fear, but that fear is replaced by a more passive, withdrawn and depressive-like response pattern when the trauma is perceived to be uncontrollable. Activation theory labels a similar biphasic pattern as 'phasic-tonic activation' (Ursin, 1980).

Each of these theories suggests that the first and second stages show different affective profiles, different behavioural responses (for example, agitated versus retarded), and different cognitive (for example, attributional, attitudinal) processes. What can be suggested is that all of these models outline a kind of go→stop process based on an invigoration–disengagement cycle (Klinger, 1975, 1977). In the first phase there is activation when the animal seeks to obtain the threatened or lost incentive. Cognitive processes are attuned to searching functions (for example, the way to escape/avoid trauma or the way to reunite with the loved object). This is followed by a disengagement phase: that is, a stop phase, when the animal's psychobiological routines close down the activity of the animal. Cognitive processes no longer search for coping options but focus on the consequences of having lost, evaluations of seriousness (globality), and future probabilities of success/failure.

These models differ on specifics and temporal dynamics and developmental processes. Some are specially related to social events; others are more general, treating various traumata as equivalent events. Nevertheless, they share a number of important elements. First, they are basically phasic models. That is, they ascribe to an unfolding and changing pattern of responses. Second, what happens during the second phase of responding (for example, during despair, defeat, disengagement or helplessness) is significantly influenced by the environmental consequences of the first phase of responding. In other words, if the go-phase succeeds in obtaining the threatened, or reinstating the lost, incentive, then the second phase (the stop/disengagement-phase) may be inhibited. However, the repetition of engagement and subsequent success of a go-state, for example a proximity seeking state (searching for or calling to the lost attachment object) may, depending on the context and the number of repetitions, significantly affect the relationship between go and stop states. For example, go states (such as protest responses) can, under some conditions, come to be easily evoked, more severe, longer lasting and more difficult to extinguish (Mineka and Suomi, 1978). Hence, many factors appear to mediate these response routines.

Hofer (1984) points out, however, that simply because one response routine follows another this does not necessarily imply that they cannot be invoked separately or for that matter that the first response routine, for example, protest, must always be evoked as the forerunner to the second response routine, for example, despair. Indeed, I shall argue shortly that the degree to which individuals will activate certain types of go–states is dependent crucially on cognitive factors. For example, to anticipate for a moment, individuals who believe that seeking out others for support is weakness or will provoke humiliation would be unlikely to engage this behavioural possibility under various stresses. Instead they will look to their own efforts to get them out of trouble.

The third element that these models have in common is that the response patterns are all, at least in crude form, evolutionarily based and have fairly specific psychobiological mediators. This can be seen to be important if we take the view that the psychobiological state of the animal will alter the encoding, retrieval and storage of information (Reus, Weingarter and Post, 1979). Moreover, these psychobiological patterns are elicited in one form or another in many different species while their sophistication, modifiability and amplification in part relate to the phylogenetic advancement and type of the species studied.

Fourth, these models share the idea that significantly different biological changes mediate the first and second (and possibly subsequent) response pattern. In other words, at some point during the unfolding and running of the first response routine to loss or stress, the nervous system appears to change course. This change is determined by a multitude of factors which include processes internal to the organism. These include the capacity to biologically handle stress (for example, innate temperament), the cognitive appraisal systems (such as 'I am winning'; 'I am losing'), and the degree to which the environment responds to the animal's efforts to secure the valued incentive. This implies that the nervous system has a blueprint, or plan, as part of a genetically determined routine (a) for dealing with specific environmental events, (b) for evaluating the success of the first strategy, and (c) for invoking a different routine if and when the first strategy is evaluated as unsuccessful. Hence, there is a highly sophisticated system of psychobiological routines which can be activated and played out according to the animal–environmental interactions. The degree of activation of these routines determines the prevailing brain state, which in turn has a significant influence on many cognitive factors including memory and attitudes (Gilbert, 1984).

The Biology of Unfolding Responses and Emotional Disorders

To put a little flesh on these theoretical skeletons, it is useful to go into some details about what the neurophysiological changes are in these different states. Since we cannot here examine each theory we will focus on just three: a general theory (learned helplessness), and two social theories (abandonment and status defeat).

Learned Helplessness
The learned helplessness model suggests that when trauma first occurs there is an invigoration of psychomotor and psychophysiological activity which may be loosely labelled as 'fear'. This response pattern facilitates (in most but not all cases) the animal's ability to control or escape adversity. If the animal's efforts are unsuccessful the response routine may show a radical change to a pattern closely resembling depressive passivity. This should not necessarily imply that the animal now ceases to be anxious since both anxiety and depression probably co-exist. What is important is that the unfolding of the helplessness or depressive-like routine is marked by appetitive changes, reduced aggressiveness, weight loss, psychomotor retardation, major difficulties in active avoidance learning and noradrenaline depletion. Whether or not one believes that helplessness is learned, and there is some controversy over this, clearly, certain symptoms (such as sleep disturbance, weight loss, diurnal variation and so on) are not learned but manifest as part of an invocation of an evolved psychobiological response routine. To put this more crudely, if noradrenaline depletion occurs as a result of the invocation of helplessness, then various vegetative functions which rely on the integrity of the noradrenergic system will be affected. Moreover, it is most unlikely that cognitive functions are not affected by noradrenaline and other biological changes. Hence, switches in attention and encoding strategies are likely to be consequences of changes in brain state (Gilbert, 1984).

Considerable research has examined the underlying neurochemical changes that occur during both the fear stage and the helplessness stage in uncontrollable stress (Anisman, 1978; Anisman and Zacharko, 1982; Weiss et al., 1979). In general terms, when stress is first encountered there is a faster turnover of noradrenaline in various brain areas together with a possible inhibition of monoamine oxidase activity. This psycho-biological routine enables synthesis and availability to match increased release of noradrenaline (Anisman, 1978). The increase in release and availability of noradrenaline probably facilitates and encourages some elements of invigoration, such as searching behaviour and cognitions for the response(s) needed for escaping. Under some conditions however, this invigorated response may be overridden by the switching in of an inhibitory response system, probably involving acetylcholine and 5-hydroxytryptamine (Gilbert, 1984).

Be this as it may, the capacity to increase noradrenaline activity at the synapse is not unlimited over time and eventually various factors such as the availability of tyrosine hydroxylase (an important enzyme in the production of noradrenaline) may decline. Equally, changes at the receptors may occur in response to the increased noradrenergic activity at the synapse. Thus, at some point in the response routine factors of biological significance come into play to alter the balance between go and stop processes: that is, a shift in brain state occurs (Gilbert, 1984 and in press). The most significant cognitive correlate of this shift is that the animal stops exploring active solutions to overcoming trauma.

If stress continues without a successful coping response being apparent, deficits in the transmission of noradrenaline occur. The exact mechanisms responsible for this switch from baseline to hyperfunctioning through to hypofunctioning of noradrenergic neurones is more complex than we need outline here. Moreover, noradrenaline is only one of the many neuro-transmitters involved in these brain state changes. Nevertheless, the idea that stress first engages an invigorated noradrenergic response which is followed by a hypofunctioning noradrenergic response is important. For cognitive psychologists, the questions are far-reaching: 'What kinds of memories, attitudes and styles of information-processing are activated in these different states during the searching mode; what is the person searching for: a reliable other, success, achievement? Does the person expect to fail? Is such a failure perceived as carrying significance to many of life's incentives or just a few?'

This general model of invigoration–disengagement (or go→stop) is probably involved in most emotional disorders. But general process models do not distinguish between social and non-social events. Without this distinction it is impossible to know what an individual will actually do under threat (for example, seek out or avoid others). The next two models examined attempt to provide more specific insights to these issues.

The Separation–Abandonment Model

The models of emotional disorder derived from attachment theory (Bowlby, 1969, 1973) are more specifically social models in that it is specifically interpersonal events which are believed to start the go→stop cycle off. This theory also suggests a biphasic response to loss (Bowlby, 1973; McKinney, 1977; Mineka and Suomi, 1978; Gilbert, 1984). When separation first occurs, the pattern of behaviour is labelled 'protest'. This is marked by increased psychomotor activity and object proximity searching. In other words, the animal seeks and calls to the lost object. After a period of time, however, this gives way to a pattern of activity marked by behavioural withdrawal and passivity. McKinney (1977) and Coe et al. (1985) offer a good discussion of complications and species differences to this pattern. It is far more complex than has been suggested here. Kraemer and McKinney (1979) have shown how a number of factors such as previous learning history and social housing conditions interact with the physiological responses of protest–despair produced with a challenge (via drugs) to monoaminergic pathways. Coe et al. (1985) have demonstrated that social factors (such as being separated from mother but with significant others) have significant effects on the cortisol response to separation. In general, this theory also sees increasing and decreasing alteration in noradrenaline as playing a central role in the switching of protest (go) to despair (stop) states.

Status

In primitive organisms without social hierarchies competitiveness often involves simple contests and guarding behaviour (territory, mates, etc.). The ability to exert a direct effect on the environment is therefore central to competitive competency. With the evolution of social hierarchies, animals come to pay greater attention to the activities and competencies of other group members. This involves various cognitive mechanisms which allow the animal to compare the strength of self in relation to others, and hence evaluate whether a challenge can be coped with or not, what the outcome of defeat or success will be and so on. Control over resources now involves control over potential competitors. In most mammal-like species this is usually acquired by status. In humans status has come to involve considerable levels of complex symbols aimed at signalling competency, talent, skill, knowledge, power, etc. Individuals will work for many years, for example, to obtain qualifications that act as symbolic representations of status, rights to belong to certain groups and claims to material resources.

There is considerable evidence that low status animals behave in very different ways to high status animals (Price, 1972; Crook, 1980; Price, 1982). The acquisition of status seems to operate through similar go→stop (invigoration–disengagement) processes which may loosely be regarded as challenge–withdrawal. During the acquisition and holding of status, animals exhibit characteristic behaviours. These include various increases in approach behaviour to survival-relevant resources (mates, food, territory), preparedness to challenge others with relevant and often aggressive or threatening displays, a more upright posture, preparedness to stare at potential competitors and so on. In general, they exhibit an increased preparedness to meet and respond to challenge. Defeated animals, however, show far fewer approach behaviours, tend to be more timid, respond to challenge with appeasement (grin), submissive postures (gaze avoidance) and increases in various (social) avoidance behaviours. In humans, affect will vary from winners' elation to losers' depression. Consider the comments of world chess champion, Gary Kasparov:

Usually I win. If I win a tournament or match or the world championship there is great celebration. But I do not lose myself in happiness because maybe someone else will go in front of me very soon...If I lose, it is very bad. I can't eat, can't sleep and I must understand why this has happened...but I never blame my coaches or anyone else because I know it is my fault. Maybe I say to myself some bad words. (Kasparov, 1986: 50)

These comments speak for themselves and encapsulate the issues including the vegetative disruption of defeat. At the present time our understanding of the psychobiology of status behaviour is vague. However, go→stop processes are certainly involved. Major falls in blood levels of 5-HT have been found in dominant monkeys removed from their group (Raleigh et al., 1984). Tyrosine hydroxylase in some brain areas may correlate with status position and various catecholamine changes occur in parallel with changes in social position (Weiss et al., 1982). There are also major changes in various stress related and sex hormones following changes in status (Henry and Stephens, 1977; Leshner, 1978; Price, 1982). Helplessness may be a powerful variable in these changes (Seligman, 1975). Defeated animals lose the power to influence others and also their control over various social and survival-relevant resources. MacLean (1985) noted how defeated lizards lost their colours and died shortly thereafter.

All in all, then, like loss of attachment objects, loss of status is behaviourally and physiologically very disruptive. To what extent these biological changes interfere with an individual's capacity to recruit coping cognitions and memories is unknown, but it is obviously the case that these changes in brain state have some profound implications for how therapists approach the suffering of clients. These implications are considered in more detail elsewhere (Gilbert, in press).

The Models Compared

Each of the three models suggests that there is a go→stop *sequence* of responding which is mediated by neurophysiological changes. In fact, this is a rather old idea (Whybrow, 1984), but is important for an understanding of emotional disorders since these neurophysiological changes have important effects on cognitive processes (Gilbert, 1984). There are, however, notable differences between the separation and defeat models, and the learned helplessness model. These concern the pattern of emotional expressions, the types of behaviour and the content of cognition in each phase. For the learned helplessness theory, depressed affect appears only to occur in the second (helplessness) phase, yet this phase is accompanied by many symptoms normally associated with endogenous depression (Depue and Monroe, 1978). This is a limitation of the theory and arises because it does not address social issues. Consequently, the theory cannot deal with data relevant to emotions as important mediators of social communication.

Such a limitation is not evident in the separation or defeat models. During protest, labile mood, which may include episodes of dysphoria, crying, anxiety and anger, may also be present. The protest pattern is designed to both signal distress and facilitate social reunion, and also to facilitate exploration and object seeking. In the learned helplessness model it is only what the animal itself does that makes a difference. However, in the social models certain responses may be emitted, in order to invoke responses from others. It is the responses of others (caring, nurturing, retreating or challenging) which are important for the termination or amplification of distress. The pattern of emotions, viewed in part as social signals, which manifest during the activated or go-state, may be a more useful model for considering neurotic depressions, anxious or aggressive states involving changes in many affective systems.

In this scheme of things, then, the emotional–behavioural dimension of protest involves a social communication where the infant or mother seeks to re-unite and call to the lost object. Hence, dysphoria, far from being related to the more classical depression state, may actually be a positive emotion in the sense that it represents a state of activation or a state of go.

Despair however, is more marked by psychomotor and psychobiological retardation. The animal gives up and stops signalling–communicating. Indeed, slowness of speech and impoverished facial muscle activity are marked in retarded depression. In other words, the stop-state seems to represent the inhibition of a number of affective and behavioural systems. Many patients in serious retarded depression describe the experience as one of inner deadness, emptiness and an incapacity to experience any emotion at all. The loss of positive feelings for persons previously loved can fuel beliefs of self as empty or bad. Hence, there are probably qualitative differences in the experienced pattern of affects dependent on whether the individual is in go- or stop-state.

In 1984, I put forward this sequential model to suggest how patients can show mixed syndromes. This is because individuals may be at different points in their go→stop cycles and because go and stop (Activated and Retarded) states may be mediated by different psychobiological systems. In consequence, it can be suggested that these neurochemical changes mediating go→stop processes may be seen as controlling, overlapping but also potentially independent response routines (Gilbert, 1984). The first routine is a fast developing state to facilitate protest, invigoration, go- or activated states so that the animal is able to mobilize its own resources and attempt to mobilize the (social) environment on its behalf (for example, to elicit care or get others to back down). But a failure to secure these outcomes and/or changes in neurochemical pathways activate a slower-building inhibitory state which is uncovered as the first state wanes. This view has much in common with Solomon's (1980) opponent process model, a model favoured by Mineka and Suomi (1978) to explain protest–despair patterns.

The essentials of this model, then, without going into more neurophysiological detail is simply go → stop: that is, activated–retarded states. But what is essential is to consider how cognitive factors activate go-states or activate stop-states. Moreover, given that neurophysiological parameters mediate these different states, and given the importance of state dependent learning, it may be that as individuals switch between states we will see different styles of encoding and appraising environmental stimuli, different memories coming on line and so on (Gilbert, 1984). This may offer some explanation to Beck's concept of latent schema (Beck, 1967). Latent schemata may be as much activated by neurophysiological cueing as by cognitions. In other words, the neurophysiological changes that mediate the activation of go- or stop-states are likely to shift attentional, encoding and retrieval processes in state specific ways. Cognitive appraisal may determine what is stressful to whom, how and why, but the physiological changes engaged by such appraisals will further alter many cognitive and behavioural processes. Hence, perhaps cognitive schemata do not so much represent enduring structures within the CNS, but rather, are elements of patterns of *psychobiological activity* (see Iran-Nejad and Ortony, 1984 for an interesting discussion of these issues).

By understanding the psychological rules and models of relationships that people carry in their heads, we may come closer to understanding how some psychological styles specifically activate different patterns of brain activity, and how, once these patterns of brain activity are switched on, they will feed in a state dependent learning way the maladaptive schema: that is, a vicious circle is set up. In the next few sections, we will look at this issue and note that some advances have been made in identifying the personal styles which predispose to vulnerability of emotional disorders. These styles are seen to operate through attachment systems and dominance-status systems.

Abandonment Schemata

The psychobiological routine (protest–despair) which is evoked by abandonment, threats and losses arises from the evolution of attachment and affectional systems. Cognitive schemata which are capable of activating this psychobiological routine relate to appraisals that significant others are necessary to achieve important life goals and incentives. There are a number of theorists who believe that dependency on another to achieve incentives predisposes people to certain types of psychopathology. Existential psychotherapist Yalom (1980) refers to this dependent style as the Pursuit of the Ultimate Rescuer. This style is believed to underpin many forms of emotional disorder, not just depression. Ego analytic theorists

(Arieti and Bemporad, 1980) refer to this vulnerability as the pursuit of a Dominant Other. Analytic theorists call this dependency anaclitic and relate it to the oral stage of dependency in the Freudian model (Blatt et al., 1982). Bowlby (1973, 1980) regards these individuals as being highly reliant on others. Gilbert (1984 and in press) has referred to such individuals as predominantly care elicitors. Beck (1983) calls this style the socially dependent or sociotropic style. From a cognitive point of view he has outlined many of the salient characteristics in the cognitive domain. Since Beck outlines these in a highly concise form they are quoted in full here. The socially dependent type is believed to show the following characteristics:

1   'Needs' people for safety, help, gratification.
2   Wants stability of relationship to ensure steady flow of supplies and other interpersonal factors.
3   Depends on relationship to ensure safety and prevent the pain of social isolation (therefore requires stability and predictability).
4   The concerns regarding health and fears of getting lost require an access to a nurturant figure.
5   Rejection is worse than aloneness – particularly if loneliness can be compensated through some access to some nurturant figure. Rejection represents severing of tie to the nurturant figure (abandonment).
6   Needs reassurance continually to make sure that the pipeline is still open and operating ('Do you love me?'; 'Can I call you when I need you?').
7   Cannot take any risks that might lead to alienation and closing down of pipelines (e.g. asserting self with significant others)
8   Rejection by another person leads to loss of confidence in opportunity or ability to get supplies. It also diminishes self-esteem in that the individual sees self as having lost the attributes that will attract people to provide what he feels he needs.
9   Inclined to take out insurance to protect against alienation, isolation, and sickness, etc. (e.g. wide circle of friends, acquaintances, associates who are pledged to come to his assistance).
10   Does not want to take chances because he does not feel that he can cope with unexpected eventualities. (Therefore, avoids 'strange places'; is reluctant to express hostility or simple assertion.)
11   Obtains pleasure from receiving.
(Beck, 1983: 274–5)

As is clear from the term 'socially dependent' these individuals are highly dependent on significant others. In this sense they can be seen as using schemata deeply embedded and encoded within attachment systems. This vulnerability has significant overlaps both for certain types of depression and for certain types of anxiety such as agoraphobia and panic disorder (Beck, Emery and Greenberg, 1985). In general, the motto here is: 'I need others to survive'. The prominent concern is to maintain proximity and reduce interpersonal distance in both emotional and sometimes physical terms. When anxiety is prominent the main concern is to avoid being 'beyond help'.

Consider the client who had gone to see a friend's mother who was dying in a hospice. He found it a very depressing experience and on leaving the hospice could not get it out of his mind. He said he felt that something had snapped inside of him. As he pondered her state he realized that she was now 'beyond help', to use his words; she was going to die. He managed to clear the idea from his mind eventually although he found the image of her lying in the bed dying a troublesome one. Two weeks later, when his wife had gone away for the weekend and he was at home alone, he suddenly became aware of his heart racing. He phoned his doctor immediately because he thought he was going to die. Reconstruction of the event showed that at the point he had his first panic attack he was feeling particularly lonely. Subsequently, he would get panic attacks in situations where he was frightened of being beyond help. For example, while out in his boat fishing one day, he suddenly thought, 'God, if anything happens to me here no-one will ever get to me.' He rowed for the shore as quickly as possible.

In anxiety, these individuals normally have specific fears of abandonment, illness or death and believe that significant others can be used to help, protect, rescue or save. In depression, however, the focus is less on being beyond help but more on a general loss of interpersonal relationships. That is, depression does not necessarily have specific fears associated with it. (Having said this, anxious depressions are very common and hypochondriasis may be a prominent feature of some depressive conditions. In severe depression patients may believe they are going to die and complain of rotting brains or bowels, or believe they have cancer. Hence, both depressive and anxiety concerns can be present.)

Sometimes no actual loss may have occurred but the person usually reports a feeling or evaluation of a widening or a change in an important relationship. Often the loss is symbolic (Beck, 1987).

A typical example here is of the woman who marries and then finds that her husband spends increasingly long hours away from home. As she looks at her life she begins to feel that it is empty and the close affectional bonds she thought she was acquiring through marriage seem to become increasingly stretched. When her husband returns home tired he pays her less and less attention as time goes on. She begins to worry that she has lost her power to attract him and elicit caring, nurturing behaviours from him. This may be followed by dysphoric feelings during the day and episodic tearfulness which she may not fully understand. From a psychobiological and social signalling hypothesis this tearful dysphoria can be regarded as a form of care eliciting, triggered by (a perceived) increase in interpersonal distance (see Hofer, 1984 for a psychobiological view).

Beck, Emery and Greenberg (1985) have outlined the cognitive distinctions between depression and anxiety and suggest that depressive attributions are more global, stable and exclusive. They suggest that the anxious patient does not self-blame. However, in my experience this is a matter of degree since some anxious patients do self-blame for being anxious. Beck, Emery and Greenberg (1985) also suggest that threat, rather than loss, is the hallmark of the anxious, while loss relates more to depressive disturbances. While I agree with this formation a number of cautions are in order.

It is worth remembering two things. First, these kinds of depression usually focus on more global, interpersonal or emotional concerns. It is the loss or threat to a relationship which will activate tearful dysphoric states. If we regard protest as a social signal, then clearly, tearfulness, lability of mood and dysphoria may be regarded as a form of protest. But the depressed patient may not perceive any specific danger. Rather it is a more global, interpersonal threat, distance or loss to attachment bonds. In other words, dysphoric states can manifest to the threat to attachment bonds and not simply to the loss, especially if the person perceives him/herself to have lost control over his/her significant other and may be abandoned, and unloved. Threat is perceived as a widening in the interpersonal relationship. This is described as 'I don't feel my spouse is as close to me as she/he was: I don't think he/she loves me as she/he did.' This means of course, that certain kinds of depression can be regarded as go- or activated states.

Also, tearful dysphoria, pining and loved object seeking may be significantly involved in grief (death of a loved one). Even though a person may say, 'I know rationally that my spouse is dead' they may still be bombarded with fantasies and images of reuniting with the lost person. They may search in various rooms or places, and be unable to part with clothes or other objects because they believe the dead person may somehow return, or it is all a bad dream (see Parkes, 1986 for a fascinating discussion of searching in grief). This may be an example of where biology is more powerful than psychology. I would suggest that it is the biological activation of protest which invokes these images, beliefs and ideas of looking for, and searching. This view is in accord with state dependent learning. The activation of protest states will activate searching behaviour and cognitions. It is as if the activation of these searching functions in cognitive processes has more power than rational evaluation. Hence, when the biology of protest is activated, the individual struggles with what he/she knows to be true but cannot accept. Other affects, such as anger, which relate to protest may also be manifest.

As the protest state wanes, however, the person becomes more able to emotionally 'believe' that the loss has occurred and is irrevocable. Then begins the swing down into a more retarded form of grieving. It is now a matter of theory as to whether we believe that this downswing is produced cognitively or biologically. My own view is that it is a highly interactive system; different sides of the same coin. If the loss is now seen as removing significant components of the incentive structure, in the absence of a supportive social environment the individual may become severely depressed. Horowitz et al. (1980) suggest that grief becomes more depressive when loss of a significant other reinstates old, unresolved negative views of self and role relationships. The negative views remained latent while the relationship prospered. Alternatively, in brain state theory, we would say that the negative views of self were not active in the non-alone (not abandoned) state, but became so with the activation of the psychobiological changes associated with loss and perceived isolation.

In general, socially dependent types develop cognitive schemata that are very attuned to the protest–despair psychobiological patterns. When depressed, they may criticize themselves for lacking socially desirable attributes. Their evaluation of vulnerability focuses heavily on emotional phenomena: for example, needing love, inability to suffer anxiety or pain, the search for meaning in the loved other, fears of not being cared for or nurtured. In fact, these individuals suffer problems in accepting uncontrollability. For example, a patient of mine believed that if she looked like a famous film star then I would love her. She had difficulties in accepting that people were autonomous. She blamed herself for her divorce when, in fact, her husband had frequently had affairs and used alcohol to a significant degree. For some time she persisted in her belief that if she had been different then he would have loved her and been a perfect husband. In cases of grief, individuals may search in themselves for qualities that might have prevented the death. Here again, this searching is often related to difficulties in accepting that death is, in reality, uncontrollable.

To sum up, then, we now understand a little of the biology of go-states which, in the case of the socially dependent type, is normally protest. When these states are activated they will cue searching and explorative cognitive-behavioural patterns. The classical searching behaviours of the recently bereaved are examples of this (Parkes, 1986). This search may also involve looking for attributes of self that will maintain supplies and the individual may engage in various seeking out and attention attracting behaviours. Sometimes it is a specific fear that evokes the searching for others, in which case the problem is normally one of anxiety. On the other hand, sometimes searching involves looking for characteristics of self which, if possessed, would bring about a loving, meaningful relationship. If, as time goes by, the individual becomes progressively more global and more hopeless that a loved object can be obtained then depression may become more severe. Hence, individuals may start off in the early part of their lives with a proneness to manifesting primarily anxious depressions.

With the passage of time their episodes show more retarded types of symptomatology as they see themselves as less attractive or potentially less able.

Defeat Schemata

In contrast to abandonment schemata there exists defeat schemata.[1] The psychobiological routines which underpin defeat schemata evolved out of the context of competing for resources. The dimension here is not one of abandonment concern but of loss of status. In other words, this is the dimension of dominance–submission evaluations. Abandonment fears may become an issue during therapy with patients who use these kinds of schemata if it transpires that achievement was sought to win the love of parents. Normally however, patients with these kinds of problems do not present with abandonment difficulties as their primary problem in the first instance. What is presented is the fear of exclusion, attack, humiliation, rejection or loss of prestige. Here again, the individual is concerned with how he looks in the eyes of others but this is related to his talents and skills for doing, competing and being seen as someone to look up to. These individuals are prone to activate psychobiological routines which relate to dominance-status changes. Cognitive schemata capable of activating this psychobiological routine therefore relate to threats or losses of status.

Again, many authors have noted this type of vulnerability. In family therapy intrafamilial struggles for power are believed to be central concepts responsible for generating neurotic behaviour (Sloman, 1981). At the individual level, Yalom (1980), an existentialist psychotherapist, labels those concerned with status and power as pursuing specialness. Ego analytic therapists regard this kind of vulnerability as relating to dominant goals: that is, the individual regulates his or her self-esteem through achievement (Arieti and Bemporad, 1980). In a slightly different context, Bowlby (1973, 1980) argues that these people are compulsively self-reliant. Gilbert (1984) suggests that these individuals evaluate themselves according to what they can do, and in relationships to what they are able to give to others. Their concern is to be of value to others and to have something to offer them. Beck (1983) calls this kind of style the autonomous style. He argues that the following characteristics identify the autonomous style in the predepressive stage. These are people that have the following characteristics:

1   Has own set of internalized standards, goals, criteria for achievement and highly specific set of self-rewards or acceptable rewards from others. The standards and goals are different from and often higher than the conventionally accepted norms. This person may thus judge himself more stringently than he does other people.

2   Is less susceptible to external feedback than the socially dependent person; thus is less influenced by praise or criticism.
3   Is less sensitive to other people's needs and wishes (although he may *believe* that he is aware of other people's feelings and cares about them). Does not rate well in accurate empathy.
4   Is action oriented; emphasizes DOING rather than THINKING.
5   Is less reflective than the dependent type.
6   Is focused on getting positive results and places less weight on possible negative consequences of action.
7   Tends to be direct, decisive and positive, often dogmatic and authoritarian.
8   When not depressed has high level of self-confidence and self-esteem.
9   Wants freedom to initiate action, dislikes being held back, blocked or deterred from doing what he wants to do.
10 Strongly prefers that his options are open rather than making permanent commitment.
11 Adapts better than socially dependent person to situations or relationships in which there is a good deal of variability and/or ambiguity.
12 Dislikes externally imposed directives, deadlines, demands or pressures.
13 Most common 'cause' of rupture of interpersonal relations is a belief that he or she is trapped or forced to do something against his or her will.
14 Dislikes asking for help.
15 Self-esteem based on attributes that facilitate independence, action and versatility.
16 Unless has a serious physical illness is less concerned than average about physical illness or death.
17 Judges own worth by success in fulfilling specific role expectations (student, employer, employee, parent, child).
18 Obtains pleasure from 'doing' and reaching goals.
(Beck, 1983: 273–4)

Ethological research has suggested that in status fights serious fighting is rare. Rather contestants engage in bluff and counter-bluff using social (visual–auditory) displays to signal threat and status. Furthermore, the loser in such a contest may often run away, but if this is not possible he or she has a repertoire of responses to signal submission. This repertoire is usually exhibited through body postures and is not learned but innate. These signals are innately coded and context triggered. To what extent then do cognitive schemata parallel these evolutionary processes? It would seem that cognitive processes do indeed track these underlying biological predispositions fairly closely. Individuals whose brain states are primarily set in the autonomous-self mode are most concerned with humiliation, loss of status, respect and prestige. Beck, Emery and Greenberg (1985) referred to this as evaluation anxiety. Attentional mechanisms are, as it were, on the look out for these possibilities. These individuals tend to see others as evaluators (competitors who can add to or take away from status). As in the context of most social competition, (which involves significant degrees of 'bluff'), these individuals can become concerned and preoccupied with being a fake or being discovered as less competent than they are attempting to display to others. To counter this, they go all out to prove their value, either to others, or to prove their autonomy and superiority over others.

Like protest–despair, under challenge or threat to the autonomous style a go- or activated searching state is invoked. What is searched for is rather different from the socially dependent type who seeks out significant others. Autonomous individuals will not distress call or seek out significant others for emotional support, since they believe that the exhibition of emotion could be seen as a weakness inviting attack. Hence, they look to improve their own performance. Anxiety in these states is about not being good enough, falling short of standards, and concerns with showing submissive behaviour. Beliefs like 'I have to succeed; I have to win' become amplified. Perfectionistic obsessionalism may also be activated. Here, the aim is to make performances so competent that the individual is always 'beyond attack', 'beyond rebuke'. In the work situation, these individuals often have unrealistic dreads of making an error and can respond to minor criticisms with withdrawal or considerable rage.

Invigoration or go-states may bring on line a more competitive, aggressive style. Here, the individual is prone to be overly rigid and use dominant or submissive evaluative schemata in many interpersonal domains. In an ambiguous world where interpersonal events can be evaluated in various ways the autonomous individual tends to use competitive schemata. This would be marked by the classical type A behaviour which involves (a) ambitiousness, (b) setting excessively high standards, (c) hard driving behaviour, (d) competitiveness, (e) aggressiveness, (f) time urgency, (g) impatience and irritability, and (h) speech and motor behaviours mostly of an activated form (Price, 1982). Price offers a very informative and interesting cognitive and social learning theory of Type A behaviours.

This invigorated competitiveness can cut across many situations: for example, driving a car can be pursued as a competitive exercise. Spouses, work colleagues and/or work subordinates of these individuals when they are in these states can have a hard time of it. The autonomous person in a go-state may be prone to look for weakness in others and may be cynical, sarcastic or outright other-downing. This tends to accentuate marital problems where the individual may retreat into becoming more autonomous due to the difficulties in interpersonal relationships that this type of behaviour produces. Hence, a vicious circle is set up. These individuals may also show considerable aggression towards themselves (Gilbert, 1984 and in press).

If the individual evaluates that he has failed to reach standards, and that major components of his life may be viewed as failure, he will be inclined to access submissive defeat processes. Cognitive processes are then focused on the lack of competency and the perception of self as a failure. Here again, ethological research suggests some interesting observations for cognitive psychotherapists. When an animal loses status following contest, there is a hypoactive, depressive-like phase that manifests (Price, 1972). This phase stops the animal from recuperating and rechallenging. The capacity for continual rechallenge would lead to continued conflict and lack of social cohesion and stability. The shift to a more retarded state may be a biologically triggered response in the context of social defeat, designed to facilitate social cohesion. It is possible, therefore, that the shift to a negative cognitive style, which involves accessing memories and interpretations of defeat in these individuals when depressed, may relate to the activation of this underlying psychobiological process. This psycho-biological routine which involves inhibiting the animal from rechallenging may be prominent when the individual is depressed.

Comparison and Summary

To sum up then, socially dependent types tend to activate searching and inhibitory functions arising from the evolution of attachment systems. The psychobiology of these routines relates primarily to object-attachment loss. The socially dependent respond to threat by invigorated searching aimed at eliciting help from a significant other or others. There is a prominent concern in their affective (social signalling), cognitive (needs for love, protection and help) and behaviour (proximity seeking) systems – all designed to elicit caring agents or closing interpersonal distance at either physical or emotional levels. In anxiety conditions the concern is to avoid being 'beyond help'. The main concern when depressed is the loss or lack of attributes that would be socially desirable to others. Individuals may have some illusion of control, believing that love/help would be guaranteed if they had these attributes.

Autonomous types, however, do not trust others but see them as evaluators. They activate psychobiological systems which evolved in the context of competition for resources (for example, challenge/withdrawal and dominance/submission systems). These biological processes are usually operated by schemata concerned with evaluative issues such as the acquisition of status, respect and prestige. Autonomous types respond to threat and challenge with invigorated searching behaviour. In anxiety the concern is with the possibility of defeat, and the perception that others are evaluators and competitors who can add things (often of a symbolic nature) or take them away. They search and continually check for possibilities of attack or humiliation. This leads to perfectionistic obsessionalism. Here, the concern is to be beyond attack and beyond rebuke. Aggressive Type A behaviours may also be a hallmark of these activated states. In depression, a hypofunctioning state seems to be switched on which focuses the individual on his or her lack of competency, negative expectations about the future which may have evolved to inhibit continual rechallenging. The cognitive processes here are particularly attuned to having been defeated and having been found to be incompetent. This, of course, may not actually be true but it is how the individual sees it.

The cognitive model may be considerably strengthened by a greater understanding of how cognitive processes tap into, modify, yet are also amplified by, the activation of underlying psychobiological routines. State dependent learning has focused principally on mood states (Reus et al., 1979; Bower, 1981). As mentioned at the beginning of this chapter, however, the selection of mood as an independent variable is questionable. The view proposed here goes considerably beyond that of state dependent learning and suggests that brain states are, in part, related to the operation of particular seeking (go, invigoration) and inhibitory (stop, disengagement) processes which are available as innately organized psychobiological routines. These psychobiological routines were specifically evolved to deal with certain classes of social behaviour and interactional events. Gardner (in press) has further proposed that evolution is principally concerned with linking and spacing functions between species members. He prefers to think of psychopathological states primarily in terms of the activation of underlying communicative processes. Gardner's fascinating work may offer a significant contribution to those interested in the psychobiology of cognitive theory.

Personal Thoughts on Psychotherapy

1   In our technological age psychotherapists are becoming more pre-occupied with techniques, rather than with theory and deeper understanding of the disorders of human nature. However, if one has no underlying theory then symptoms tend to be treated as individual 'bits' of the person for which the therapist searches in his bag of tricks to confront. This can be useful but is also limited. The arbitrary matching of symptoms to techniques, started by the behaviourists, was a response to a quite reasonable desire to develop exposure procedures for behaviour theory. But the refusal to believe that symptoms were anything more than what they appeared and were an inconvenience to be done away with is a limited view. In cognitive psychotherapy there is much greater concern with understanding a person's base schemata. Base schemata are like the trunk of a tree which will feed up many branches that affect many aspects of the person's life. Getting caught up in the branches and attempting to change them one by one may be less effective than working with the trunk itself. In brain state theory, these schemata can be considered as particular patterns of psychobiological activity that have been amplified by experience.

2 My general view of psychotherapeutic procedures is a developmental one. Recently, Kegan (1982) has offered an interesting perspective on a cognitive developmental approach to psychotherapy. Hence, in psychotherapy the question is: what does this person need to develop? Cognitive psychotherapy has become aware of the fact that disputing negative cognitions may be less effective than enhancing positive ones. So, developmental processes seem important. The socially dependent person seems to have a developmental difficulty in competing and becoming autonomous. Therefore helping these individuals learn to be alone, to develop assertiveness and a sense of autonomy can be very productive. It can be suggested that these processes involve the individual becoming more confident and at home with alternative psychobiological patterns. Sometimes, people who have been divorced will in retrospect report that the time they spent alone was at first very painful but subsequently immensely strengthening. This takes us to a common therapist dilemma (Dryden, 1985). When do therapists battle to save a marriage and when do they help to end it? Therapists with very religious views may relate rather differently to clients than those who follow strictly cognitive and rational-emotive therapy philosophies.

In the autonomous individual the developmental arrests lie in other directions. Here, the need is to facilitate the recognition that nobody is perfect: 'If I get stuck I can go and get help.' Teaching these individuals that they do not always 'have to be strong and confident', that they can elicit care without distracting from competency in different arenas of life, can be a very productive procedure. Homework assignments for these individuals tend to be more concerned with the expression and sharing of positive feelings in marriages (Powell and Friedman, 1986). A recent patient was encouraged to ask work colleagues whom he respected for help when he got stuck on particular projects. He found this difficult at first, believing he should know all the answers, but subsequently he found it quite rewarding to work as part of a team. The individual whose competitiveness has been developed from a fear of being unloved can be allowed to engage these central concerns in therapy.

3 I have found that a number of autonomous depressed patients prefer to be left alone for a good part of the time. This is a tricky area, especially if therapist and spouse feel impelled to 'do something'. Autonomous individuals can actually become more stressed by people 'fussing' over them and some discussion with other family members to respect interpersonal boundaries and the nature of the autonomous conflicts is useful. One lady felt that being cared for was 'humiliating' and increased urges to run away. Another patient wanted to hide in his room alone. Too much 'caring' attention can therefore be stressful. Hence, careful negotiating, with the patient feeling in control, is important. On the other hand, too much distance and the person may become more depressed and suicidal.

At present, more work needs to be done on interpersonal spacings that are helpful or hindering for different types of patient.

4   Psychotherapy relates to educating context appropriate behaviours to increase the conceptual repertoire of patients in therapy. For example, love making can become more than just an act of dominance or self-esteem. 'Screwing' can become more than just a preoccupation with performance. Further, because some autonomous individuals are low on empathy, questions like 'How do you think others think/feel when you criticize them that way?' can be quite important in directing the person's attention to the fact that they have significant effects on those individuals to whom they relate. In Leary's (1957) model, hostility usually provokes hostility. In autonomous individuals hostility may arise from a desire to demonstrate superiority and control. These individuals may become quite perplexed by the hostile responses they invoke in others. This of course tends to strengthen their belief that they must 'defend themselves'.

5   The activation and expression of emotion in psychotherapeutic encounters can have very different meanings in a socially dependent type to an autonomous type. In autonomous individuals the expression of emotion in therapy can be a highly significant event and may need to be dealt with in a different way than if the patient were a socially dependent individual. Autonomous individuals may admit that they have never shown emotions before and the therapist must be careful that they are not repressed again. In other words, these individuals need to conceptualize and learn about their emotions. Allowing emotions to be active and present in the therapy may facilitate a patient's reconceptualization of the meaning of emotion. Here, then, allowing emotional expression with the simple evaluation that it has not ended in rejection, it has not lowered their worth or removed their competency, can be a most illuminating experience.

6   Insight into psychotherapeutic procedures can be greatly advanced with ethological approaches. Using such an approach Kennedy and MacKenzie (1986) have demonstrated that in group psychotherapy, the group's relational style goes through certain stages. In the first stage the group attempts to harmonize its relationship and find common ground and goals. Ideas like: 'I didn't think anyone else could have such thoughts; it's a great relief to know I'm not the only one' (1986: 627) emerge. These are expressed and are correlated with the cognitive dimension of reassurance, no-threat, 'I'm one of you' responses. In my view, socially dependent types are particularly prone to get stuck at this stage. At stage two, the distinctiveness and individuality of group members becomes more apparent. This is marked by increased competitiveness for attention, time, care, admiration, etc. The autonomous type will now bring to bear all the old well-tried ways of dominating others or withdrawing if he/she is not the centre of

attention. Alliances may also be formed at this time as groups settle down into a dominance hierarchy. Cognitive psychotherapists should be mindful of these underlying dynamics and focus on cognitive processes that inhibit the socially dependent type from challenging, or inhibit the autonomous type from listening to or helping other members.

A group therapy client of mine who was also having some exposure therapy from a nurse behaviour therapist revealed the following event. While in a shop she had been temporarily separated from the nurse. It made her very cross because she thought the nurse should have been more careful. But when the nurse eventually found her she did not express anger but considerable anxiety over the separation (guilt inducing?). When the group asked her what she would do if this were to happen again she rather illuminatingly said: 'Oh, I would get very anxious and hope the nurse could see how bad I was feeling and would come and rescue me.' In group therapy she was reluctant to compete for time but would wait to be asked or take up submissive or slightly agitated postures to provoke care. This lady had considerable moral dilemmas and confusions of her right to make requests and demands. This is an example of the importance of considering some pathological states as those of social communication.

7 Grief is often, although not always, involved in psychotherapeutic procedures. In order to grow and mature something must be given up for something to be gained. The socially dependent type learns to give up maladaptive dependency on a significant other. This will remove the burden that he/she places on his/her attachment (protest–despair) system. In therapy, this involves working on separation anxiety and the ability to take the not always easy road to greater self-determination. The autonomous type, on the other hand, must give up his belief that he/she is, or is potentially, superior or more special than others. In one interview a rather autonomous individual broke down in tears saying, 'But I always wanted my parents to see me as special then I knew they would always love me as something they valued. They hardly ever did of course but I always believed I could crack it if I just tried harder.' Accepting that this may not be the best road to adult love, and being given space and time to grieve and to reconceptualize past patterns of relating, was important to this person. As in standard cognitive psychotherapy, 'have to be loved' and 'have to be strong' ideas were examined but the grieving process was important. Recognition of context appropriateness and inappropriateness of certain behavioural styles was also necessary for this person to learn in order to facilitate his maturity. As individuals become more context appropriate – being able to elicit care appropriately, support others appropriately and compete appropriately – there is less stress placed on defeat activated mechanisms. The individual comes to appreciate that the implications of possible defeat are limited.

Various forms of cognitive psychotherapy are sometimes rather hard on emotion even though it is with problematic emotions that patients usually come to therapy for help. Descriptions in the literature of people behaving like 'love slobs' or acting like 'fucking babies' (especially from the RET literature) seems to me to miss the point. These individuals have developmental arrests and are prone to overly activate attachment loss, or defeat mechanisms. In my view, it is only through a trusting and empathic relationship that the developmental arrest can be restarted. This opens up the patient to greater potentials within their own nature. In Jungian terms it means activating archetypal potential. However, this is not the place to engage in debate on the role of the therapeutic relationship in cognitive psychotherapy, an important and neglected area though it is.

Conclusion

This chapter has argued for a recognition of a preparedness for psychopathology. Syndromes of disorder cannot be fully understood in cognitive–behavioural terms alone. The evolution of social behaviour and the cognitive, behavioural and affective systems that go to co-ordinating such behaviour is important. When we add the biological dimension it becomes possible to recognize how cognitions both evoke and are amplified by biological processes in state dependent ways. In this presentation I have argued in terms of underlying go–stop states which evoke searching behaviours on the one hand and retarded behaviours on the other. Seligman (1975) demonstrated that once an animal had become helpless, even dragging it back and forth in the experimental chamber was not too productive. Clearly, the capacity to 'learn' is influenced by physiological state. As pointed out elsewhere certain classes of coping responses can be extremely difficult to learn in certain brain states (Gilbert, 1984).

I would urge cognitive psychotherapists to take more time out from their technique-oriented approaches and consider what it is to be a human being. It is suggested here that the incentive structure, as it relates to personality characteristics (sociotropic vs autonomous) determines the kinds of events that individuals find stressful. These styles in turn activate invigoration–disengagement processes which have particular effects on cognitive, behaviour and affective systems. Crucial, however, is the issue of what gets activated during go-invigoration processes. It is suggested that go usually evokes searching in both cognitive and behavioural domains. But what is searched for and the manner in which this search is conducted depends critically on the incentives pursued. Sociotropic individuals activate patterns of 'other' searching under threat, whereas autonomous individuals activate efforts to acquire status – involving the repertoires of innately available assertive (dominance) displays, and avoidance of humiliation or others getting 'one over on them'.

Individuals who, early in life, have been thwarted in the acquisition of one (for example, close attachment bonds) may pursue the other (for example, status) with some vigour, and vice versa. However it is also possible that status may be pursued by an autonomous individual in order to ensure a flow of social affiliative opportunities. In this case, the individual may have both highly amplified status needs and also have fears of the potential separation and loss that success and self-assertion might bring. This would represent the style of needing to be needed (Gilbert, 1984). In other words, as Price and Sloman (1984) point out, the competition model and abandonment model should not be seen as mutually exclusive but probably interactive. Therefore, individuals may be vulnerable to psychopathology (a) because being dependent on others they are vulnerable to the psychobiological consequences of loss and interpersonal disruptions, (b) because being dependent on status and autonomy they are vulnerable to the psychobiological consequences of defeat and loss of control over others and resources or (c) because fears of separation may have indeed facilitated the pursuit of autonomy yet to achieve autonomy is to be separate; this is a situation of conflict.

Note

The extensive quotations from Beck (1983) are included by kind permission of Raven Press.

1 Remember, in brain state theory schemata are not structures but are patterns of encoding, storing, retrieving and appraising information guided by psychobiological routines.

References

Anisman, H. (1978) Neurochemical changes elicited by stress: behavioral correlates. In H. Anisman and G. Bignami (eds), *Psychopharmacology of aversely motivated behavior*. New York: Plenum Press.

Anisman, H. and Zacharko, R. M. (1982) Depression: the predisposing influence of stress [plus commentary]. *Behavioral and Brain Sciences*, 5: 89–137.

Arieti, S. and Bemporad, J. (1980) The psychological organisation of depression. *American Journal of Psychiatry*, 137: 1360–5.

Beck, A. T. (1967) *Depression: clinical, experimental and theoretical aspects*. New York: Harper & Row.

Beck, A. T. (1976) *Cognitive therapy and the emotional disorders*. New York: International Universities Press.

Beck, A. T. (1983) Cognitive therapy of depression. In P. Clayton (ed.), *Treatment of depression: old and new controversies*. New York: Raven Press.

Beck, A. T. (1987) Cognitive models of depression. *Journal of Cognitive Psychotherapy*. 1: 5–37.

Beck, A. T., Emery, G. and Greenberg, R. (1985) *Anxiety disorders and phobias: a cognitive perspective*. New York: Basic Books.

Beck, A. T., Rush, A. J., Shaw, B. F. and Emery, G. (1979) *Cognitive therapy of depression: a treatment manual*. New York: Wiley.

68   *Paul Gilbert*

Blatt, S. J., Quinlan, D. M., Chevron, E. S., McDonald, C. and Zuroff, D. (1982) Dependency and self criticism: psychological dimensions of depression. *Journal of Consulting and Clinical Psychology*, 50: 113–24.

Bower, G. H. (1981) Mood and memory. *American Psychologist*, 36: 129–48.

Bowlby, J. (1969) *Attachment. Attachment and loss, vol. 1.* London: Hogarth Press.

Bowlby, J. (1973) *Separation: anxiety and anger. Attachment and loss, vol. 2.* London: Hogarth Press.

Bowlby, J. (1980) *Loss: sadness and depression. Attachment and loss, vol. 3.* London: Hogarth Press.

Boyle, G. J. (1985) Self-report measures of depression: some psychometric considerations. *British Journal of Clinical Psychology*, 25: 45–60.

Coe, C. L., Weiner, S. G., Rosenberg, L. T. and Levine, S. (1985) Endocrine and immune responses to separation and maternal loss in non-human primates. In M. Reite and T. Field (eds), *The psychobiology of attachment and separation.* New York: Academic Press.

Crook, J. H. (1980) *The evolution of human consciousness.* Oxford: Oxford University Press.

Depue, R. A. and Monroe, S. M. (1978) Learned helplessness in the perspective of the depressive disorders, conceptual and definitional issues. *Journal of Abnormal Psychology*, 87: 3–20.

Dryden, W. (1985) *Therapists' dilemmas.* London: Harper & Row.

Ellenberger, H. F. (1970) *The discovery of the unconscious: the history and evolution of dynamic psychiatry.* New York: Basic Books.

Ellis, A. and Grieger, R. (eds) (1977) *Handbook of rational–emotive therapy.* New York: Springer.

Gardner, R. (1982) Mechanisms in manic-depressive disorder: an evolutionary model. *Archives of General Psychiatry*, 39: 1436–41.

Gardner, R. (in press) Psychiatric syndromes of infrastructures for intraspecific communication. In M. R. A. Chance (ed.), *Social fabrics of the mind.* London: Lawrence Erlbaum.

Gilbert, P. (1984) *Depression: from psychology to brain state.* London: Lawrence Erlbaum.

Gilbert, P. (in press) *Human nature and suffering.* London: Lawrence Erlbaum.

Henry, J. P. and Stephens, P. M. (1977) *Stress, health and the social environment.* New York: Springer-Verlag.

Hofer, M. A. (1984) Relationships as regulators: a psychobiologic perspective on bereavement. *Psychosomatic Medicine*, 46: 183–97.

Hollon, S. D. and Kriss, M. R. (1984) Cognitive factors in clinical research and practice. *Clinical Psychology Review*, 4: 35–76.

Horowitz, M. J., Wilner, N., Marmar, C. and Krupnick, J. (1980) Pathological grief and the activation of latent self-images. *American Journal of Psychiatry*, 137: 1157–62.

Iran-Nejad, A. and Ortony, A. (1984) A biofunctional model of distributed mental content, mental structures, awareness and attention. *Journal of Mind and Behavior*, 5: 171–210.

Kasparov, G. (1986) A life in the day of Gary Kasparov. *Sunday Times colour supplement.* 10 August: 50.

Kegan, R. (1982) *The evolving self: problem and process in the human development.* Cambridge, Mass.: Harvard University Press.

Kennedy, J. L. and MacKenzie R. K. (1986) Dominance hierarchies in psychotherapy groups. *British Journal of Psychiatry*, 148: 625–31.

Klinger, E. (1975) Consequences and commitment to aid disengagement from incentives. *Psychological Review*, 82: 1–24.

Klinger, E. (1977) *Meaning and void.* Minneapolis: University of Minnesota Press.

Kraemer, G. W. and McKinney, W. T. (1979) Interactions of pharmacological agents which alter biogenic amine metabolism and depression. *Journal of Affective Disorders*, 1: 33–54.

Lazarus, R. S. (1982) Thoughts on the relations between emotion and cognition. *American Psychologist*, 37: 1019–24.

Leary, T. (1957) *Interpersonal diagnosis of personality*. New York: Roland Press.

Leshner, A. I. (1978) *An introduction to behavioral endocrinology*. New York: Oxford University Press.

McKinney, W. T. (1977) Animal behavioral–biological models relevant to depressive and affective disorders in humans. In M. S. Schulterbrandt and A. Raskin (eds), *Depression in childhood: diagnosis, treatment and conceptual models*. New York: Raven Press.

MacLean, P. D. (1985) Brain evolution relating to family, play and the separation call. *Archives of General Psychiatry*, 42: 405–17.

Mineka, S. and Suomi, S. J. (1978) Social separation in monkeys. *Psychological Bulletin*, 85: 1376–1400.

Parkes, C. M. (1986) *Bereavement: studies in grief in adult life* (2nd edn). Harmondsworth: Penguin.

Powell, L. H. and Friedman, M. (1986) Alteration of Type A behavior in coronary patients. In M. J. Christie and P. G. Mellett, (eds), *The psychosomatic approach: contemporary practice of whole person care*. London: Wiley.

Price, J. S. (1972) Genetic and phylogenetic aspects of mood variation. *International Journal of Mental Health*, 1: 124–44.

Price, J. S. and Sloman, L. (1984) The evolutionary model of psychiatric disorder [Letter]. *Archives of General Psychiatry*, 41: 211.

Price, V. A. (1982) *Type A behavior pattern: a model for research and practice*. New York: Academic Press.

Rachman, S. (1978) *Fear and courage*. San Francisco: Freeman.

Rachman, S. (1981) The primacy of affect: some theoretical implications. *Behaviour Research and Therapy*, 19: 279–90.

Rachman, S. (1984) A reassessment of the 'Primacy of Affect'. *Cognitive Therapy and Research*, 8: 579–84.

Raleigh, M. J., McGuire, M. T., Brammer, G. L. and Yuwieler, A. (1984) Social and environmental influences on blood serotonin concentrations in monkeys. *Archives of General Psychiatry*, 41: 405–10.

Reus, V. I., Weingartner, H. and Post, R. M. (1979) Clinical implications of state-dependent learning. *American Journal of Psychiatry*, 136: 927–31.

Seligman, M. E. P. (1971) Phobias and preparedness. *Behavior Therapy*, 2: 307–20.

Seligman, M. E. P. (1975) *Helplessness: on depression development and death*. San Francisco: Freeman.

Selye, H. (1979) The stress concept and some of its implications. In V. Hamilton and D. M. Warburton (eds), *Human stress and cognition*. Chichester: Wiley.

Sloman, L. (1981) Interfamilial struggles for power: an ethological perspective. *International Journal of Family Psychiatry*, 2: 13–33.

Solomon, R. L. (1980) The opponent process theory of acquired motivation: the cost of pleasure and the benefits of pain. *American Psychologist*, 35: 691–712.

Tomkins, S. S. (1981) The quest for primary motives: biography and autobiography of an idea. *Journal of Personality and Social Psychology*, 41: 306–29.

Ursin, H. (1980) Personality, activation and somatic health. A new psychosomatic theory. In S. Levine and H. Ursin (eds), *Coping and health*. New York: Plenum Press.

Weiss, J. M., Glazer, H. I., Pohorecky, I. A., Bailey, W. H. and Schneider, L. H. (1979) Coping behavior and stress-induced behavioral depression: studies of the role of brain catecholamines. In R. A. Depue (ed.), *The psychobiology of the depressive disorders*. New York: Academic Press.

Weiss, J. M., Bailey, W. H., Goodman, P. A. et al. (1982) A model for neurochemical study of depression. In M. Y. Spiegelstein and A. Levy (eds), *Behavioral models and the analysis of drugs action*. Amsterdam: Elsevier.

Whybrow, P. (1984) Contributions from neuroendocrinology. In K. R. Scherer and P. Ekman (eds), *Approaches to emotion*. Hillsdale, NJ: Lawrence Erlbaum.

Yalom, I. D. (1980) *Existential psychotherapy*. New York: Basic Books.

Zajonc, R. B. (1980) Feeling and thinking: preferences need no inferences. *American Psychologist*, 35, 151–75.

Zajonc, R. B. (1984) On the primacy of affect. *American Psychologist*, 39: 117–23.

Zilboorg, G. (in collaboration with Henry, G. W.) (1941) *History of medical psychology*. New York: W. W. Norton.

4

From a Linear to a Contextual Model of the ABCs of RET

Russell M. Grieger

When he first conceived of rational–emotive therapy (RET) in 1955, Albert Ellis formulated the ABC paradigm to explain human emotional disturbance and to direct psychotherapeutic efforts at change (Ellis, 1958, 1962). Simply and brilliantly, the ABC paradigm articulates the basic tenet that cognitions mediate and are central to the causation and amelioration of emotional, behavioural, and interpersonal disturbance. In this paradigm, A (an activating event in the world) does not directly produce or cause C (the cognitive, emotional, and/or behavioural consequences); rather, it is the Bs (mediating thoughts, attitudes, or beliefs about A) that cause C.

Over the last three decades, the influence of Dr Ellis's work on both the theory and practice of psychotherapy has become increasingly profound and pervasive. The premises posited by Ellis have spawned an enormous body of research and theoretical literature and have contributed immeasurably to the development of cognitive-behavioural psychotherapy and to its emergence as a dominant force in psychology. A recent survey (Smith, 1982) concluded that the 'cognitive-behavioral system represents one of the strongest, if not *the* strongest, theoretical emphasis today'. Furthermore, the survey indicated that of the 10 individuals reported to have most powerfully influenced today's clinical trends, Albert Ellis ranked second, and five were either strongly or moderately identified with cognitive-behavioural therapy (Ellis, Wolpe, A. Lazarus, Beck, and Meichenbaum).

As the amount of research on and conceptualization of the role of cognition on human psychology and psychopathology has grown, however, a parallel recognition has emerged regarding the need for greater understanding and more precise delineations of what constitutes the Bs in the ABC paradigm (Bernard, 1980; Eschenroeder, 1982; Huber, 1985). Ellis himself has stated that the ABCs 'are oversimplified and omit salient information about human disturbance and its treatment' (1985).

Partially in response to this recognition, a number of rational–emotive therapists have expanded the ABC model in attempts to describe more completely what takes place within humans that causes them to respond as they do (Diekstra and Dassen, 1979; Maultsby, 1975). A particularly impressive effort has been made by Wessler and Wessler (1980), who outline an eight-step model of an emotional episode: (1) a stimulus, which begins the episode; (2) selection of some aspects of the stimulas based on neural and physiological processes; (3) perception and symbolic representation of the stimulus; (4) cognitive interpretation of nonobservable aspects of the perceived stimulus; (5) cognitive appraisal or evaluation; (6 and 7) affective arousal, and an action tendency caused by the appraisal; and (8) functional feedback (such as positive reinforcement) that affects future action. Among the attractive features of the Wessler and Wessler model is that it includes the focus of most all cognitive-behavioural therapies and provides the therapist with the opportunity to assess and intervene cognitively at any or all of the eight steps.

In Ellis's (1985) expanded ABC model, he distinguishes between such various Bs as non-evaluative observations and perceptions (cold cognitions), positive and negative preferential evaluations (warm cognitions), and positive and negative absolutistic evaluations and demands (hot cognitions). Most innovative, however, are his observations about how people's As, Bs, and Cs reciprocally influence and 'cause' each other. For example, he states that people are 'prone to seek out and respond to their 'As', that they 'largely bring their beliefs to A, and they prejudicedly view or experience As in light of these biased beliefs', and they 'partly create the activating event at A'.

As a practitioner and teacher of RET, I commend these rational–emotive therapists for their efforts in expanding the ABC model. At the very least, their efforts recognize the complexity of human thinking, provide the therapist with a framework from which to decide which cognitive-behavioural strategies to employ and in what order, and offer a basis for the integration of the various cognitive-behavioural therapies into an eclectic whole.

It is with this indebtedness that I offer my thinking on what I call the contextual ABC model of RET. Piggybacking on those who have already expanded the ABCs, I too wish to acknowledge the mutual influence among A, the Bs, and C, to underscore the individual's ability to choose consciously, to act creatively, to take responsibility, and to emphasize the distinction between thinking that is specific to a particular situation and beliefs, philosophies, or life principles that are central to a person's way of functioning in the world across situations.

Despite the greater refinement and descriptiveness of the expanded ABC models just discussed, they remain essentially linear and therefore relatively static in nature. What appears to be missing from the RET and, indeed, from the cognitive-behavioural literature is a more complete, graphic, dynamic, and three-dimensional model that more accurately captures the intricacies of the ABC process. This is the gap that the contextual ABC model attempts to fill. Specifically, in moving from a linear to a contextual model, it becomes increasingly possible to visualize and conceptualize the complexities of B, the reciprocity among the components of human functioning, and the power of the individual to create Cs, Bs and even As independent of any environmental event.

What follows, then, is the contextual ABC model. First will be presented a section on the nature of activating events (As), followed by a discussion of the nature of human cognition. After this I will describe how human cognitions variously influence and create action, feelings, thinkings, and even activating events. Finally, the chapter concludes with some implications for the practice of RET.

The Nature of Activating Events: 'The' Reality versus 'Our' Reality

The contextual ABC model begins with the proposition that there exists a real world of objects and events; whether or not a person is physically present or mentally alert to experience what is there is irrelevant. In reality, literally, there is both a solid mass of, and a continual series of, available 'things out there' that a person can select, perceive, symbolically represent, interpret, and evaluate.

A central distinction is made in RET between the circumstances *in* one's life (the As) and the experiences one has *about* those circumstances (the Cs). I argue that it is also crucial in RET to draw the distinction between the circumstances *in* one's life and the experience one has *of* the circumstances. While there is indeed a real world of circumstances (matter and events) that does exist 'out there' (*the* reality), this real world differs from the one to which we relate and respond. What we as humans deal with are the circumstances as interpreted by us (*our* reality). In other words, as Mahoney (1980) has indicated, it is our representation of environments to which we respond, not the environments themselves.

As with the experiences people have *about* activating events, the experiences people have *of* activating events (their reality) is also mediated by the person's Bs. Coexistent with the fact that it is virtually impossible for people to not think, people are 'thrown' to operate automatically, actively, and immediately on the real events they encounter, that is, to attend selectively, to perceive, to represent symbolically, and to infer about the events. In doing this, people 'create' a reality of activating events for themselves that may be, but probably is not, identical to the real reality. In actuality, nothing exists *for us* without this selection/filtering/interpretation process; the rub is that people are usually unaware of that process and assume that what they 'see' accurately represents what exists 'in the world'.

This re-creation of reality is represented in Figure 4.1, where A represents

A → B₁ → A′ → B₂ → C

'creates' (B₁ → A′)

'creates' (B₂ → C)

Reinforces the experienced reality

Reinforces the interpretation

A	B₁	A′	B₂	C
Activating real event	Interpretative thinking about A	Perceived or experienced reality of activating event, as created by person	Evaluative thinking about A′	Emotional/behavioural reactions to A′

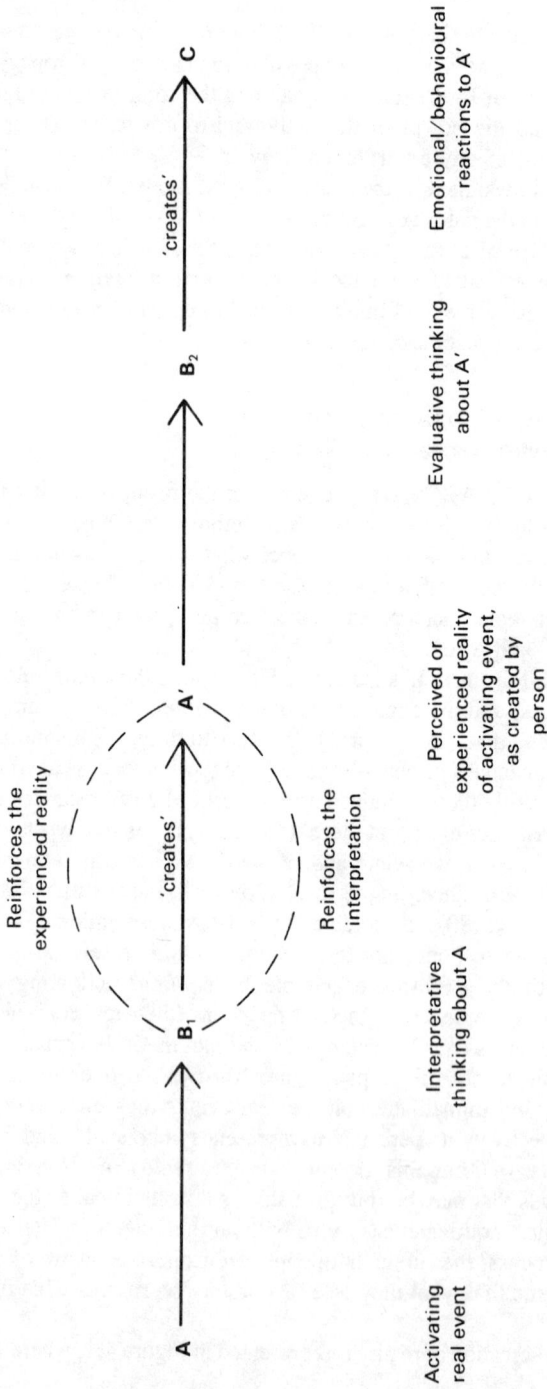

Figure 4.1 *The creation of reality*

the actual events in the real world; B_1 represents the cognitive operations, including interpretations, that 'create' the reality as experienced by the person; and A' represents the experienced or perceived events, as 'created' by the person. I hypothesize that a very interesting, reciprocal process occurs at this point, in that the cognitive activity at B_1 and the experience of the event at A' mutually reinforce and ingrain each other. That is, after several such 'creations' of the experienced event (A') by the cognitive activity at B_1, the two become yoked such that the presence of one confirms to the person the validity of the other. The perceived reality confirms and reinforces the validity of the cognitive process that generated the event, and the interpretation, in turn, confirms and reinforces the reality of the event. Then, finally, picking up the sequence in typical RET fashion, the person again operates on the new, perceived reality (the A') with evaluative thinking (B_2) to 'create' the emotional and behavioural consequences of reactions at C.

Thus, people not only create their Cs, but they create their As as well. In the contextual ABC model, it is logical to help people understand and change the ways at B_1 that they create their reality of events, as well as to help them change the ways at B_2 that they create their feelings and behaviours at C.

The Nature of Human Cognition

Among the objects in the universe are, of course, people, one such person represented in Figure 4.2 by a circle. Like all people, this person possesses a multitude of traits and attributes, including, among others, physical, interpersonal, intellectual, sexual, and cognitive ones. Imagine the person, the circle, filled with thousands of dots, each representing a separate attribute of the person. Among the various attributes people possess, the ones most uniquely significant for human functioning are those that are cognitive.

Central to the contextual ABC model is the premise that human cognition may be delineated by a number of categories that can be arranged, at least for the sake of discussion, from the most general and philosophical to the more specific. From this statement, three things are assumed: (1) the more general and philosophical the cognition, the more likely the cognition is to be unarticulated or beyond awareness; (2) the more general and philosophical the cognition, the more pervasively the cognition is likely to influence the person's life; and (3) the interplay of these various types of cognitions to a large extent directs what a person does in any given situation or about any given event.

In the contextual ABC model, three categories of cognition are delineated (see Figure 4.2); Life Positions (Bp), Values (Bv), and Interpretational Habits (B_I). Each will be briefly presented, proceeding from the most

Life positions (**Bp**)

Values (**Bv**)

Interpretation (**B₁**)

(1) Active–reactive
process

(2) Active–active
process

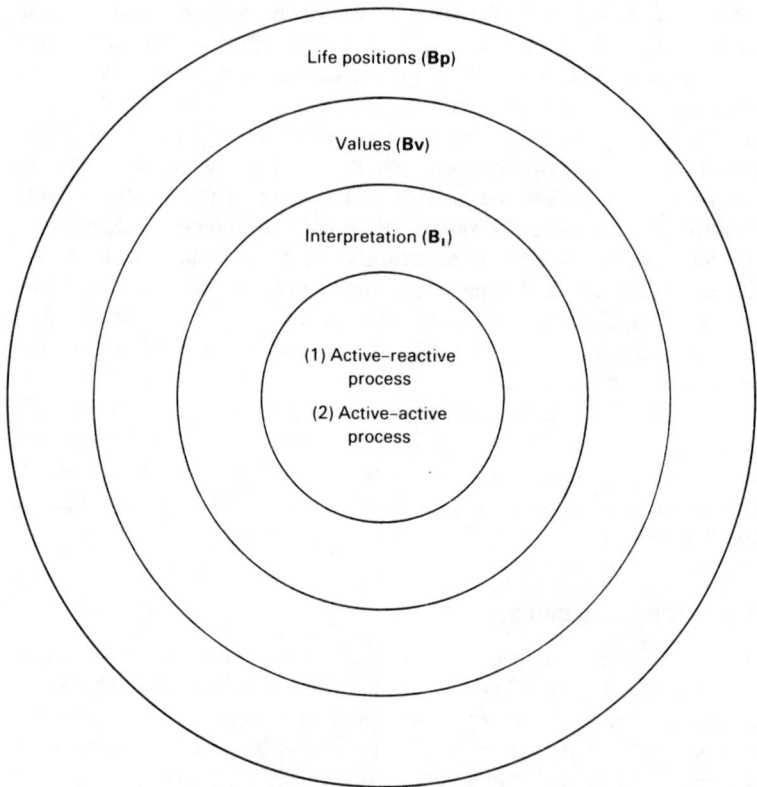

Figure 4.2   *Person in the world (the page represents the world filled with objects and events, and the circle represents a person)*

general and philosophical to the more specific. This is not meant to suggest a rigid progression from one to the other in human functioning, but rather that the more general cognitions form a backdrop or context that influences the less general ones, and, conversely, that the less general cognitions are influenced contextually by the more general ones.

Life Positions (Bp)

Most basic to all human beings is the existence of fundamental life positions. These positions, probably adopted when we are young, determine the scope and boundaries of both how we experience the world and how we act in it. These positions are not what we think, do, or feel on a moment-by-moment basis; rather, they are generalizations or abstractions, often unrecognized and unarticulated, that guide and set the boundaries of our thinking, doing, and feeling. They are the most basic assumptions, the context that most fundamentally guides our lives (Earle and Regin, 1980). I will delineate four life positions that have both the scope and the power to colour virtually all of a person's life. Each of the four can be stated as a dichotomy between two poles, with no middle ground; the person at any moment stands either at one pole or the other, but rarely if ever with a foot in both.

Demandingness versus affirmation   The first of the four dichotomous life positions comes primarily from RET and Albert Ellis (1962, 1971, 1974b, 1977, 1979) and can be termed *demandingness versus affirmation*. I direct the reader to almost any of Ellis's writings for an exposition of demandingness. Suffice it to say that, at the pole of demandingness, the person takes the childish, egocentric stance that the world automatically *must* be the way one wants and *must not* include what one does not want. It is, at one and the same time, an insistence for certain things to be ('I demand', 'It must', 'You should', 'I have to') and a resistance to and a protestation against other things being as they are ('No! It mustn't be that way.'). As the crux of most emotional disturbances, demandingness embodies the insistence that life be the way we want it, rather than the insistence that it be exactly the way it is.

At the polar opposite to demandingness is what I call affirmation. It is a rather complicated position that includes two subparts. Affirmation, first, includes being displeased in an anti-awfulizing way when something is not the way one wants it to be, preferring or desiring in a nondemanding way for something to be different than it is, and being willing in a nonself-pitying way to act to get what one wants regardless. So, affirmation is not a mere passive acceptance of what is, but an active position of power and potential action to get what one wants in the future. Second, affirmation includes, at any given moment in time, regardless of what that moment holds for a person, saying 'Yes' or 'I insist' to what, indeed, is there. Beyond acceptance, it is 'choosing' what is there and what is not there. It is taking what one gets when one gets it, and not taking what one does not get when one does not get it (Rhinehart, 1976). This was stated well by a man serving a rather long prison term:

> Some days, my mind just can't stop wishing I were out. So then I say, 'Why wish to be out there when I can't. No amount of resistance will change that. Now you have a choice. You can keep resisting and bitch about it, or you can choose it.' I go through that maybe ten times a day and pull myself out of it. But it works. I tell myself, 'This is all there is right now so just relax and quit fighting because you can't do anything but worry yourself to death trying to make it something it isn't.' (Bry, 1976: 120)

Self as object versus self as context   Rational–emotive therapy shares with all of psychology, and indeed with Western civilization, a view called *'self as object'*. In this view, 'the self is an abstraction that an individual develops about the attributes, capacities, objects, and activities which he possesses and pursues' (Coopersmith, 1967: 20). Different from the object of observations – the person – the self is a conceptualization *about* the object. Self as object is represented graphically in Figure 4.3, in which the large circle represents the person, the small circles represent the various roles the person plays in life (for example, wife, mother, friend), and the dots represent the various attributes and performances of the person. Self, then, or self-concept, is the sum of the dots known to the person.

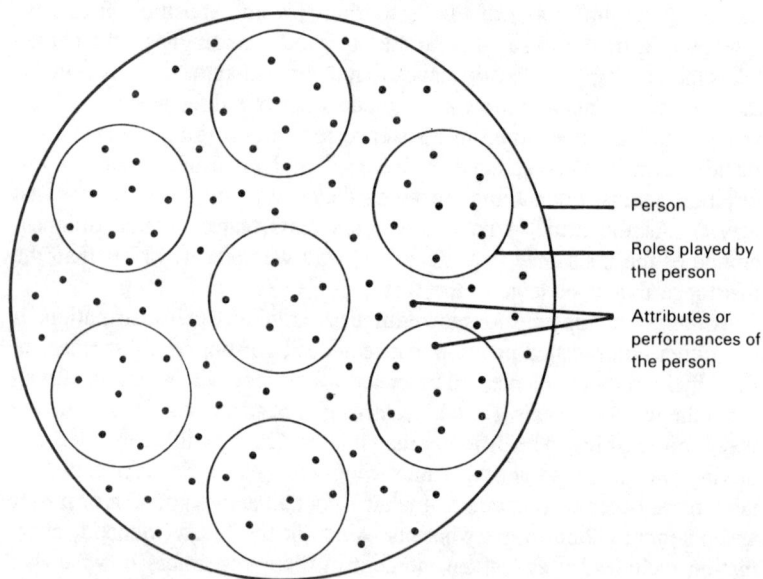

Figure 4.3   *Self as object*

With a self-as-object model, it is easy for a person to identify his or her self as a role (for example, psychologist), as an attribute (for example, selfish), or as a particular behaviour (for example, an angry outburst). Thus, people identify themselves as such things as their jobs, their matehood or parenthood, their money, their education, their physical appearance, their good or bad deeds, and so on. From this process of identification, a person is likely to go the next step and evaluate or rate his or her self as being either bad or good.

RET has made an enormous contribution in helping clients to stop this self-defeating process by making the important distinction between self-esteem and self-acceptance (Boyd and Grieger, 1982; Ellis, 1972, 1974a, 1974b; Ellis and Harper, 1975; Grieger, 1975). Self-esteem refers to the individual's evaluation or rating of self as being either good or bad, based on the presence or absence of certain traits, behaviours, or attributes (dots). RET advocates self-acceptance rather than self-esteem, based on the proposition that human beings are simply too complex to be accurately rated. It is recommended that people rate their individual performances but that they entirely dispense with rating their selves. What is suggested, instead, is that people decide to accept themselves, *a priori*, as fallible human beings who, like all human beings, do some things particularly well, some things poorly, and many things adequately.

Despite the obvious advantages in RET of advocating self-acceptance over self-esteem, the self-as-object model is still retained. I contend that there are problems inherent in the self-as-object viewpoint that can be avoided with an alternative framework. First of all, with this model, it is an easy progression from self-identification to self-esteeming or self-rating, a stance highly associated with a wide array of emotional and behavioural disturbances (Ellis, 1972). Second, in holding oneself to be what one does or what one has (one's dots), it becomes very difficult to avoid taking a variety of seemingly self-protective but actually self-defeating stances, such as justifying oneself as being right and thereby invalidating others, dominating and avoiding domination, and creating the extremes of euphoria and depression. Third, and perhaps most important, there is limited power to the person locked into the self-as-object viewpoint, for, in holding oneself as an object (a mass comprised of perceived attributes and performances), one easily sees oneself as what one already is. That is, one easily sees oneself as static, formed, inert, immovable, and unchangeable, and such a perception certainly creates barriers to therapeutic growth and change. In essence, then, with a self-as-object concept, one becomes a victim of one's own self-concept, which greatly diminishes the likelihood of acting creatively, courageously, and newly.

An alternative view of self, here called *self as context* or *self as potential*, is, I believe, a much more useful one, and one that contributes significantly to the contextual ABC model to follow. This view starts from the perspective that the self is *not* what one has or does; that is, it is not one's behaviour, it is not one's traits; it is not one's intelligence; it is not one's body, hair, or other physical attributes; nor is it the roles one plays. A person certainly has and does all these things, but the person is *not* these things.

What, then, does the construct *self as context* mean? Very simply stated, self in this view is not a thing or an object; it has no substance, nor is it measurable. Rather, it is metaphysical. It, the self, is held as the background, the context or backdrop, out of which what the person has or does emerges. Referring again to Figure 4.3, self in this view is all of the empty space inside the person (the space between the dots), which always has the potential to be filled and that spawns the person's attributes and performances (the dots themselves). Rather than being an identity, self is the source of identities; rather than being the sum of one's attributes, self is the space in which attributes show up and develop; rather than being one's behaviour, self is the clearing from which behaviour comes; rather than being one's philosophies, values, and commitments, self is the place from which these emerge, flourish, and decline. Self as context, in sum, is 'the context in which content is crystallized and process occurs, and it is not any individual content or process' (Bartley, 1978).

The importance of such a conceptualization will be seen further as the contextual ABC model is developed. For now, suffice it to say that the self-as-context viewpoint has several important benefits to it. First of all, it preserves and even enhances the self-acceptance position. Since one simply is not what one does or has, self-rating becomes blatantly non-sensical. Second, this model of self obviates the concept of self-identity, or the 'Who am I?' issue. 'Who a person is' is defined as potential – a clearing, an opportunity, a context – so that what one *does* and what one *wants to do* emerge as the central issues. Third, since self is seen as potential, the door is opened to creation, to taking the stance that 'I can create my own beliefs, feelings, and behaviours out of an act of will (just because I want to), because there is the room and potential to do so.' Fourth, self as potential conveys the position that change, psychotherapeutic or otherwise, is always possible and hence provides hope and motivation to the individual.

Living psychologically versus living philosophically   The third of the four dichotomous life positions contrasts *living psychologically* with *living philosophically* (Siegel, 1984). At the pole of living psychologically, people identify themselves as exclusively psychological beings; they see themselves *as* their psychological attributes, as being their feelings, attitudes, wants, and goals, rather than seeing themselves as merely *containing* or *having* these *attributes*. The upshot of this position is that people become trapped by their psychological make up. Since they hold that their psychology is who they are, they assume that they have no choice but to respond according to how they feel and think. Thus, for example, a person living psychologically might have the intention of working on a project in the evening, then become anxious about something during the day, and conclude that it is not possible to work because of this anxiety.

The position of living philosophically does not deny the existence of psychological events, nor does it deny the coerciveness of these events. Living philosophically, however, is a position that has the effect of undeifying one's psychology; that is, it notes one's psychological state but puts it aside. Living philosophically means that one holds one's word, or one's promises and commitments, as being of paramount importance, regardless of how one feels at a given moment in time. In this rather unique philosophical position, one has declared that the stand one takes or the promises one gives are eminently more important than how one feels or even what one desires. Thus, when one makes a promise ('I will meet you for lunch at 12:00 p.m. on Tuesday'), one follows through despite how one feels ('I'm depressed, *and* I'll keep my word'), or what one wants ('I'd rather go jogging, *and* I'll keep my promise'), or what is convenient ('I'll get up an hour earlier to get paperwork done in order to keep my commitment to have lunch with her'). In genuinely taking this life position, a person can overcome procrastination, irresponsibility, and a whole hoard of passive, helpless stances in life.

Being at effect versus being at cause The fourth and final of the dichotomous life positions has been termed *being at effect versus being at cause* (Rhinehart, 1976). Being at effect is a position in which one believes that the circumstances in one's life control one's destiny and well-being. If articulated, this position would sound something like, 'My well-being, my happiness, my goals getting met, are dependent on circumstances, by chance, working out.' With such a philosophy, it is easy to imagine a person feeling like a leaf ready to be blown about at random, a hapless victim who is likely to respond with helplessness and depression, anger, and bitterness, when circumstances happen to be adverse.

The contrasting position, being at cause, starts from a position of personal responsibility for one's own well-being, for how one responds to events, and for the choices one makes in life, regardless of the circumstances. Responsibility, in this view, does not include credit or blame, right or wrong, good or bad; it is the 'point of view' in which one 'chooses' not to see oneself as a victim, but as being bigger than the circumstances. If articulated, being at cause would sound like this: 'No one or no thing is put on this earth to make my life work; I am totally responsible for my own well-being, and I take that responsibility. Even though I may not know what to do to overcome this adverse circumstance, I am committed to doing whatever is necessary to make life work. I may now have this bad thing in my life, and I may not be able to change the circumstances, but I will go about living positively and hopefully anyway.' To continue the analogy of the leaf, in this position the person holds him/herself as the wind, or 'cause in the matter', not as some helpless object buffeted by uncontrollable forces. In taking this position, a person is less likely to whine or to experience depression, rage, extreme frustration, low frustration tolerance, or other symptoms of emotional disturbance when circumstances are adverse.

It is my observation that most people, particularly those who have an emotional disturbance, take the first pole of each of the four dichotomies just discussed. They tend to endorse demandingness, self as object (accompanied by self-esteeming or self-rating), living psychologically, and being at effect. Until they become aware of the positions they hold and of their impact on their functioning, and until they take responsibility for them, they are likely to operate as victims who believe that they cannot bring about significant change in their lives.

Values (Bv)

I share with Ellis (1974b, 1985) the view that human beings are naturally motivated and goal oriented, but, in contrast with Freudians and others who hold that human motivation is largely biological, instinctual, and unconscious, I believe that motives can be understood best in terms of values (Petersen, 1968). That is, people come to value certain outcomes and so they are motivated to act by the values they hold. For example, if I value basketball and not opera, I will be spurred to attend basketball games rather than operas; if I value a single intimate relationship over several more casual ones, I will act to get and maintain a committed relationship; if I value doing psychotherapy over psychological research, I will spend a great deal of time doing therapy and little or no time in conducting research.

According to Ellis (1985), human beings almost always hold the basic values of (1) remaining alive and (2) being happy while alive. Under the rubric of being happy, it seems that human values can be grouped in terms of (a) friendship, affection, and love, in both intimate relationships and more casual associations, (b) success in work and similar pursuits, (c) fun or pleasure in recreational activities and hobbies, and (d) comfort or ease in the general flow of life.

In the contextual ABC model, exactly how values influence actions depends on their interaction with the life positions a person holds, particularly vis-à-vis the demandingness–affirmation dichotomy (see previous section). When a person endorses the affirmation life position, values tend to be experienced and expressed in such terms as desires, wishes, wants, and preferences, such as 'I want (or prefer) you to like me'. With values held in this way, one is motivated to seek what is valued and, depending on whether or not the valued outcome is attained, is either pleased/happy or displeased/sorrowed. In endorsing the demandingness life position, values are held and expressed in terms of shoulds, oughts, musts, have tos, and needs, as in the statement 'I need you to like me' or 'You must like me'. Values held this way are characterized by absoluteness, necessity, all-or-noneness, and either/or-ness, and they have been shown to be associated with desperation for what is valued; depression, guilt, and anger over being thwarted in attaining what is valued; and anxiety over getting and keeping what is valued.

Interpretational Habits (B$_I$)

The third and last of the categories of cognitions delineated in the contextual ABC model are interpretational habits (B$_I$). Contained contextually within people's life positions (Bp) and values (Bv), these have to do with the inferences and conclusions people make about the unobserved aspects of encountered objects and situations.

It is an assumption of the contextual ABC model that people naturally and regularly make situational interpretations. What is important here, however, are the *habitual, recurring* interpretations people have learned and make across situations, which colour or create their 'view of life'. Furthermore, *interpretation* here refers both to a person's habitual style of processing data (such as, general versus specific, logical versus non-sequitorial, realistic versus minimizing or magnifying) as well as to the content of the conclusions a person habitually draws. Examples of the latter include (1) internal versus external locus of control (Rotter, 1966) in which people either assume that a thing that happens to them is directly due to their actions (internal locus) or to luck, chance, or fate (external locus); (2) self-efficacy expectations (Bandura, 1977), the 'conviction that one can successfully execute the behavior required to produce the outcomes' (p. 194); (3) outcome expectancy (Bandura, 1977), or a person's estimate that a given behaviour will lead to certain outcomes; (4) a view of the world as friendly, supportive, and good versus overwhelming and making exorbitant demands (Beck, 1967); and (5) a view of the future as hopeful and positive versus bleak and difficult (Beck, 1967).

Cognitive Creation of Consequences

Thus far in the contextual ABC model, two major elements have been delineated: (a) a real world that contains an unlimited number of potential activating events and that provides a 'playground' for people to attempt to fulfil their goals or values; and (2) a person who, through the course of living, has acquired and retained a relatively stable variety of cognitive attributes that remain fairly constant across situations, the most important ones in determining one's experience in life here distinguished as life positions, values, and interpretational habits. I will now discuss the interaction of the two in the production of human actions and reactions, abstracted either as an *active–reactive* process or an *active–active* process. These processes are shown in the centre of the person in Figure 4.2, are elaborated in Figures 4.4 and 4.5, and will be discussed in turn.

The Active–Reactive Process

After Ellis (1976, 1979, 1985), the contextual ABC model asserts that people can be understood best as trying to fulfil what they value in environments that contain numerous potential activating events. People do

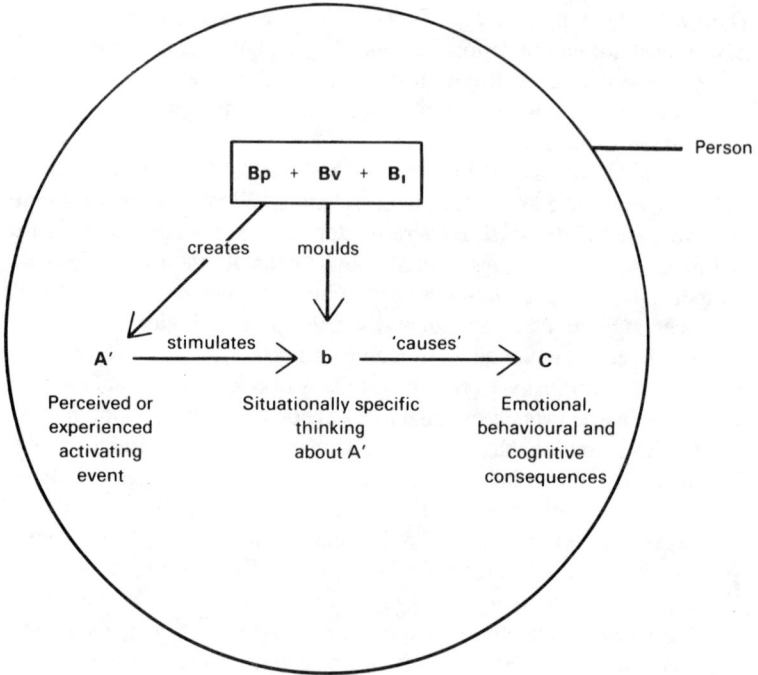

Figure 4.4   *The active–reactive process* (**Bp** = *life positions*, **Bv** = *values*, **B$_I$** = *interpretational habits*)

not merely react passively to the events they encounter, however; as discussed earlier, they actively operate to create their environments and then actively operate on their created environments in a way that 'causes' their reactions.

This process can be seen in Figure 4.4, which is a blow-up of the centre part of the person depicted in Figure 4.2. First, in part as a result of trying to satisfy their values (Bv), people seek out environments or parts of environments (As) they think will fulfil their values. For example, people go to parties, bars, and other social places because they value fun, attention, or stimulation. Then, in bringing their values (Bv), their life positions (Bp), and their interpretational habits (B$_I$) to these environments, they also selectively attend to and prejudicially perceive and interpret what they encounter. So, to begin with, people really create the activating events (referred to as the perceived or experienced activating event and designated as A') that they eventually operate on in causing their emotional and behavioural reactions.

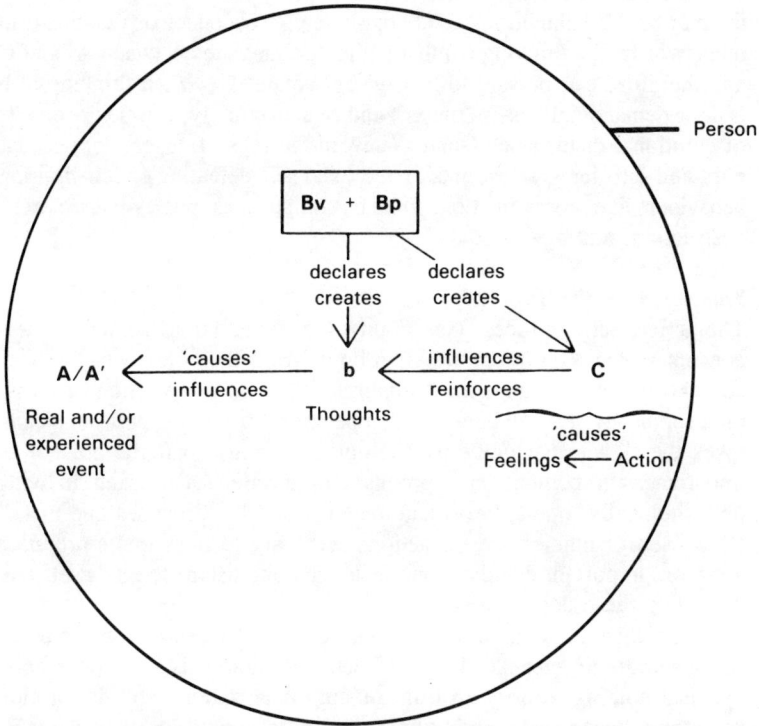

Figure 4.5 *The active–reactive process (here,* **Bv** + **Bp** = *life position of living philosophically)*

As a next step in the process, people think about the experienced activating event (A'). Yet, while people can have any number of thoughts about their experienced activating event (A'), these thoughts are rarely random or accidental). To the contrary, the thinking that people do about A', designated in Figure 4.4 as b, is strongly moulded by their higher-order cognitions, most prominently by their life positions (Bp), values (Bv), and interpretational habits (B$_i$). Most notable at b, then, are either preferential or demanding thinking (reflecting the life position of either demandingness or affirmation), either evaluative or nonevaluative thinking about oneself or other selves (self as object versus self as context), and either thinking that reflects a belief in one's being powerful and in control (the life positions of being at cause and living philosophically) or a belief that one is relatively powerless and helpless (being at effect and living psychologically). Thus, the thinking that goes on about any particular experience or event (A') may be unique and random but more probably is moulded or formed by more basic, enduring cognitions carried with the person across situations.

Finally, following RET, the interaction of A' and b strongly influences the emotional, behavioural, and cognitive consequences or reactions. In other words, the thinking (b) that people do mediates between A' and C and therefore can be said to 'cause' or 'create' C. When thinking at b is done demandingly (as in 'musts') and/or self-ratingly, C usually consists of emotional disturbance (such as severe feelings of anger, depression, guilt and self-denigration, and anxiety; and self-defeating or self-limiting behaviours like procrastination, phobias, compulsions, possessiveness, self-destruction, and aggression).

The Active–Active Process

The active–active process (see Figure 4.5) is, as far as I know, a new concept in the RET literature. It follows from the construct of self as context or potential and, most importantly, from the position of living philosophically. As will be recalled, a person who is living philosophically takes the stance that one's psychological response patterns are not as important as the commitments, promises, or declared stands taken. In living philosophically, one *believes* and *declares* that the promises one makes (to oneself or others) and the actions necessary to fulfil one's promises are more important than how one feels, and one listens to one's self-talk regarding these declarations.

In the active–active process, then, the concept of a *declaration* is crucial. In the spirit of the contextual ABC model, a declaration is an act of creation that has nothing to do with truth or empirical validity; by declaration something becomes so simply because a person says so, or declares it. Examples of declarations include the following: a judge declares a defendant guilty; a baseball umpire calls a strike; a parent names a child 'Todd'; a priest pronounces someone married; a person forgives himself for a wrongdoing; a person says, 'I love you', to someone else. All of these outcomes happen or become real simply because someone with authority says so.

The importance of the declaration process is that people, by endorsing the position of living philosophically, have the power to create out of their own self-initiated declarations how they will act, feel, and think without any immediate or prior stimulating event or condition needed. It may very well be that, once one declares that one will act a certain way and follows through on the declaration, a process of feeling and thinking consistent with the action occurs; that is, the self-initiated act will 'cause' feelings and thoughts congruent with the action (see Figure 4.5). Furthermore, it also may very well be that events in the environment, formerly thought of as activating events, begin to respond in a way that is consistent with this process. The person, in the long run, has actually influenced the occurrence of events in the environment. Thus, these events become the consequences of the individual intervening directly at point C so that it is possible for the process to occur from C to B to A, rather than the usual A–B–C one.

Take, for example, a husband who is in a marriage that is conflictual and in crisis; he is often angry with his wife, he frequently acts ungraciously and hostilely toward her, and he regularly participates with her in bickering. Amidst this situation he may take the stance that she is at fault in the conflict and, furthermore, that she causes him to feel and act as he does (he believes that A causes C). Or, he may even go so far as to take responsibility for his actions and feelings (holding that his Bs cause C), but he nonetheless believes that he has no choice but to act and feel as he does until he changes either her actions, his own thinking, or both (living psychologically). Either way, he will continue his marriage-defeating behaviour.

Now, imagine a whole new scenario in which this same man lives philosophically: he believes that his commitments are more important than how he feels, and furthermore he believes that he can choose to act in certain ways simply because he declares he will. So, wanting to try to make his marrage once again viable, he *declares* that he will act in considerate, respectful, and even kind ways to his wife, even though his feelings or attitudes toward her are not consistent with this; in effect, he creates these behaviours at C from nothing except his value for the marriage and his self-generated declaration (see Figure 4.5). Imagine, further, that this husband also *declares* that he will mostly think about his wife's good attributes, that he will frequently remember the good times they had together, and that he will regularly imagine having fun with her in the future. Now he has created thoughts at b, with no activating event present or necessary to stimulate them. Before long, he will 'cause' himself to feel in ways consistent with his actions, and he will influence and reinforce, by his positive actions and feelings, the positive thoughts, memories, and fantasies he has about his wife at b. What is likely to happen, as is often observed in marriage counselling, is that when one spouse (here, the husband) sustains positive behaviour toward the other spouse, the spouse (here, the wife) tends to come around and act in ways consistent with the positive behaviour she gets. In RET terms, this husband created the A. So, by creating C, he influences b, and both C and b 'caused' A.

Some Implications for Psychotherapy and Wellness

The contextual ABC model is *not* a new model of psychotherapy; rather, it is the ABCs of RET expanded in a way that represents the complexities of human cognitions; the diverse and fluid interrelationships among the As, the Bs, and the Cs; and the power that people have to influence and even to create their beliefs, actions, and feelings, regardless of the external reality. This model is intensely cognitive and philosophical at its core and, as such, completely endorses and seeks to further the fundamental premises and techniques of rational–emotive therapy. Consistent with the goals and aims of RET, then, some of the contextual ABC model's implications for psychotherapy are as follows.

Forwarding Elegant Change

A feature that distinguishes RET from other cognitive-behavioural therapies is its preferred goal of elegant change (Ellis, 1971, 1974b, 1977, 1979; Grieger and Boyd, 1980). *Elegant change* means first to lessen or reduce client endorsement of disturbance-producing cognitions, rather than mere symptom removal or environmental problem solving; moreover, elegant change means to lessen or reduce dysfunctional evaluative attitudes or beliefs (for example, 'I *must* be liked') rather than inaccurate, non-evaluative interpretations (for example, 'No one likes me'), although the latter are still deemed appropriate grist for the therapeutic mill.

The contextual ABC model goes beyond the exploration and ameliora-tion of situational-specific b's to the uncovering and modification of the most profoundly held and enduring Bs (life positions, values and inter-pretational habits). By inviting clients to discover their (often unconscious) Bs and by teaching them the enormous impact of those Bs on how they perceive and respond to the events in their lives, and thus how they colour the very quality of their lives, the 'need' for elegant change of the most profound order is made absolutely clear and palpable.

Forwarding Philosophical Change

Closely related to and even concurrent with the endorsement and furthering of elegant change is the forwarding of philosophical change. Ellis (1962, 1971) has long contended that RET is much more a philosophical than a psychological endeavour, in that emotional and behavioural problems are essentially the result of holding dysfunctional or self-defeating beliefs or philosophies. Successful therapy therefore involves giving up these philosophies and replacing them with more workable ones. Indeed, most skilled RET practitioners spend a high percentage of time with their clients in philosophical exchanges.

The contextual ABC model is deeply wedded to this perspective. A rereading of the section in this chapter on life positions will show that each of the four dichotomies described are philosophical stances that can be said to guide and set the boundaries of our thinking, doing, and feeling. These form the backdrop or context out of which everything else comes. In the contextual ABC model, then, it would behove the therapist to focus on the most elegant and far-reaching outcomes, that is, to make the correction of life positions (Bp) the first order of business, with inter-pretation (B$_1$) and thinking (b) change following.

Furthering Self-acceptance

A particularly powerful and unique aspect of RET is its endorsement of self-acceptance (*a priori*, non-evaluative acceptance of self) over self-esteeming (a criterion-based, conditional process of valuing the self). People are encouraged to rate their performances honestly but not to extend this to rating themselves (Ellis, 1971, 1972, 1974a, 1974b, 1977).

In articulating the concept of the self as context (or as potential), rather than as an object, the contextual ABC model provides an even clearer opportunity for clients to liberate themselves from self-assessment. For, when self is conceived as the potential *out of which* what one does and has emerges, but is not what one does or has, the absurdity of self-rating leaps out and we are left with the only viable alternative, a self-acceptance model.

Allowing Emotional Disturbance to be Irrelevant

A phenomenon noted by many RET therapists is what has been called a 'second-level problem' (Ellis, 1971, 1974a, 1977, 1979; Ellis and Harper, 1975; Grieger and Boyd, 1980). What this means is that, once people develop an emotional problem, a social phobia for instance, they often develop another emotional problem *about* the original problem, like depression or anger about being phobic. In RET we often find it necessary to help clients get rid of the second problem before tackling the original one.

The contextual ABC model takes this practice one step farther by advocating that people adopt and practice the life positions of living philosophically and being at cause. In deciding that they are ultimately responsible for what happens to them in life, despite barriers and adverse circumstances, and by determining that they will uphold their commitments regardless of how they feel at a particular moment in time, clients have the power to make their emotional problems irrelevant. These emotional problems then simply become barriers, circumstances, or psychological states, like many others, that can be overcome or even disregarded as clients continue to work toward creating satisfaction and happiness in their lives.

To illustrate this concept briefly, take the case of a 50-year-old woman who became rather depressed about several severe compulsions she developed following the untimely death of her 20-year-old daughter. While working on the irrational belief underlying her compulsions, I taught her the two life positions of living philosophically and being at cause. She, with encouragement, used them in her life successfully. To use her words, she convinced herself to take the following attitude: 'These compulsions are stupid and are an annoyance in life, but they only occupy a part of my time. I'm determined to enjoy myself at times when I don't act this way, and I will actively find ways to do so despite them. My life is bigger than these compulsions.' In no time her depression lifted and she and I are now concluding the therapy on her compulsions. The important point, however, is that, even if she is unable to rid herself completely of her compulsions, she can still have a happy life, so long as she keeps this attitude. In effect, then, she has made her compulsions irrelevant to her enjoyment of life.

Moving toward a Wellness Model
While we all would probably agree that there is a lot more to mental health than the absence of symptoms (Ardell, 1979; Ellis, 1980a, 1980b; Phares, 1979; Rogers, 1961), most of the field of psychotherapy is locked into a disease model that emphasizes the remediation of emotional, behavioural, and/or social symptomology. Although RET is certainly noteworthy for its didactic methods, its appeal to the masses through self-help literature, and its willingness to use radical vehicles to reach large groups of people (such as Ellis's famous Friday Night Workshops), it by and large fits into the remediation framework. An alternative approach is embodied in the wellness or holistic health movement, in which therapy is defined as 'any attempt to help the patient achieve a high level of wellness' (Kaplan, Saltzman, and Ecker, 1979). Treatment then focuses on health care instead of, or in addition to, disease care.

It seems to me that the contextual ABC model lends itself to the conditions of the wellness model quite nicely. In addition to doing psychotherapy with 'sick' people, the model suggests ways to help people achieve high levels of wellness, including teaching them healthy life positions (for example, affirmation instead of demanding; being at cause rather than being at effect), specific healthy attitudes (for example, 'I do not need to always succeed'), and various helpful life skills (for example, communication skills, skills in self-analysis), as well as self-acceptance and anti-awfulizing stances.

Enhancing Personal Power
Most people who try to define a mentally healthy or 'fully functioning' person include terms that convey a person's ability to act independently, freely, self-directedly, and powerfully. Examples include Rogers's (1961) concept of inner directedness, Wessler and Wessler's (1980) focus on a person's ability to make choices freely, and Ellis's (1980a) criteria of self-interest, self-direction, commitment, and risk taking.

If these features indeed characterize healthy people, then the contextual ABC model provides a unique framework from which to help people attain these attributes. For, in addition to helping people to rid themselves of irrational demands and self-ratings, the therapist can help clients and others to adopt the living philosophically and being at cause life positions, thereby teaching people how to live creatively and declaratively, regardless of the inner or outer circumstances of their lives. By adopting these positions, people act because they determine that they do so, not because it does or does not feel good or because others will or will not approve; that is, they come from positions of personal power, freedom, and complete autonomy.

Conclusion

The contextual ABC model represents a departure from the traditional ABC paradigm of RET. While in no way denouncing the theory or practice of RET, its intent is to capture in a three-dimensional and dynamic way the intricacies of human feeling, thinking, and acting and the complexities of human cognitions. Distinctions are made between situation-specific thoughts, ideas, and beliefs (small b's) and relatively enduring and constant philosophies and styles (large Bs). The latter include life positions (expressed via the dichotomies of demandingness versus affirmation, self as object versus self as context, living psychologically versus living philosophically, and being at effect versus being at cause). The other Bs are values and interpretational habits. Also delineated are the active–reactive and the active–active processes. The former relates to the power of Bs to mould and create both the events in the world as perceived by the person and the situational-specific thinking a person does about these perceived events. The latter relates to the power a person has to create actions, feelings, and thoughts independently of a stimulating event.

It is hoped that the concepts and constructs presented in the contextual ABC model will further the basic goals of rational–emotive therapy, which are the promotion of elegant and philosophical change, the elimination of second-level problems or emotional problems about emotional problems, and the enhancement of personal wellness and power. Reactions and comments to this chapter are welcome, in the spirit of the continuing development of RET.

Note

This chapter was first published in the *Journal of Rational–Emotive Therapy*, 1985, 3(2): 79–99. I want to express my deep appreciation to Ingrid Grieger for the many helpful suggestions she made on this chapter and for the many hours she spent in editorial work.

References

Ardell, D. B. (1979) *High level wellness*. Emmaus, PA: Rodale Press.
Bandura, A. (1977) Self-efficacy: toward a unifying theory of behavioral change. *Psychological Review*, 84: 191–215.
Bartley, W. W. (1978) *Werner Erhard: the transformation of a man; the founding of EST*. New York: Carkson N. Potter.

Beck, A. T. (1967) *Depression: clinical, experimental, and theoretical aspects.* New York: Hoeber.

Bernard, M. E. (1980) Private thought in rational–emotive psychotherapy. *Rational Living,* 15: 3–8.

Boyd, J. and Grieger, R. (1982) Self-acceptance problems. In R. Grieger and I. Z. Grieger (eds), *Cognition and emotional disturbance.* New York: Human Sciences Press.

Bry, A. (1976) *EST.* New York: Avon Books.

Coopersmith, S. (1967) *The antecedents of self-esteem.* San Francisco: W. H. Freeman.

Diekstra, R. and Dassen, W. F. (1979) *Rationale therapie.* Amsterdam: Swets and Zeitlinger.

Earle, M. and Regin, N. (1980) *A world that works for everyone.* San Francisco: The EST Enterprise.

Ellis, A. (1958) Rational psychotherapy. *Journal of General Psychology,* 59: 35–49.

Ellis, A. (1962) *Reason and emotion in psychotherapy.* Secaucus, NJ: Lyle Stuart.

Ellis, A. (1971) *Growth through reason.* North Hollywood, CA: Wilshire Book Company.

Ellis, A. (1972) Psychotherapy and the value of a human being. In W. Davis (ed.), *Value and valuation: aetiological studies in honor of Robert A. Hartman.* Knoxville, TN: University of Tennessee Press.

Ellis, A. (1974a) *How to stubbornly refuse to be ashamed of anything.* Cassette recording. New York: Institute for Rational–Emotive Therapy.

Ellis (1974b) *Humanistic psychotherapy: the rational–emotive approach.* New York: McGraw-Hill.

Ellis, A. (1976) RET abolishes most of the human ego. *Psychotherapy: Theory, Research and Practice,* 13: 343–8.

Ellis, A. (1977) The basic clinical theory of rational–emotive therapy. In A. Ellis and R. Grieger (eds), *Handbook for rational-emotive therapy, vol. 1.* New York: Springer.

Ellis, A. (1979) The theory of rational–emotive therapy. In A. Ellis and J. Whiteley (eds), *Theoretical and empirical foundations of rational–emotive therapy.* Monterey, CA: Brooks/Cole.

Ellis, A. (1980a) An overview of the clinical theory of rational–emotive therapy. In R. Greiger and J. Boyd, *Rational–emotive therapy: a skills-based approach.* New York: Van Nostrand Reinhold.

Ellis, A. (1980b) Rational–emotive therapy and cognitive behavior therapy: similarities and differences. *Cognitive Therapy and Research,* 4: 325–40.

Ellis, A. (1985) Expanding the ABCs of RET. In M. J. Mahoney and A. Freeman (eds), *Cognition and psychotherapy.* New York: Plenum.

Ellis, A. and Harper, R. A. (1975) *A new guide to rational living.* Englewood Cliffs, NJ: Prentice-Hall.

Eschenroeder, C. (1982) How rational is rational–emotive therapy? A critical appraisal of its theoretical foundation and therapeutic methods. *Cognitive Therapy and Research,* 6: 381–92.

Grieger, R. (1975) Self-concept, self-esteem, and rational–emotive theory. *Rational Living,* 10: 12–17.

Grieger, R. and Boyd, J. (1980) *Rational–emotive therapy: a skills-based approach.* New York: Van Nostrand Reinhold.

Huber, C. H. (1985) Pure versus pragmatic RET. *Journal of Counseling and Development,* 63: 321–2.

Kaplan, R., Saltzman, B. and Ecker, L. (1979) *Wholly alive.* Millbrae, CA: Celestial Arts.

Mahoney, M. J. (1980) Psychotherapy and the structure of personal revolutions. In M. J. Mahoney (ed.), *Psychotherapy process.* New York: Plenum.

Maultsby, M. C. (1975) *Help yourself to happiness*. New York: Institute for Rational–Emotive Therapy.

Peterson, D. R. (1968) *The clinical study of social behavior*. New York: Appleton-Century-Crofts.

Phares, E. (1979) *Clinical psychology: concepts, methods and profession*. Homewood, IL: Dorsey Press.

Rhinehart, L. (1976) *The book of EST*. New York: Holt, Rinehart and Winston.

Rogers, C. (1961) *On becoming a person*. New York: Houghton-Mifflin.

Rotter, J. B. (1966) Generalized expectances for internal versus external control of reinforcement. *Psychological Monographs*, 80 (1, whole no. 609).

Siegel, A. (1984) *Ideas*. Paper presented at The Forum Conference, San Francisco, CA, July 2–6.

Smith, D. (1982) Trends in counseling and psychotherapy. *American Psychologist*, 37: 802–9.

Wessler, R. A. and Wessler, R. L. (1980) *The principles and practice of rational–emotive therapy*. San Francisco, CA: Jossey-Bass.

Comments on Grieger's Contextual Model of the ABCs of RET

Windy Dryden

In this chapter several features of Grieger's contextual model of the ABCs of RET are criticized. It is argued that (a) Grieger fails at various points to give due regard to the interactive nature of evaluative and interpretive thinking and that he fails to show clearly how people's evaluative thinking can colour the interpretations that they make about A; (b) Grieger fails to distinguish clearly between the terms 'create' and 'influence'; (c) Grieger's claim that Life Positions are dichotomous is not valid; (d) the Life Position of Living Psychologically implies a philosophy toward psychological events, a point neglected by Grieger; (e) Grieger's statements about individuals being totally responsible for their wellbeing are overgeneralizations; (f) Grieger fails to show clearly how some invalid and unempirical 'declarations' can be signs of emotional disturbance; and (g) Grieger's view that emotional disturbance can be seen as *irrelevant* encourages clients' indifference rather than rational concern. Nevertheless, Grieger has introduced an interesting and thought-provoking model into the RET literature. Several suggestions are made to improve the model.

Grieger has outlined a complex model of the ABCs of RET which he terms 'contextual'. It is in many ways an excellent and ambitious model which will, as he hopes, promote much debate among rational–emotive theorists and therapists. However, in my opinion, the model has certain deficiencies and in response to his request for comments on his paper, I will outline these and will indicate how his model could be improved.

Thinking about A and its 'Creation'

Grieger correctly distinguishes between actual events in the real world (A) and the perceived reality of these actual events (A'). He argues that a person 'creates' A' by means of interpretative thinking about A. However, he does not, at this point of his article, emphasize sufficiently that such interpretations are often based on the person's evaluative thinking which he or she brings to A.[1] Thus, if I believe that I *must* be approved by my professional colleagues, I will more likely predict that Grieger will dislike me for writing this critique than I would if I believed that I want to be approved by my colleagues, but that I don't have to be. My interpretation is coloured by my evaluation.

In his Figure 4.1 (p. 74) Grieger outlines in *linear* form a process whereby A occurs which the person then interprets to create A' which is then evaluated to 'create' the emotional/behavioural reactions to A'. This assumes that interpretative thinking about A occurs before evaluative thinking and constitutes a major weakness of this part of his model, since it seems to not only (a) downplay the role played by evaluative thinking in colouring the kind of interpretations the person brings to A, but also (b) de-emphasize the interactive interplay between evaluative and interpretative thinking processes (Ellis, 1984). These are also major weaknesses of Wessler and Wessler's (1980) eight-step model of ABCs.

I suggest that Grieger's model can be improved, then, by (a) showing that humans *bring to* situations their tendencies to make evaluations which often influence the kinds of interpretations they make, and by (b) stressing that, in reality, interpretative and evaluative thinking interact.

Later in the article, Grieger discusses a case where a husband by sustaining positive behaviour toward his spouse 'creates' A whereby his wife 'tends to come around and act in ways consistent with the positive behaviour she gets. In RET terms this husband *created the A'* (p. 87, italics added). This is incorrect since it omits the wife's own interpretations and evaluations about her husband's behaviour. It would be more accurate to say that the husband's behaviour *influenced* A rather than *created* it. Grieger's model would be improved at this point were he to distinguish accurately between the processes of creation and influence.

The Validity of the Dichotomous Nature of Life Positions

Grieger outlines four major Life Positions (Demandingness vs. Affirmation; Self as Object vs. Self as Context; Living Psychologically vs. Living Philosophically; and Being at Effect vs. Being at Cause) and argues that 'Each of the four can be stated as a dichotomy between two poles, with no middle ground, the person at any moment stands either at one pole or the other, but rarely ever with a foot in both' (p. 77). Taking Demandingness vs. Affirmation as an example, this is in direct opposition to Ellis's (1979) statements that we have *both* rational and irrational beliefs about A and that particularly when our desires are strong we often 'escalate' our desires into demanding musts. This escalation process implies that at a given point in time we have *both* musts *and* desires about a given event rather than either–or. Grieger's dichotomies may, in practice, discourage clients from changing their evaluative thinking by leading them to believe that they had better *only* adhere to one pole completely.

In addition, Grieger's dichotomies appear to conflict with Ellis's (1963) position on the difference between intellectual insight (a weak and context bound belief) and emotional insight (a strong and generally held belief). According to Ellis, changing from intellectual insight to emotional insight appears to occur along a continuum and does not result, as Grieger's model implies, from making a leap from one pole to the other. If Grieger would show that we can, in fact hold two Life Positions simultaneously, albeit at different degrees of strength, the model would then allow for clients to weaken an irrational belief while *at the same time* strengthening a rational belief. Another advantage of showing that the Life Positions are not dichotomous would be that it would bring more flexibility to Grieger's model. Dichotomous thinking appears to run contrary to the relativistic philosophy of RET.

Living Psychologically vs Living Philosophically: Two Philosophies not One

Among the four 'Life Positions', Grieger presents *Living Psychologically* where 'people identify themselves as exclusively psychological beings' (p. 80) which he contrasts with *Living Philosophically* where psychological events are not denied but are put aside. Grieger notes that 'Living Philosophically means that one holds one's word, or one's promises and commitments, as being of paramount importance, regardless of how one feels at a given moment in time' (p. 81). These positions, of course, approximate to Ellis's (1979) concepts of short-range and long-range hedonism. However, they do not, in my opinion, represent an advance over Ellis's concepts because they imply that only one position, Living Philosophically, represents a philosophy. I disagree. A person who is Living Psychologically is indeed choosing to adopt a *philosophy* of short-range hedonism, whereby that person *chooses* to abandon important commitments in favour of satisfying less important (from a long-term perspective) but more immediately pressing psychological desires. Grieger's concept of Living Psychologically, then, obscures the fact that in *both* Life Positions, a person has a philosophy towards immediate psychological events that 'determine' how that person will feel and act, in the face of events. Showing that *both* positions imply a philosophy would strengthen the model here and help clients to understand better that they may, for example, actually choose to act according to the philosophy of long-range hedonism even though they may want to act according to a philosophy of short-range hedonism.

Being at Effect vs Being at Cause and the Concept of Total Responsibility

Grieger contrasts Being at Effect, whereby 'a person believes that the circumstances in one's life control one's destiny' (p. 81), with Being at Cause which 'starts from a position of personal responsibility for one's own well-being, for how one responds to events, and for the choices one makes in life *regardless of the circumstances*' (p. 81, italics added). While this is an interesting distinction (although I note again that these positions are best viewed as opposite poles of a continuum rather than dichotomous), Grieger goes on to say that Being at Cause includes the belief that 'I am *totally* responsible for my own well-being' (p. 81). This, in my opinion, is an invalid overgeneralization and stems from the worst excesses of 'est' philosophy which has influenced (but not created!) Greiger's views (Rhinehart, 1976). Although Grieger terms his model 'Contextual' he, in fact, appears to underestimate the effect that one's context may have in constraining (but not, of course, completely determining), one's well-being. Contexts, particularly harsh ones like an earthquake and a nuclear holocaust, as Ellis (1984) has noted, have an important influencing effect on one's well-being and had better be given due regard in any model of the emotions rather than held as unimportant as in Grieger's amplification of Being at Cause (see above, particularly the phrase 'regardless of the circumstances'). I suggest that Grieger's model can be improved by showing that people are mainly (but not totally) responsible for their well-being and that circumstances do have an influence on their well-being.

Invalid and Unempirical Declarations as Disturbance

Grieger introduces a new concept into the RET literature termed the 'active–active process' which describes how people can create feelings, thoughts and behaviours independent of any prior activating stimuli. He argues that the concept of a *Declaration* is crucial in the process which he defines as 'an act of creation that has nothing to do with truth or empirical validity' (p. 86), *but fails to show how some declarations that are invalid and unempirical can often be a feature of emotional disturbance.* Burns (1980), in contrast, has shown that 'emotional reasoning' (for example, 'since I feel it (declaration) it must be so'), is a cognitive distortion that is often a feature of such disturbance. According to Ellis (1979), healthy individuals strive to test out the validity of their 'declarations' and employ the logico-empirical methods of science in the process. A person who Lives Philosophically based on an invalid declaration appears healthy according to Grieger's criteria but would be judged emotionally disturbed by Ellis (1979). Showing that some unempirical declarations may encourage psychological disturbance would give Grieger's model greater clarity on this issue.

Emotional Disturbance as Irrelevant
– a Denial of Desire

In discussing some of his model's implications for psychotherapy and well-being, Grieger argues that it allows emotional disturbance to become irrelevant. Thus, individuals who adopt and practise the Life Positions of Living Philosophically and Being at Cause 'have the power to make their emotional problems irrelevant' (p. 89). Here, as elsewhere, Grieger ignores the fact that people have desires and while it is true that they can commit themselves to following long-term projects despite their emotional problems, it does not follow that their emotional problems thus become irrelevant. Such people will often prefer not to have these problems. They are not indifferent to them and I am concerned that Grieger may here be reinforcing a basic tendency of clients to change their philosophy of demandingness ('I must not have such emotional disturbances') to one of indifference ('It doesn't matter at all if I have them'). This would encourage clients to deny their rational desires – hardly a highly recommended principle of RET! So Grieger could improve his model by showing that emotional disturbance *is* relevant to clients' well-being in the sense that it very often matters to them whether or not they have disturbed feelings. I agree with Grieger, however, that they do not have to be slaves to their disturbed feelings and can work toward creating satisfaction and happiness in their lives *despite* such feelings.

In conclusion, while Grieger's contextual model of the ABCs of RET contains, in my opinion, the above deficiencies, he is to be congratulated for introducing an interesting and thought-provoking set of ideas into the RET literature. If he revises his model along the lines outlined above, then I believe that his contribution to RET theory will prove to be outstanding!

Note

1 The hypothesis that evaluations colour interpretations is an important one in RET theory that has not been directly tested empirically. I am, at present, conducting a series of studies specifically designed to test this hypothesis.

References

Burns, D. D. (1980) *Feeling good: the new mood therapy.* New York: Morrow.
Ellis, A. (1963) Toward a more precise definition of 'emotional' and 'intellectual' insight. *Psychological Reports*, 13: 125–6.

Ellis, A. (1979) The theory of rational–emotive therapy. In A. Ellis and J. M. Whiteley (eds), *Theoretical and empirical foundations of rational–emotive therapy*. Monterey, Calif.: Brooks/Cole.

Ellis, A. (1984) Expanding the ABCs of RET. *Journal of Rational–Emotive Therapy*, 2(2): 20–4.

Rhinehart, L. (1976) *The book of EST*. New York: Holt, Rinehart & Winston.

Wessler, R. A. and Wessler, R. L. (1980) *The principles and practice of rational–emotive therapy*. San Francisco: Jossey-Bass.

Comments on Grieger's Contextual Model of the ABCs of RET

Albert Ellis

Grieger's contextual model of the ABCs of RET is well conceived, presents some fascinating and provocative ideas, includes some original suggestions, and adds some theoretical and practical points that may well prove valuable to RET practitioners. It raises some important questions, as Dryden has indicated, and I largely agree with his criticisms. Rather than repeat what Dryden has said, let me make some additional comments that largely concern the therapeutic aspects of Grieger's suggestions.

Demandingness vs Affirmation

Grieger fully endorses RET's stand against demandingness and musturbation (Ellis, 1962, 1979, 1985; Ellis and Harper, 1975) and opts for Affirmation, 'an active position of power and potential action to get what one wants in the future' (p. 77). RET has always advocated action to effect change by emphasizing its own version of Reinhold Niebuhr's serenity prayer: 'Let me grant myself the courage to change what I can change, the serenity to accept what I cannot change, and the wisdom to know the difference between the two.' Grieger (p. 77) seems to go beyond this by defining Affirmation as ' "choosing" what is there and what is not there. It is taking what one gets when one gets it and not taking what one does not get when one does not get it (Rhinehart, 1976).' I frankly did not quite understand this when I read it in Rhinehart who originally 'got it' from Werner Erhard; and I am still not sure that I do. It implies that (1) we have no choice but to 'choose' what *now* exists, and (2) we need only accept it *after* we act against it and still find that we cannot change it. RET endorses the second position but it is still not clear whether Erhard, Rhinehart, and Grieger also endorse the first. Some clarification is in order here.

Self as Object vs Self as Context

Grieger clearly points out that when we view ourselves as objects we easily and self-defeatingly evaluate our 'self' as being either bad or good, and he notes that 'RET has made an enormous contribution in helping clients to stop this self-defeating process by making the important distinction between self-esteem and self-acceptance.... It is recommended that people rate their individual performances but that they entirely dispense with rating their selves' (p. 79).

In his next paragraph, however, Grieger holds that 'Despite the obvious advantages in RET of advocating self-acceptance over self-esteem, the self as object model is still retained' (p. 79). I fail to see how he comes to this conclusion. If RET entirely dispenses with rating people's selves – as, indeed it does! – how does it retain the self as object model? As I have pointed out to my clients and workshop audiences since 1962, 'If you insist on rating your "self", you had better say, "I am good just because I exist".' Then you won't get into any trouble. But this is philosophically unsound, because your self-statement is unprovable and unfalsifiable. Someone could just as accurately say, 'You're no good because you exist.' Therefore, it would be wiser if you say, 'I exist. I want to continue to exist and to be happy. I will therefore only rate my acts and traits in regard to remaining alive and enjoying myself; and I refuse to rate my "self", my "essence", or my "being" at all.' In this RET formulation, as far as I can see, the self as object model is avoided.

Self as Context vs Self as Potential

Grieger advocates seeing the self as context – as 'the background, the context or backdrop, out of which what the person has or does emerges ... "Who a person is" is defined as potential – a clearing, an opportunity, a context' (p. 80). This definition of 'self' is intriguing and seems fairly sensible. It is similar to one of the common RET arguments that you cannot really rate yourself because you are a process, an ongoing entity, with a past and with a future, and therefore you cannot accurately rate this ever-changing *process* (as if it were a *product*).

The problem with the terms that Grieger uses to define the 'self' is that they mostly seem to be rateable and can consequently lead to seeing and rating the self as object. Thus, your *potential* as a human may be good or bad. If you are deaf, dumb, and blind, you have less *potential* for life and for happiness than if your senses are in good condition. Your *opportunity* for life and joy may also be fine or poor. If you are poor, old and ill, you have much less *opportunity* than if you are rich, young and healthy. Your *context* may also be measurable, in that if you live in a desert or in a community where there is little law and order, you may have considerably less chances of remaining alive and happy than in a moderate and orderly environment. Defining your 'self' in terms of *potential*, *opportunity*, or *context* may therefore lead you to see your 'self' as good or bad. In RET, we would not try to define your 'self' at all, but merely to say that your *aliveness* or *existence* is 'good' or 'better' when it leads to prolonged life and happiness and that it is 'bad' or 'worse' when it leads to shorter life and unhappiness.

Living Psychologically vs Living Philosophically

Grieger notes that Living Philosophically is 'a position that has the effect of undeifying one's psychology; that is, one notes one's psychological state but puts it aside. Living Philosophically means that one holds one's word, or one's promises and commitments, as being of paramount importance, regardless of how one feels at a given moment in time' (p. 81). RET has always, of course, opposed deifying one's feelings, failing to keep commitments because of present moods, and giving in to short-range rather than long-range pleasures. But Grieger's way of de-escalating Living Psychologically can be taken to antihedonistic extremes in several respects:

1   If you note your psychological state and 'put it aside', you are in danger of ignoring your rational *preferences* and *wishes* along with your irrational *demands*. If you really love a person and marry him or her, you may later *rationally* prefer and *appropriately* desire not to be with him or her.
2   No matter how strong your commitment to someone or something may be, if you make it 'of paramount importance' you may prevent your giving equal or greater importance to sensible noncommitment. If the mate you committed yourself to marry and have children with acts very abusively to you and your children you may sanely decide to uncommit yourself, to sue for divorce, and to ask for custody of the children.
3   'Living Psychologically' invariably *includes* your goals, purposes, and desires that you normally *bring* to the ABCs of RET – as I show in the expanded model of these ABCs (Ellis, 1984a). You only irrationally disturb yourself – at points B and C – because you *desire* to gain some pleasure and/or to avoid some pain and because you then *command* that you *have to* get what you want and avoid what you don't want. Living Psychologically (as well as Philosophically) shows you what your goals and wishes are. RET teaches, therefore, that you had better not live *too* psychologically, nor *too* philosophically. It advocates both/and rather than either/or.

Being at Effect vs Being at Cause

Grieger opposes Being at Effect, 'a position in which one believes that the circumstances in one's life controls one's destiny and well-being' and he espouses Being at Cause, 'a position of personal responsibility for one's well-being, for how one responds to events, and for choices one makes in life, regardless of circumstances' (p. 81).

Once again, following Werner Erhard's position, Grieger takes things to extremes that RET avoids, especially when he notes that 'I am totally responsible for my own well-being.' RET holds that you are far from totally responsible for your own well-being, since that depends on many environmental and innate factors – such as the conditions under which you live, your physical and mental heredity, the rules and regulations of your community, etc. As Bertrand Russell (1950) once wisely said, anyone who believes what happens solely comes from within had better be condemned to spending a night in rags in a raging storm in sub-zero weather!

RET, along with practically all cognitive-behavioural therapies, hypothesizes that your Belief System (B) *largely* determines your *disturbed* emotional Consequences (C) after obnoxious Activating Events (A) have occurred in your life (Beck, 1976; Ellis, 1958, 1962, 1971, 1973, 1985; Meichenbaum, 1977; Mahoney and Freeman, 1985; Grieger and Boyd, 1980). But it does not insist that your Bs are *completely* self-chosen, since it acknowledges that what you believe is usually strongly influenced (though not entirely mandated) by your social learning, by your innate predispositions to think in certain ways, by changing conditions in your life, etc. What Grieger calls Being at Cause really seems to be Being at Cause *and* Effect, since humans are born strongly influenceable and never seem to be *completely* independent and self-choosing in their thinking and feeling. To assume that they are can easily lead to feelings of grandiosity and pollyannaism – which many religious and mystical therapies, including est, unfortunately encourage.

The Active–Active Process and the Concept of Declaration

Grieger advocates an Active–Active instead of an Active–Reactive process and encourages people to follow it and to Live Philosophically by making a Declaration, 'an act of creation that has nothing to do with truth or empirical validity . . . People have the power to create out of their own self-initiated declarations how they will act, feel, and think without any immediate or prior stimulating event or condition needed' (p. 86).

Grieger's concept of Declaration logically follows from his concept of people Living Philosophically rather than Living Psychologically. It is an important therapeutic point, if not stated in the extreme form in which he has formulated it. For, as he indicates, humans *can* actually *declare* that they will ignore their negative thoughts and feelings about their mates, they *can* act kindly toward these mates, and in the very act of doing so they *can* create new As (remembrances of good instead of bad times they had with their mates) and also create new Cs (feelings of renewed love for these mates).

I have often quoted, in this respect, Stendhal's famous words from his book, *On Love*, published early in the nineteenth century (Stendhal, 1947): 'If you act as if you're in love, you will frequently fall in love.' I have also, using RET, induced many marital partners to *resolve* to act kindly and more sexually to their mates, to force themselves to *act* on this resolve, and thereby often to create a better marriage and the feelings of sex and love that accompany it.

So Grieger's point is a very important one. Human thought is *creative* and only *partly* depends on outside conditions and internal feelings. You can, by what Assagioli (1965) calls an act of will, significantly change your present thoughts, your feelings, and your behaviours. Similarly, as I indicated in my first RET writings (Ellis, 1958, 1962), thoughts, feelings and actions are invariably interrelated, not pure. They inevitably affect each other; and that is why RET has always been a comprehensive and multimodal form of therapy, employing many cognitive, emotive and behavioural methods (Ellis, 1962, 1973, 1984b, 1985; Ellis and Bernard, 1985).

Grieger's important point about the Declaration Process, however, holds that people 'have the power to create out of their own self-initiated declarations how they will act, feel, and think *without any immediate or prior stimulating event or condition needed* (p. 86, emphasis added). But this would mean they can hoist themselves by their own bootstraps, think and feel in a vacuum without *any* prior (or existing) environmental conditions or learning. And presumably without the physical and mental limitations that their bodies impose on them. How is this possible? How can they act, think, or feel as disembodied spirits? RET has always held that people have much *more* power over themselves (and their environment) than they choose to recognize and use. More, but hardly unlimited!

In sum, Grieger's contextual model of the ABCs of RET is very thought-provoking and presents some ideas that may well add to its theory and practice. But the manner in which its therapeutic hypotheses are presented poses serious problems to which we had better give continued thought and experimentation.

References

Assagioli, R. (1965) *Psychosynthesis*. New York: Viking.

Beck, A. T. (1976) *Cognitive therapy and the emotional disorders*. New York: International Universities Press.

Ellis, A. (1958) Rational psychotherapy. *Journal of General Psychology*, 59: 35–49.

Ellis, A. (1962) *Reason and emotion in psychotherapy*. Secaucus, NJ: Citadel Press.

Ellis, A. (1971) *Growth through reason*. North Hollywood, Calif.: Wilshire Books.

Ellis, A. (1973) *Humanistic psychotherapy: the rational–emotive approach*. New York: McGraw-Hill.

Ellis, A. (1979) The theory of rational–emotive therapy. In A. Ellis and J. M. Whiteley (eds), *Theoretical and empirical foundations of rational–emotive therapy*. Monterey, Calif.: Brooks/Cole.

Ellis, A. (1984a). Expanding the ABCs of RET. *Journal of Rational–Emotive Therapy*, 2(2): 20–4.

Ellis, A. (1984b) Is the unified-interaction approach to cognitive-behaviour modification a reinvention of the wheel? *Clinical Psychology Review*, 4: 215–18.

Ellis, A. (1985) *Overcoming resistance: rational–emotive therapy with difficult clients*. New York: Springer.

Ellis, A. and Bernard, M. E. (eds) (1985) *Clinical applications of rational-emotive therapy*. New York: Plenum.

Ellis, A. and Harper, R. A. (1975) *A new guide to rational living*. North Hollywood, Calif.: Wilshire Books.

Grieger, R. and Boyd, J. (1980) *Rational–emotive therapy: a skills based approach*. New York: Van Nostrand Reinhold.

Mahoney, M. and Freeman, A. (eds) (1985) *Cognition and psychotherapy*. New York: Plenum.

Meichenbaum, D. (1977) *Cognitive-behavior modification*. New York: Plenum.

Rhinehart, L. (1976) *The book of EST*. New York: Holt, Rinehart and Winston.

Russell, B. (1950) *The conquest of happiness*. New York: New American Library.

Stendhal, (1947) *On love*. New York: Liveright.

5

Responsibility and Therapy

Mark Glover

The quality of experience is complete from moment to moment – it cannot be accumulated over time. . . .

Krishnamurti

Responsibility is an increasingly fashionable word in psychotherapy, and clients are now frequently exhorted to 'take responsibility' for their thoughts, feelings and actions. However, it is very unclear what is communicated by this; after all, the therapist may say (or just think) that he does not mean the term in its conventional sense of *moral duty* or *blame*, but these connotations are culturally very salient, and any alternative explanation offered by the therapist is likely to be weak, inadequate and semantically superficial.

Clients are therefore likely to become confused or to revert to familiar meanings, and it is worth summarizing the reasons why the latter in particular may be therapeutically counterproductive. First, responsibility in the conventional sense is socially defined and may therefore conflict with the needs of the individual. Second, a heightened sense of responsibility is likely to make the individual unspontaneous and superego-bound. Also, having to 'account for' one's actions encourages defensive rationalization and intellectualization of behaviour (thus widening the split between acceptable and unacceptable aspects of the self, with perhaps increasing denial of the latter). Finally, it encourages destructive and paralysing feelings of guilt over one's past (or again a defensive, counter-blaming attitude).

Consequently, the concept of responsibility is not one which should be used lightly in the context of therapy, and it is somewhat surprising that the term has attracted so little critical examination in the psychotherapy literature. Perls (1969), the founder of Gestalt therapy, has perhaps been most vociferous in advocating a specifically therapeutic use of the term, with emphasis on the aspect of 'response-ability', but the implications of this have never been fully explored. Clearly, however, the central idea is of profound importance, for when the client acknowledges his/her *ability* to respond he/she is thereby acknowledging that he/she could also respond differently or not at all, and thus begins the process, in Gestalt therapy terms, of reclaiming previously disowned parts of his/her personality.

Yalom (1980), in an excellent discussion of responsibility from an existential viewpoint, bemoans the paucity of substantive reference to it in the literature, and cites Sartre's definition of 'uncontested authorship of an event or thing'. In practice, this means being 'aware of creating one's own self, destiny, life predicament, feelings and...suffering' (1980: 218). However, this approach has serious shortcomings in clinical practice, whatever its philosophical appeal. Though he/she may be said to make a very considerable *contribution* to the events in his/her life, an individual is clearly not the sole cause of them, except in the sense that he/she may be said to be the sole author of his/her *experience* of them. This kind of subjectivist reasoning is likely to lead down a rather trivial cul-de-sac in which clients attempt to manipulate their perceptions of events without altering their actual interactions with the world. Moreover, clients are often disturbed precisely because they attempt to fulfil misplaced, over-extended responsibilities already, and a therapeutic definition of responsibility should therefore help the client to recognize the *limits* as well as the scope of personal responsibility.

Attribution theory has stimulated much research on the conditions under which events are attributed to internal or external causes, and a therapeutic approach has been suggested (Ross, Rodin and Zimbardo, 1969) in which misattributions are corrected by manipulating these conditions. For example, the client would be helped to attribute positive changes during the course of the therapy to his/her own efforts, whereas an episode of extreme emotional disturbance would ideally be attributed largely to external factors, to avoid a secondary problem of self-condemnation for weak or shameful behaviour. Once again, this approach has a fundamental flaw. A central aim (possibly *the* central aim) of therapy is to teach the client *how* to discriminate between the things he/she can and cannot be responsible for, in order to make him/her an effective interactor with the world and optimize his/her freedom of action. A therapist who manipulates this sense of responsiblity on an event-to-event basis does little to increase the client's power of discrimination.

The purpose of the present chapter then, is to present a clear and un-ambiguous definition of responsibility which is consistent with, and pertinent to, the aims of therapy, and which can readily be understood by clients (and other non-psychologists) in the context of their everyday lives.

Principles of Responsibility

Following on from Perls's notion of 'response-ability', implying a capa-bility to *choose* how to respond, the definition proposed is: *awareness of choice at the moment of action.* A responsible act occurs only when a person is (1) aware that he/she is acting and (2) aware that he/she could be acting differently. Thus any act may be undertaken with or without responsibility, the difference being only that in acting responsibly there is recognition of one's *freedom* of action. A fully responsible person would never say of his/her own actions that he/she 'had no choice' or 'was forced' to act in a particular way, as psychotherapy clients frequently do, and so it is instructive to examine the corollaries of this apparently naïve definition in parallel with some of the more frequent of clients' objections to it.

Responsibility involves choice and choice involves conscious and explicit rejection of alternative courses of action   Clients are often unaware of having a choice because they are oriented to looking for *more* options rather than identifying the options which they are *already implicitly rejecting*. The rejected options may involve putting up with uncomfortable feelings that the client considers 'intolerable', for example, 'How could I possibly (put up with the guilty feelings and) go on holiday without my mother?' Clearly, responsibility does not just concern the things you do; it concerns also the things you *could* do and don't.

Every situation contains choice   This is a rather daunting proposition, since acceptance of it calls into question all those innumerable occasions in the past when one submitted to the easy notion of having had no choice at all. Clients typically raise extreme examples such as 'What choice do you have when standing in front of a firing squad?' The answer, of course, lies in not confusing actions with outcomes: you may have no choice over being shot, but you do have some choice over dying defiantly or begging for mercy, and (if they gag you) over fidgeting or standing still. We are never, while alive and aware, *quite* deprived of all choice, and in most situations the range of choice is normally greatly in excess of that which we readily acknowledge.

Perfect choice is never available   Some clients believe they are not free because they do not have choice amongst a perfect set of options. Until a client accepts that all choices are limited and imperfect, he/she is unlikely to make the best use of whatever choices *are* available, just as the child whose favourite ice-cream is strawberry may angrily refuse to choose between chocolate and vanilla.

Choices never recur exactly   Just as every situation is unique, so the range of available choices reflects that uniqueness. It is characteristic of neurotic behaviour to respond to situations as if they were mere repetitions of earlier ones, as when the dog-phobic reacts to all dogs by escaping, or the depressive reacts to instances of social 'failure' by self-condemnation. One feature of behaviour therapy is that it seeks to re-present similar situations to clients with progressive variations (such as new coping skills); more generally, the aim of responsibility therapy would be to enable clients to respond to the *specificity* of situations, instead of by the application, as Beck (1976) has pointed out, of overgeneralized and over-defended rules to one or two salient features.

You have direct control over actions, and not over events A major reason why clients in therapy feel so helpless is that they pay too much attention to trying to alter the overall situation and too little to identifying and then altering their own *contribution* to it in terms of their own behaviour. Defining responsibility as awareness of choice at the moment of action underlines the fact that you can only be responsible for your actions, and that although you obviously hope to influence the things that *happen* in your life you have *no other* means of doing this other than through your actions. Sharpening up your sense of responsibility in this way has two important consequences: first, it puts you back in charge of that which you *do* potentially have control over; and second, it reduces futile efforts to control the uncontrollable, and enables you to accept rather than worry (or feel guilty) about negative events that occur in spite of your contribution.

Only you can be responsible for your actions, and you can only be responsible for your own actions This statement is an amplification of the one above; the need to spell it out in detail is because it is in interpersonal situations that people's sense of responsibility most easily goes awry. If responsibility is about acknowledged choice of action, then it can only relate meaningfully to the doer of the action. You can never be responsible for me, for the simple reason that you can never do my actions; conversely, you cannot make me responsible for you, because I can never do your actions. So far so good, but the general proposition still seems to fly in the face of common sense. After all, a client might argue, surely a mother would have to take responsibility for a 'helpless' baby? But actually all she can do is to take responsibility for her own behaviour in controlling/nurturing him, and in the end his own responses and actions remain (as countless parents have discovered) freely and idiosyncratically his own. What may seem like hair-splitting in this example becomes crucially important in other interactions where the client addresses such problems as how to get other people to like him/her, how to get his/her spouse to behave in the way he/she wants or how to make someone happy. All of these things are impossible, and what is more, while he/she is attempting to be responsible for other people's lives an individual will be neglecting responsibility for his/her own. It is a common clinical observation that people who try to control and dominate the lives of those around them often have chaos at the centre of their own lives.

There is, of course, a recurrent temptation to abdicate responsibility and be dependent on another person, or manipulate another person to be apparently responsible for us. Nor is this necessarily a bad thing if done temporarily and explicitly. However, it is essentially a false position, since power over your actions *cannot* be given away. Take, for example, the group member who sits in silence throughout a session, apparently letting the other members determine the direction the group takes. Although he/she may deny that he/she has influenced the group (and this may give him/her, with an inexperienced therapist, a useful trump-card if the group fails) the influence of his/her silence is in fact very powerful. Just as you cannot not communicate, since your 'non-communication' communicates something, so you cannot *not* have the choice of action, since your refusal to choose is itself a choice and leads to the unfolding of yet other choices. Denying responsibility has a number of social advantages (to be discussed later), but these usually turn out to be minor in comparison with the advantage of exercising power over your life in as direct a way as possible.

Responsibility only exists here and now, and real choice is only between options available in the present This is what might be called the 'unacceptable face of responsibility', since we are never relieved of the possibility of choice but are, in Sartre's words, 'condemned to choose' as part of the human condition. Responsibility which does not relate to present actions is spurious, and the greater the discontinuity between choice and action the more impotent the chooser becomes, whether the action is past or future.

Responsibility for an action cannot be acquired retrospectively This follows obviously from the definition of responsibility: in order to act responsibly it is necessary to acknowledge choice *at the moment of* action, and that moment cannot subsequently be 'recovered'. That is not to say that it is not useful to reflect on past actions and/or take (present) correcting action where these had undesirable results. But to think that unresponsible[1] behaviour can subsequently be invested with responsibility is a mistake which often leads clients (a) to 'lag behind' their lives, constantly patching up an endless series of completed actions, and (b) to lose touch with their present power of action.

It is important at this point to pause and consider the distinction between the conventional meaning of responsibility and its therapeutic meaning in a little more detail. The judge and the therapist are both interested in the question 'Was X responsible for some (antisocial) act he/she committed?', but the intention behind the question is very different in the two cases. In the first case, the question is in an accusatory form, and it is presumably in the individual's interest simply to defend himself by denying responsibility. The therapist, on the other hand, wishes to get the client to *embrace* his/her sense of responsibility (in future). The starting point must therefore be that responsibility is *available* to the individual for any act that he/she commits; hence if he/she says that, looking back, he/she was not aware of having any choice at the moment of committing the act, he/she certainly did not act responsibly (assuming he/she recalls correctly), and that lack of responsibility represents a lost opportunity to gain control of his/her life. Socially, we often gain by not being responsible (since we avoid being brought to justice) but personally we nearly always lose. Thus it is of little therapeutic use to ask in generalized form 'Was the concentration camp guard responsible for the death of his prisoners or not?' Of course, he *could* have identified alternative options to complying with orders (not necessarily very pleasant alternatives), and had he done so and then chosen to reject them in favour of compliance he would, in personal terms, have been acting responsibly. We might abhor his choice, and even punish him for it, but in therapeutic terms any act which is explicitly and whole-heartedly chosen is a responsible act. Conversely, if the guard did not consider his alternatives at the time, no amount of soul-searching can recover the choice.

Responsibility for future choices cannot be taken now   This is not to suggest that the future cannot be planned for, nor that commitment is useless. However, resolution and responsibility are not the same thing, and mere resolution cannot do the work of ongoing responsibility. For example, the resolution to give up smoking does not prevent a series of future situations arising in which a specific choice will need to be made not to smoke at that moment. Life would perhaps be easier if we could fix the future by means of grand resolutions, but in practice it is usually the person who makes most resolutions who is least in control of life.

The true test of any choice is whether it has any *implications for the present*; if it does not, it cannot be said to be invested with any responsibility. Of course, many decisions are about events some distance in the future, such as having a baby in a year's time or working towards some qualification. The crucial question is: what first step can I take right now towards the ultimate realization of this goal? It is the presently-available first step that represents the real choice and prevents the decision being mere empty fantasy. Clients are often very uncomfortable when faced with concrete choices of this kind, and they are stuck not because of fantasizing *per se* but because of failing to *recognize* that they are not willing to face the effort or dysphoria needed to convert wish into reality.

Responsible action is not the same as right action   Actions freely chosen do not necessarily turn out to be right in the sense of producing the best possible outcome. However, this does not retrospectively invalidate the degree of responsibility with which they were originally carried out. Responsibility has more to do with acknowledging the fact of choosing than with the method or quality of decision-making. Indeed, as Miller and Starr point out, 'it is always questionable whether the optimum procedure is to search for the optimum value' (1967: 51). Rollo May, the existential psychotherapist, makes a similar point when he states that 'The discussion of dynamisms of social adjustment. . . is over-simplified and inadequate when it omits the central fact of all – namely, the person's capacity *to be aware* at the moment that he is the one responding. . . the one choosing' (1983: 147, emphasis added). The nature of ongoing choice is that it has to be made under very imperfect conditions, including shortage of information, 'bias' introduced by immediate personal feelings, and inadequate processing time. Responsibility demands that you acknowledge your power to choose *in spite of* these limitations. It asks that your choices be whole-hearted rather than perfect-minded, and it has the generosity to acknowledge genuine error. The responsible person therefore does not waste too much time in feeling guilty about his/her past mistakes, but works instead with the new present created by these and more successful choices. Clients often take the slightest evidence of 'bad' choices as a sign that they are incapable of being responsible for themselves, when in practice the reverse is true – redoubling your efforts to be aware of choice from moment to moment will eventually, by successive approximations, lead to decisions more in line with your actual (as opposed to distortedly perceived) best interests.

Consequences cannot be guaranteed   It has been emphasized in various ways that our real options are simply behavioural alternatives and *not* their outcomes. To confuse the two leads rapidly to a perceived loss of power and eventually to helplessness. Take, for example, a man who wishes to develop friendlier relationships with his neighbours. He certainly has the option of smiling at them more, enquiring about their health, inviting them in for coffee etc., but he does not have the option of *making* them behave in a friendly way in return (though it is a likely outcome). If he made that mistake, he would soon begin to interpret any continued indifference on their part as evidence that he never really had any choice in the matter in the first place. Moreover, he will then begin to sabotage his real arena of choice by implementing his own 'friendly' behaviour in a half-hearted and resentful way, resulting in a self-fulfilling prophecy. The final outcome is likely to be a generalized loss of responsibility, a sense of being unable to change his life in any way.

   The belief that our choices should lead to guaranteed (and often immediate) successful consequences, and that otherwise choice is illusory, is a frequent, and very damaging, aspect of neurotic problems. Behaving responsibly (that is, keeping in touch with the possibility of choosing) tends to promote a person's well-being over time, but it is only a question of the cumulative balance of probabilities. Conversely, not getting your just deserts on a particular occasion is a bad reason for abandoning responsibility altogether.

Choosing does not necessarily mean taking the path of least resistance Clients commonly assert that they cannot possibly be free because, if they were, 'Do you think I would have *chosen* to make my life as difficult and unsatisfactory as this?' The answer to this is in two parts. When a person fails to exercise his/her freedom (by making explicit, direct choices) he/she is always likely to take the option that maximizes short-term gain, and this is often at the expense of considerable longer-term cost (for example, escaping from anxious situations relieves anxiety at the cost of reinforcing the phobic tendency). Conversely, when the nettle of choice *is* grasped, it does not necessarily mean making your life as easy and comfortable as possible, and in fact difficult and challenging options providing opportunities for growth and fulfilment may well be preferred to safe options which offer only repetition and stagnation. It is only from a standpoint of anxious insecurity that an existence free of risk and uncertainty seems attractive.

Every action is a reaction, therefore no distinction can be drawn between actions that are freely chosen and actions that are caused No action of an individual takes place in a psychological vacuum; every action arises from an exact combination of necessary causes, one of which is a decision (whether explicit or implicit) by the actor. This means that responsibility may be redefined as awareness of choice at the moment of reaction (though many clients find this too difficult to accept until they have worked through other aspects of the concept). A client may object that certain responses, such as the patellar reflex, are manifestly automatic and out of the subject's control. However, since such a response can be consciously inhibited, it follows that the jerk is *not caused in a one-to-one sense* by the doctor's tap, but rather by a combination of this stimulus plus the patient's decision not to inhibit it (or, on another level, the patient's decision to relax and trust the doctor).

In practice, a predominant feature of almost any form of therapy consists of the therapist in some way rebutting the client's perception that his/her reactions, and particularly his/her emotional reactions, are *caused* by others, and are therefore not his/her own responsibility. Rational–emotive therapy (Ellis, 1962) and its derivatives have been especially explicit on this point, emphasizing to the client that emotional dysfunction is caused not by events themselves but by the client's personal beliefs and interpretations about those events. Clearly, it is more difficult to be aware of choice when experiencing a sudden surge of emotion than when about to perform a 'voluntary' muscle act, but the logic of our definition demands that the individual has the *capacity* for responsibility over *any* response for which he/she can identify viable alternatives. The limits to responsibility are therefore much more likely to be set by his/her unwillingness *to look for* alternatives (or lack of persistence in acknowledging them) than by any shortage of real choice available.

The foregoing discussion is not intended to provide an exhaustive list of the implications of an existential approach to responsibility, but it does illustrate some of the main difficulties experienced by clients in applying it to particular situations in their own lives, and it hints at a number of areas in which the concept might have some clinical utility. Clearly, for example, the notions that (a) every situation offers at least some choice of action (if you are willing to look for it), and (b) every situation is unique (so that choices never recur exactly and you are never 'forced' to repeat past choices), are of central importance to the process of change.

This is not to suggest that rational discussion alone would be sufficient (or even, perhaps, necessary) to bring about therapeutic progress in the sense of an increased level of ongoing responsibility. Indeed, certain aspects of responsibility feature in such varied approaches to treatment as behaviour therapy, gestalt therapy and rational–emotive therapy, as well as humanistic/existential modes. The question therefore arises as to whether and how the existential concept of responsibility can be applied directly and made the central focus of therapy, and if so with what results.

Choice Styles and Unresponsibility

The almost universal experience of clients seeking help for personal problems is one of stuckness, inability to get out of behavioural, cognitive and emotional patterns that they feel 'compelled' to repeat, however self-defeating. There is always a point of 'no choice', whether it be the point at which the phobic feels overwhelmed by panic and 'has' to escape the situation, or when the obsessional can no longer resist checking, or when the husband feels he 'must' point out his wife's faults to her. Beyond this point the client is unwilling to risk him/herself, preferring to repeat his/her neurotic pattern of short-term gain (that is, reduction of anxiety, guilt, shame and other uncomfortable feelings) at whatever longer-term cost in ability to deal with present reality.

He/she would be surprised to have his behaviour described as 'preferred', since he/she is choosing implicitly, and dismissing the alternatives a priori as emotionally intolerable. While implicit choosing remains the dominant strategy, he/she will continue to re-enact the same choice indefinitely. Only when he/she starts to become aware of real alternatives (at the time) will he/she begin to respond to the particularity of the situation, and to realize that he/she might respond to what makes this situation different, rather than what makes it the same. Responsible choices are always *one-off* choices, so that even if the same response is chosen repeatedly it is, on each occasion, a new choice based on different circumstances; only unresponsible choices are repeated as if they were the *same* choice. One aim of responsibility enhancement, then, is to generate change by developing a sense of the newness and freshness of the choice before us now.

Clinical observation suggests that this responsiveness to present choices is impaired in systematic ways. Individuals repeat their unresponsible behaviour in ways which often relate to personality traits or diagnostic categories, and might be called 'choice styles'. Since *any* style of choosing implies prejudice and hence unresponsibility, it would be an essential part of responsibility therapy to identify and eventually eliminate the client's particular choice style.

The choice style which is obviously adopted by most of us much of the time is that of *habit choosing*: that is, going for the established option because it is easier, safer and less disruptive of our lives than untried or unfamiliar alternatives. This is not to say that all habits must be abandoned if we are to live responsible lives, or that we must be aware of choice in absolutely everything we do (habitual behaviour on one level may serve to free us to concentrate on other levels of choice). However, even the most conservative among us would accept that circumstances change and habits outlive their usefulness; responsibility is therefore needed from time to time to review habitual actions and renew choices, to see whether they are still serving our best interests.

Whereas habit choosing is largely passive, it can become elevated in the obsessional to a positive *avoidance* of behavioural variation: that is, *routine choosing*. The maintenance of routines lessons not only the risk of failure but the risk of loss of control.

However, when faced with unavoidable choice (that is, with the routine option removed), the obsessional is likely to exhibit the style of *perfect choosing*, in which it becomes so important to make the correct choice (perfect-mindedness instead of whole-heartedness) that every option is examined in minute detail, from every angle. The resultant indecisiveness means, of course, that the perfect chooser often fails to make any choice at all, and his/her decisions are made by default – the options gradually disappear with the passage of time until only one remains, leaving the chooser somewhat dissatisfied at his/her own indecisiveness but at the same time profoundly relieved at having the 'responsibility' for the decision taken out of his/her hands!

Option preservation is another unresponsible choice style, in which the chooser is mesmerized by a need to preserve his/her sense of freedom and cannot bear to take one option if it means losing the others. The option preserver is like the child in the sweet-shop who cannot bear to spend pocket-money on chocolate because it means he/she can't have crisps and vice versa. Option preservation is often seen in bright and capable people with an apparently wide range of choice, and is characterized by repeated failure of commitment to any one course of action. The 'freedom' involved is illusory because it is freedom which the client hoards but does not dare to spend; in the analysis of Fromm (1976), it is a mode of living based on 'having' instead of 'being'.

Option preservers sometimes go further and adopt a policy of *option generating*, in which the newest, most bizarre, most exciting option etc. is invariably seized upon, as if to say that ordinary reality can never be enough. The option generator is always doing something new and interesting, and as such often arouses the envy of others; however, when the constant stream of new experiences continues relentlessly on, the suspicion grows that here is a person unwilling to face the rigours of ordinary everyday life or unable to extract pleasure and excitement from the simple exercise of being.

Another kind of choosing which is apparently positive and energetic but fundamentally unresponsible is *impulsive choosing*. Here the chooser becomes anxious whenever faced with the ambiguity or uncertainty, or just the experienced burden, of choice and so chooses rapidly in order to escape these unpleasant feelings. Such choices often masquerade as 'spontaneous' or 'intuitive' (generally considered positive qualitities in these days of over-rational living), but they are inappropriate in choice-situations in which the best option might be to *withhold* a decision until more information is available or the situation matures or clarifies. Making immediate choices at times is fine; *needing* to choose immediately impedes free choosing and hence is unresponsible.

Resolution choosing is also deceptively positive. This style involves making grand statements about the future which have every appearance of being in the individual's best interests but which falter because they are really no more than ways of alleviating guilt while postponing action. Thus the person who is 'definitely going to lose weight in time for next summer' feels free to overeat right now. The postponement of present action, effort and dysphoria is similarly apparent in *fantasy choosing* in which the available options are repeatedly ignored or discarded in favour of some central fantasy in the client's life. Sometimes this fantasy involves the hoped-for return of some lost option, such as the girl you wish you had asked out but never did. Generally it involves some form of *perfect-option seeking*, and a refusal to choose from among a set of second-best options (a stance which may be valuable at times but which when it becomes a life policy degenerates into emptiness).

It can be seen from this short selection that the range of choice styles is considerable. Moreover, every style has its opposite: for example, the counterpart of the perfect-option seeker is the perfect-option *avoider*, the person who is terrified to accept what seems on the surface to be a perfect opportunity because of the terrible risk of subsequently losing it through bad luck or, worse, his/her own inadequacy. The perfect-option avoider stays within the realms of low-grade options where he/she feels safe and relatively unanxious, but the cost is often a diffuse sense of depression.

The important point to note about choice styles is that each and every one of them impedes free and independent choosing in this situation right here and now, because each style reflects a relatively fixed attitude and approach to the act of choosing itself. Therefore any form of responsibility therapy would need not only to identify particular misconceptions that a client may be entertaining with regard to the major situations in his/her life in which he/she currently feels 'stuck' and deprived of choice; it would need also to identify patterns or styles of choosing that he/she carries around from situation to situation.

Furthermore, it would need to tackle the underlying problem of why people avoid personal responsibility, or more specifically, what are the pay-offs for unresponsible behaviour in the individual case. This is of course hardly a new question in psychotherapy, and some of the secondary gains have already been alluded to above; however, it is worth summarizing some of the major (and perhaps universally experienced) gains to be derived from unresponsible living, if only to serve as a reminder of the strength of its appeal:

1 It minimizes psychological effort, by allowing others to do your thinking and choosing for you.
2 It avoids commitment, and the hard work involved in making your own choices work for you.
3 It tends to avoid any disturbance of the status quo and the easy routine of your life.
4 Avoiding making public choices avoids exposing yourself to other people's opinions of you, and enables you to keep a 'low profile' which is failure-free.
5 When all your options seem unpleasant, not facing them may seem like the only way to avoid unpleasantness.
6 Surrendering responsibility puts you in a 'weak and defenceless position' and so gives you power (albeit indirect and unreliable) over those you depend on, by manipulating *their* guilt, anxiety and misplaced sense of responsibility.
7 Taking half-measures of responsibility is a way of hedging your bets – if it turns out well you can claim the credit, if it does not you can blame someone else (thus giving you the satisfaction of being right).
8 Choices are often made not in the individual's best interests but in the (unconscious) service of indirect communication (as when the child sulkily refuses *any* ice-cream to punish his/her parent for not providing his/her *favourite* flavour).

9   The persistence of the alluring idea of an Ultimate Rescuer in life (based on the child's original myth about his/her parents) means that we still, at times, hope for a magic solution and a magician to produce it.
10 Most fundamentally, in the existential analysis, genuine choosing is by yourself and for yourself, and therefore reminds us of the profound aloneness of the human condition. (To live responsibly, or as the existentialists would express it 'authentically', means to embrace this inescapable source of anxiety and grasp the nettle of choice in full awareness of it.)

Responsibility Therapy

Given this powerful battery of reasons for avoiding responsibility, what specific approach might the therapist use to shift the client in the direction of *increased* responsibility? Clearly, since responsibility has been defined as awareness of choice at the moment of action, the key ingredient is the development of greater moment-to-moment awareness: that is, willingness to observe and acknowledge events taking place here and now, both inside (thoughts and feelings) and outside (behaviour and environmental events). This creates the conditions for changing implicit to explicit choosing, and in particular for the elimination of strategic avoidance or denial of choice.

Therapy might begin with the client identifying specific recent situations in which he/she felt he/she 'had no choice' but was compelled by circumstances to behave in a certain (usually repetitive) way. Some of the implicit options rejected in each situation can then be identified, using a creative brain-storming approach, for example by considering such questions as 'What might a more sensible/stupid/mature/childish/courageous/selfish/spontaneous person have chosen to do in this situation?'

Discussion of these options is likely to reveal something about the implicit assumptions underlying the client's denial of responsibility, and also about his/her particular pay-offs for remaining unresponsible.

The issue of assertiveness generally becomes salient at this early stage, since people often make choices that are manifestly contrary to their own well-being as a means of indirectly communicating a message which they are unwilling to communicate directly (for example, your partner arrives late for an evening out; even though it is a good film you sulk for the whole evening to indicate how displeased you are, and to let him/her know that he/she is not going to get away with it). Direct communication obviates the need to make self-damaging choices that convey such messages as:

I'm *very* annoyed with you
Now look what you've done to me
Poor, long-suffering me

Help me, you can see I can't cope
I'll make you suffer/regret the way you behaved
You'll definitely owe me for this
You will *not* tell me what to do.

Discussion of past situations cannot recover lost opportunities for choosing, but it can point the way to dealing with future situations differently: the client is encouraged to recognize that choice is available in every situation, to identify more of the available options in the situation itself, and to explore both the scope and limits of his/her power to influence situations by means of valid behavioural experiments (including variations introduced by the use of direct assertive behaviour and emotional self-management techniques). In the process, untapped or suppressed aspects of the client's personal resources may be revealed and integrated into his/her overall capability. The ideal outcome would be a maximization of the client's personal power (not an unrealizable exaggeration of it), along with a minimization of neurotic anxiety and guilt; also, a personal perspective that allows self-exploration and self-*construction* through active participation in new experience.

The emphasis throughout is on action and behavioural options, because responsibility is about our potential for interaction with the world and can only be realized in this process; moreover, valid personal experiments are more easily conducted in the behavioural mode, since there is greater scope for objectivity in controlling the independent variable and measuring the dependent variable. The ability to identify options in a given situation in explicit, operational, behavioural terms is crucial to the development of responsibility. However, the fundamental aim is cognitive: that is *awareness* of moment-to-moment behavioural *capability*. (Skill training may be helpful in some cases, but denial of responsibility more often concerns simple behaviours already well within the client's repertoire.)

It is also worth noting that responsibility therapy focuses much more on the development of options than on the process of choosing itself. Since we are concerned with ongoing choice, the quality of decision-making is of secondary importance to the acknowledgement of the power to choose. In fact, high-quality decision-making is quite inappropriate, since it is very time-consuming and would therefore result in a loss of synchronicity between situations and our reactions to them. Moreover, laboured rationality is likely to produce the 'wrong' choice, since ongoing choices tend to reflect personal issues. An intuitive approach to choosing is therefore encouraged, *once* the options have been drawn up, for example, by asking 'Now which of these options do I *really* want to take?' This may well lead to numerous instances of error and self-deception (such as a strong tendency to choose the easy option), but the point is that making the choice an explicit one transforms it into a learning situation, so that the self-deception is eventually exposed.

Suppose, for example, I am in the habit of taking a long coffee-break every morning. One day, I decide to look at the options, and realize that I could spend part of the time improving some rather unsatisfactory lectures I have been giving. I choose to continue drinking my coffee. Next time I give a lecture, it is still unsatisfactory, but I can no longer tell myself that it is not my fault because I have too much work to do. Next time I have a coffee-break, I am faced with a more aware choice. When a series of choices is made explicit in this way, the result is *progressive* access to feelings and motivations, and progressively fine tuning of behaviour in the direction of the individual's real interests. I may, of course, continue to take long coffee-breaks and give unsatisfactory lectures, but it will eventually be whole-heartedly or not at all, rather than uneasily and bolstered with rationalizations.

Once the client has become attuned to the basic idea of monitoring choice-situations as they happen, regular feedback and review of his/her *ongoing* behaviour become an essential feature of the weekly therapy session. This is vitally important not only in helping him/her to clarify his/her resistances to becoming more responsible but also in demonstrating, *as they unfold*, the undesirable consequences of unresponsible actions. It allows a direct practical comparison of the pay-offs for responsible and unresponsible behaviour.

It would be unwise to assume, for example, that a client will necessarily agree, after a lifetime of developing skills in (and becoming relatively successful at) manipulating others into taking responsibility for him/her, that it is in his/her interests to start managing his/her own life. However, as his/her unresponsible choices begin to unfold, he/she may begin to see how restrictive, unreliable and unwieldy this method of steering one's life really is. The advantages of a more direct approach based on self-acknowledged choosing and *assertion* of the power to choose (in terms of material results but also of spin-offs like self-respect and improved relationships) may then become apparent.

The language the client uses in talking to the therapist, but more importantly in talking to him/herself, can be very revealing. Denial or subversion of responsibility is generally accompanied and rationalized by semantic evasion (indeed semantic evasion has become the cultural norm). Most of us have practised subtly unresponsible and inaccurate language throughout life, and these linguistic habits colour and distort our perceptions and attributions on many levels. We substitute verbs of compulsion and certainty (need, can't, have to, know) for verbs of volition and uncertainty (want, won't, choose to, believe). We use the third person or the general 'you' or 'we' ('It made me angry', 'You just don't do things like that') for the first person singular ('I got angry', 'I don't do things like that').

We substitute passive verbs ('Disagreements get ignored in our family') for active verbs ('We ignore disagreements'). And we have a preference for conjunctions that excuse ('I'd like to go *but* I've got some ironing to do') over conjunctions that are neutral ('I'd like to go and I've got ironing to do').

Evasions of this kind can usefully be highlighted during sessions, but the client should also be encouraged to work at using direct, personal and responsible language in everyday self-talk (albeit that it may sound strained and artificial, an indication of its cultural scarcity). Gestalt therapists have been foremost in exploring the therapeutic implications of language, and a good account of this approach can be found in Passons (1975).

By now the client's preferred choice style will be starting to reveal itself, and the fears and anxieties that lie behind the strategy can begin to be analysed. However, sight should not be lost of the repetitive damage caused by the style itself, and the client should be encouraged to experiment with the use of a contradictory or incompatible choice style as a precursor to eliminating choice style altogether. For example, the perfect chooser would be instructed to make impulsive choices (for example, by shopping at double speed and not picking up any brand that he/she normally buys). The perfect-option avoider would be encouraged to tell him/herself that he/she deserves the best, and to experiment in small ways by selecting the best rather than indulging his/her usual systematic mediocrity. The impulsive chooser would be assigned the task of choosing not to choose; the habit chooser would be instructed to choose with maximum variety, or even randomly by the throw of a pair of dice. In such cases, it is the way that choices are made, rather than the specific choices made, that is at issue. The ultimate aim of prescribed counter-styles is to break down such prejudiced responding altogether.

Another technique which can be used to invest the client's choices with extra responsibility is that of first-stepping. This can be done initially as a pencil-and-paper exercise in which the client brain-storms a number of options that he/she has with regard to a particular situation and then alongside each writes the immediately available first step which he/she can take with respect to each option. Practice at generating options is itself invaluable (beginning with the realization by the client that for every action he/she always has at least a second option of *not* acting); however, generating future options that have no implications for the present does not increase responsibility, and the process of 'tracing' future decisions back into the present demonstrates this very clearly.

One client raised the rather extreme example of his long-standing desire to travel to the moon: is this mere fantasy or a responsible decision? With guidance, he was able to trace the following sequence. Going to the moon requires transport; you need either to build your own moonship (unlikely) or join an existing space-programme; you therefore need to consider what qualifications you would require to make a successful application to become an astronaut; if you are deficient in certain areas, such as fitness, knowledge of physics, eye–hand coordination, you would need to correct these deficiencies before applying; your first steps (albeit very remote from the ultimate goal) might therefore include such mundane actions as going jogging, phoning the Adult Education Centre to find out about elementary science courses, etc., etc. Willingness or unwillingness to take the mundane first step thus discriminates very effectively between future-based fantasy and present-based responsible action.

Of course, in most situations, the options we recognize are closer to the present and more realistic; nevertheless it still holds true that it is only the presently available first steps that represent the responsible choice. Suppose, for example, I wake up on a Sunday morning and think about what to do for the day. I might come up with several options: a cycle ride, cleaning the house, reading a book, visiting a friend. But the bike needs repairs, cleaning the house needs a change of clothes, I've forgotten where I left the book, my friend lives so far away that I would need to leave now and miss breakfast. My present options thus look rather different: fix bike, change into old clothes, search through old boxes to find book, leave house right now.

Notice, incidentally, the severe *limitations* of these immediate options. It was suggested earlier that a critical element of becoming more responsible involves recognition of the limits as well as the scope of available action, and these limits are set by the fact that you can only be in one place at one time and can only impinge on your environment in quite limited ways from that unique vantage-point. Even the most brilliant life, broken down into its first steps, would be seen to be limited in the same way.

The operational transformation of first-stepping does not eliminate the need for planning and longer-term decision making, but it *is* an essential feature of responsible living which is about harnessing present opportunities. Initially used as a pencil-and-paper exercise to illustrate the process, the aim is eventually to incorporate it into the fabric of living. Since we so often act habitually and with minimum awareness of this kind, some cueing device may be helpful to serve as a reminder to initiate the processes of option-generating and first-stepping.

The appropriate cues vary from person to person (depending, for instance, on choice style), but the following are often useful: being aware of repeating a tired old habit; repeating an unsatisfactory behaviour that you promised yourself you would change; becoming aware that your attention has wandered from what you are doing; feeling resentful, coerced, frustrated; experiencing any sharp change of mood. A variety of artificial and external cues can also be used: every time you change environment (such as home, train, office, park); every time you look at your watch; every two hours, etc.

In this way the client discovers at first hand the liberating effects of constantly striving to become aware of the kaleidoscope of ongoing choices; he/she is repeatedly brought back to focusing on the leading edge of his/her life, so that his/her power to effect changes in his/her own circumstances is restored. Taken to the limit, this would be a daunting prospect indeed (Sartre's 'condemnation to choose'), since it would demand tremendous psychological stamina to keep the choice-process active and never to relax one's vigilant focus on present reality. However, most clients in psychotherapy are engaged in a very determined attempt to fix the future according to their particular expectations of failure, rejection, abandonment, pain and misery, and even an occasional injection of indeterminacy into this scenario of fixed expectations is worthwhile.

Indeterminacy is the price of freedom; the future cannot be fixed. One implication of this is that the positive therapeutic changes which the client makes are no less vulnerable to erosion and change than the problems he/she originally sought help for. The client will not remain immutably 'unwell', but (and this is the 'unacceptable face of therapy'), nor can he/she arrive at a fixed state of 'wellness'. Failure by the therapist to acknowledge this explicitly may be one reason for the client's plunging back to 'square one' at the first set-back.

Another implication of the indeterminacy principle is that the responsible *person* does not exist. According to the existential definition, responsibility is not a stable characteristic of the individual, but refers to the quality of awareness invested in a given action in a specific situation. Hence we can only meaningfully refer to responsibility A of action B by person C in situation D. This serves as a useful reminder to anyone who claims to have arrived at a responsible state: responsibility is to be exercised, not achieved! There is hope, but never certainty, for all of us.

Concluding Remarks

The concept of responsibility is a difficult and potentially hazardous one within the context of psychotherapy, and asking clients to take responsibility for their thoughts, feelings and actions may be therapeutically counterproductive if responsibility is understood in its conventional sense connoting duty, proper behaviour, accountability and blame. Attempts to define responsibility in an alternative, specifically therapeutic way have been insufficiently thorough. However, an existential treatment of the concept, leading to a definition of 'awareness of choice at the moment of action', seems to offer the prospect of both clarity and utility and hence merits further development.

Responsibility is necessarily related to choice and therefore, in some sense, to freedom, which has not generally been considered a proper subject for psychologists to discuss, at least in the scientific climate of post-Freudian clinical psychology. There are probably two major reasons for this: (1) the philosophical debate about free will vs. determinism has been notoriously inconclusive (see, for example, Trusted, 1984) and in psychological terms quite sterile; (2) freedom is (almost by its very nature) a notion too vague and unmanageable to be susceptible of systematic investigation.

Nevertheless, in clinical practice psychologists *are* concerned, fundamentally and inescapably, with issues of freedom; in the words of Yalom (1980: 401), 'the goal of psychotherapy is to bring the patient to the point where he can make a free choice'. Freedom as a hypothetical concept may be elusive, but the client's degree of *perceived* freedom, and the effects on his/her life of making a policy of acting 'as if' he/she were free, are of considerable if not critical interest and importance.

Significantly, Yalom's computer search yielded no empirical studies of either freedom or responsibility, and it is probable that attribution and locus-of-control research come closest to addressing the problem. These are, however, blunt instruments for the measurement of responsibility, for while it is true that altering the balance of internal/external attributions has a beneficial effect on many clients, it is the power to *discriminate* what you are and are not responsible for within a given situation, the ability to discern your *contribution* to the situation (rather than a single either/or perception of causation) that constitutes responsibility. Only a thorough exploration of the boundaries as well as the scope of your field of choice and action will ultimately yield a more self-directed life. In real life (as opposed to experimental situations), responsibility is not all or nothing – on the contrary, it is always available (for your actions) and always incomplete (for the situation as a whole), and indeed this essential ambiguity and the attendant uncertainty constitute a major source of anxiety, which leads to responsibility avoidance, in many clinical cases.

In as much as responsibility is about *contiguity* of choice and (re)action in the experiential flux of the moment, it represents a point of convergence between existential, cognitive and behavioural approaches. The existentialist position emphasizes the realization of authentic living through interactions with the real world, and this is underlined in the present analysis by the proposition that true options are presently available behavioural alternatives. Otherwise 'choice' becomes mere empty fantasy (as in the worst excesses of dynamic psychotherapy in which therapy 'substitutes' for real life). On the other hand, action without acknowledged choice leads to resentment and half-heartedness or subversion (as in the worst excesses of prescriptive behaviourism in which behaviour change is undermined by the client himself). Responsibility is thus neither a cognitive nor a behavioural phenomenon: it is a product of the relationship between the two.

There has, of course, been a significant trend since the early, heady days of cognitive therapy away from 'pure' cognitive approaches and towards combined cognitive-behavioural methods, in recognition of the fact that it is often easier to 'act yourself into a new way of thinking than to think yourself into a new way of behaving'. (In practice, the debate about which way the original causal link operates is of little relevance since vicious circles are quickly established; what matters is finding the most effective way of breaking the circles.)

Marzillier (1980) has noted three distinct usages of the term 'cognition' in cognitive therapy, to mean structures, processes and events. The early work of Ellis (1962) and others focused on identifying and altering certain core attitudes and beliefs so fundamental as to colour and distort people's lives in very pervasive ways (for example, the belief that one must be perfect in everything one does). The later writings of Beck (1976) emphasized more specific types of error in cognitive processing (such as selective abstraction, polarization and overgeneralization) which still have a degree of generic applicability. More recent developments, dating perhaps from the coping-skills procedures of Meichenbaum (1977), have concentrated increasingly on the manipulation of discrete cognitive events occurring in specific situations.

This last trend towards specificity and immediate, practical utility may be an inevitable concomitant of the increasing emphasis on cost–benefit analysis and the economics of mental health service provision. It is nevertheless unfortunate if it means that the client misses the opportunity to learn something at a superordinate level about the reclamation and exercise of his/her freedom.

The concept of self-efficacy (Bandura, 1977) deserves a special mention in this context. At first sight, it may seem as if perceptions of one's ability to execute behaviours likely to produce desired outcomes would bear a definite relationship to responsibility, but on closer examination the connection is untenable. Within our definition, responsibility does not depend on competence to perform complex behavioural sequences, though it does depend on being able, and more important *willing*, to identify viable first steps in any situation. Hence responsibility does relentlessly insist that however incompetent you feel you can *always make a start* (and in that sense it is perhaps likely to lead towards behavioural experimentation and eventual competence). It is a question of moment-to-moment self-*direction* rather than accumulated competence (if this were not so, responsibility would not be possible in new situations we find ourselves unexpectedly 'thrown' into, the most dramatic example of which might be our own impending death).

Another sense in which the two concepts differ is that in terms of self-efficacy the therapeutic aim has almost invariably been *maximization* (that is, the more competent you feel the better), whereas in terms of responsibility there is an *optimum* level beyond which it is impossible, and counterproductive, to exercise valid choice (for example, choosing another person's happiness). This distinction may, however, be a slightly spurious one resulting from the nature of research investigations into self-efficacy, most of which have deliberately selected therapeutic situations in which a greater degree of competence *is* clearly possible and desirable (such as phobic avoidance). In other, particularly interpersonal, situations it can be seen that even perceived self-efficacy has its limits; an overblown sense of self-efficacy would result initially in grandiose behaviour, then frustration, and finally perhaps a total collapse of the core perception of self-competence.

A limitation common to all the cognitive therapies has been their focus on identifying and correcting *individual* patterns of maladaptive cognitions (whether in core attitudes, cognitive processes or specific thoughts). Thus the *universal* cognitive problems associated with the human condition itself have not been addressed. We are all 'condemned to choose' and we are all faced with the possibility of authentic living (action based on explicit choices) or its opposite. So-called cognitive therapies that have nothing to say about the inescapable facts of self-conscious life – aloneness, meaning-lessness, the certainty of ending etc. – seem fundamentally deficient, since these facts form the backdrop to our everyday cognitive experience. Even Ellis's list of the basic irrational beliefs only hints at them.

The existential concept of responsibility is not offered as a new psycho-therapeutic panacea. Nevertheless, a more careful and thorough analysis of the meaning of responsibility (of which this is just a start) does seem to promise a number of advantages: firstly, an increase in clarity of communication between therapist and client, and a more genuinely shared language; secondly, an integrating concept linking humanistic, cognitive and behavioural approaches; thirdly, a manageable and systematic means by which clients can be helped to gain greater control over moment-to-moment functioning; and fourthly, a means by which freedom as a psychological issue can begin to be systematized and studied. If it achieves only a small fraction of all this, the exercise will have been worthwhile.

Note
•
1 The neutral term 'unresponsible' is used throughout this chapter in preference to the conventional term 'irresponsible', the negative moral connotations of which would be misleading in the context of this discussion.

References

Bandura, A. (1977) Self-efficacy: towards a unifying theory of behavioral change. *Psychological Review*, 84: 191–215.

Beck, A. (1976) *Cognitive therapy and the emotional disorders*. New York: International Universities Press.

Ellis, A. (1962) *Reason and emotion in psychotherapy*. New York: Lyle Stuart.

Fromm, E. (1976) *To have or to be*. New York: Harper & Row.

Marzillier, J. (1980) Cognitive therapy and behavioural practice. *Behaviour Research and Therapy*, 18: 249–58.

May, R. (1983) *The discovery of being*. New York: Norton

Meichenbaum, D. (1977) *Cognitive behaviour modification: an integrative approach*. New York: Plenum Press.

Miller, D. and Starr, M. (1967) *The structure of human decisions*. Englewood Cliffs, NJ: Prentice Hall.

Passons, W. (1975) *Gestalt approaches to counseling*. New York: Holt, Rinehart & Winston.

Perls, F. (1969) *Gestalt therapy verbatim*. Moab, Utah: Real People Press.

Ross, L., Rodin, J. and Zimbardo, P. G. (1969). Towards an attribution therapy: the reduction of fear through induced cognitive-emotional misattribution. *Journal of Personality and Social Psychology*, 12: 279–88.

Trusted, J. (1984) *Free will and responsibility*. Oxford: Oxford University Press.

Yalom, I. (1980) *Existential psychotherapy*. New York: Basic Books.

PART TWO   APPLICATIONS

6

The Management of Angry Aggression: a Cognitive-Behavioural Approach

Kevin Howells

Like milder forms of anxiety and depression the emotion of anger is a normal feature of everyday life for most people. The experience of anger is not only common but is also relatively easily described. I asked a group of medical students to provide written accounts of a recent experience of anger. The two following accounts were typical:

> (1)   The house we had just moved into was promised to be ready for the start of term by the landlady. But the downstairs was still undecorated and this was causing us a lot of inconvenience. What made me angry was the fact that the things we had been promised had not occurred. The landlady always had some poor excuse as to why things were going wrong. I get fed up with her excuses. I felt my blood boiling. It didn't last long because I started to laugh and then I calmed down. I thought to myself it's no use getting annoyed over the situation because that wouldn't help matters and I cooled down.

> (2)   I was sitting in a coach, while the bus driver was collecting the tickets. When he came to the back seat there were three black guys and one white guy sitting there. They couldn't find their tickets straight away, and fooled around a bit while looking for them. Suddenly the bus driver stated he had had enough of their fooling around and ordered them off the coach, threatening them with the police if they refused. I couldn't believe my ears at first then I started getting really upset – I was almost on the point of physically showing my anger.

More systematic attempts to gather information about anger experiences can be found in the literature, ranging from Hall's early survey in 1899, of 2184 people, to Averill's (1982) comprehensive questionnaire study.

As with anxiety and to some degree depression, the emotion of anger is not inherently a problem requiring therapeutic intervention. Anger may be functional for the person and also for social institutions in general. Novaco (1975, 1985) has drawn attention to the role of anger as a mobilizing, energizing state and as an instigator of corrective actions. A person never moved to anger might never be sufficiently motivated to stop provocation from another person or to right some evident injustice. The conscience and commitment of many social reformers appear to have been fired by intense experiences of anger and moral outrage when faced with injustices and unnecessary human suffering. Adams (1986) has described how many social activists, including Mahatma Gandhi, Bertrand Russell and Martin Luther King have used their sense of outrage to refine their consciousness and to stimulate creative political action. Nevertheless, anger can become a problem of a clinical nature. I shall argue later that the criterion for a therapeutic approach is that the way in which anger is experienced and expressed is self-defeating, in the sense of impeding the individual's achievement of their personal goals. From this perspective the regulation of expression of anger can be viewed as an 'affective skill'. Individuals may be skilled in the sense that their anger expression works for them (even though what is personally effective may sometimes be unacceptable to others). Others may be affectively unskilled, being unable to use the emotion to promote their short- or long-term goals.

Theoretical Issues

Therapeutic interventions with people with angry-aggression problems require some understanding of theoretical formulations of anger and related forms of behaviour.

Conceptual Distinctions

This area of work abounds with conflicting definitions and conceptual confusions. It is useful to distinguish 'anger', 'hostility' and 'aggression'. Anger refers to a subjective state of emotional arousal typically labelled as 'anger', 'annoyance', 'fury', 'rage', or by related terms. This state often has physiological and facial accompaniments. Hostility is sometimes used synonymously with anger but this is unhelpful. Hostility is better defined as an attitude or a longer-term negative evaluation of people or events. Aggression, on the other hand, refers to overt behaviour involving the infliction of harm on another person. Although anger, hostility and aggression are often interrelated, and seen by some authors as an integrated 'syndrome', they can be desynchronized. Thus a person may be temporarily angered by someone without having any long-term hostile evaluation of them. Equally, hostile judgements do not necessarily entail angry experiences. Anger and hostility may or may not induce behavioural aggression. Finally aggression can occur without any emotional antecedent. A number of authors have distinguished, for example, angry and instrumental aggression, the latter involving the use of aggression in a non-emotional way to secure some environmental reward, for example the use of a firearm in the course of a robbery (Buss, 1961; Bandura, 1973). The clinician concerned with anger-problems will encounter many clients whose anger has become a problem because of its role in inducing aggressive behaviour (for example violence to a spouse or child). For this reason I will pay particular attention to anger–aggression links in my discussion of anger in the rest of this chapter.

Relevance of Anger to Social and Medical Problems
Although there have been few, if any, attempts systematically to assess what proportion of violent assaults and violent crimes are anger-mediated (rather than being instrumental in nature), it is reasonable to infer from studies of various forms of violence that anger-mediation is common (Stuart, 1981; Feldman, 1982). Severe forms of violence (such as homicide), in particular, are likely to be induced by intense feelings of anger and rage. Averill's (1982) analysis of anger in relation to the law suggests that 'voluntary manslaughter' is the most common form of homicide in the United States and that such homicides are typically 'crimes of passion', the passion being that of intense anger. Averill goes on to suggest that the attribution of anger is vital to the assessment of responsibility for homicide in a court of law. Sexual violence also may be preceded and determined by anger arousal in some offenders. Groth (1979) has categorized 40 per cent of rapists as anger rapists. The clinical description of this type of sexual offender suggests that the sexual assault may be preceded by the kinds of frustrations and stresses and the kinds of emotional experience that also typify non-sexual violence.

Anger is central to many forms of violence within families. Violence by men towards female partners is usually preceded by arguments and conflicts (Dobash and Dobash, 1984) suggestive of anger and resentment in the assailant. The antecedents of violence towards children include social isolation, general stress, mental conflict, social deprivation, aversive crying or other behaviours on the part of the child (Gardner and Gray, 1982). This again suggests a state of irritation and negative affect in the violent parent. Micro-analyses of social interactions between abused children and their parents confirm the importance of angry affect and of irritable behaviour in the social sequences leading to physical violence to the child (Patterson, 1985; Reid and Kavanagh, 1985). Frude (1987) has put forward a model of the causation of physical abuse of children which has anger as a central component.

Most of the social problems associated with anger which I have discussed so far are instances of deviant or antisocial behaviour. In recent years a new dependent variable has been isolated in considering individual differences in anger responsiveness – that of physical ill-health. Heart disease and hypertension (Julius, Schneider and Egan, 1985; Gentry, 1985; Manuck et al., 1985; Cottington et al., 1986; Schneider et al., 1986) have been the conditions of most interest to researchers. There is a long history of research into the relationship between coronary heart disease and Type A personality (Rosenman and Chesney, 1982) and there are some indications (Matthews et al., 1977) that it is the anger/hostility component of the Type A syndrome which may be the crucial one. The development of work on anger in a behavioural medicine context marks an important extension of applied anger research away from the focus on 'offending' behaviours.

Theoretical Formulations of Angry Aggression

Theories of emotion in general appear to be prone to periodicity (Averill, 1983) with particular classes of causal variable becoming the focus of attention for a while, then declining and often re-emerging in some different guise. Thus emotion and, by implication, anger, has been accounted for in biological, psychophysiological, cognitive and behavioural terms (Averill, 1982, 1983). The purpose of this chapter is not to discuss and compare these different theoretical formulations but to derive some concepts that might have some clinical usefulness in understanding and helping angry-aggressive people.

The pioneer in the clinical application of theoretical ideas about anger in the form of anger-management therapy has been Raymond Novaco, working in the United States, and much of what follows in this chapter has its roots firmly in Novaco's work (Novaco, 1975, 1976a, 1976b, 1977a, 1977b, 1978, 1979, 1985). Novaco (1978) has put forward a model of anger which allows a systematic approach to the assessment of anger problems and also to their therapeutic management. The model suggests that there are four major components to the anger syndrome and that these components have recipro-cal, bidirectional relationships. The components are (1) external events (henceforth the 'triggers' for anger); (2) cognitive processes (cognition occupies a central place within Novaco's theory); (3) anger arousal (involving physiological arousal and the labelling of that arousal); and (4) behavioural reactions. These four components provide a useful way of construing and organizing the growing literature on anger and its therapeutic treatment.

Triggering Events

Angry aggression is typically preceded by particular kinds of environmental event. There have been a number of attempts to describe the nature of triggering events. Not all triggers for anger are 'frustrations' (the failure to achieve an accustomed reward or to reach a valued goal), though frustrations are one type of anger-instigation. Berkowitz (1982, 1983) has argued that the stimuli which induce angry aggression are simply 'aver-sive', thus being thwarted or frustrated induces anger to the extent that this experience is aversive for the person. Laboratory work (Berkowitz, 1982, 1983) indicates that a range of aversive events can instigate angry aggres-sion including pain, unpleasant odours, high temperatures, 'disgusting' visual stimuli and noise, and that by a process of classical conditioning stimuli associated with such aversive events can acquire the same capacity.

There are dangers in overgeneralizing from laboratory studies where the aversive events are often impersonal. The major triggers for anger in everyday life are predominantly social and interpersonal (Averill, 1982). G. S. Hall in his early account of the causes of anger (1899), found that the thwarting of expectation or purpose, 'invasion or repression of the self', slights to pride, injustices and jealousy were important. Striking in Hall's account is the anger-arousing potential of idiosyncratic variation in personal appearance. He reports that for 130 out of the 679 women he studied 'ear-rings in men...are objects of intense and very special annoyance' (1899: 543). McKellar (1950) analysed his own anger experience continuously over a period of 47 days and subsequently studied 200 subjects. His results led him to suggest two categories of triggering events: (1) 'interference with the pursuit of a goal, under the influence of some primary or secondary need' (1950: 107), in which category McKellar includes events such as missing a bus or train; (2) 'a felt encroachment upon values, possessions, status or habitual relations and attitudes towards other persons' (1950: 107). This category includes criticism of one's ideas, work, clothing or friends. We might relabel this second category of McKellar's as 'threats to the self-system'. Long-term hostility and hatred, McKellar found, were particularly likely to be induced by these threats to self. 'Humiliation' for example, was the most common cause of a long-term hostile attitude.

There may be correspondences between the stimuli that elicit anger in humans and those that induce offensive attack in a number of non-human species. Blanchard and Blanchard (1984) have argued that animal aggression can be categorized as either defensive or offensive. Whereas the former is elicited by threat and danger, the latter is elicited by dispute over control of resources and by problems in the establishment or maintenance of within-species dominance relationships. The Blanchards suggest that many elicitors of anger in humans can be construed as fitting the general pattern established by evolution in lower species. In humans, they propose, it is a challenge to more abstract 'rights' and 'prerogatives' that elicit anger rather than disputes over resources.

Cognitive Processes

The 'cognitive revolution' of the last 15 years has deepened the appreciation of clinicians and researchers of the role of cognition as a determinant of social problems and particularly of problematic affect. The bulk of this work has been in relation to anxiety and depression (Salkovskis, 1986; Clark, 1986; Beck, Emery and Greenberg, 1985). Cognitive processes are also an important feature of most contemporary analyses of anger and of anger-management treatments.

In the previous section I reviewed evidence that aversive events are triggers for anger. The cognitive perspective would qualify this proposition.

It is in the way in which such events are construed and appraised that determines whether the affective reaction is an angry one or of some other kind.

Novaco (1978) highlights three facets of cognitive processing that may be relevant: expectations, appraisal and private speech. In Novaco's analysis expectation influences anger in three ways: (1) high expectations of favourable outcomes that do not ensue can produce frustration; (2) expectation of aversive behaviour by other people may reduce the threshold for anger; (3) low expectations of self-efficacy can lead to anger and aggression as attempts to gain control over the situation.

The appraisal processes that turn aversive events into provocation have received attention in experimental social psychology. Attribution theorists draw attention to the importance of *perceived causality* for the aversive event (Dyck and Rule, 1978; Kremer and Stephens, 1983; Nasby, Hayden and De Paulo, 1980).

The potential power of attributions in determining anger can be illustrated by a simple example. If I were to be knocked down by a car while cycling home from work, the affective reaction to this aversive event is likely to be different if (1) I attribute the accident to my own clumsiness; (2) attribute the accident to the driver (his carelessness); (3) attribute the accident to the driver, but to his deliberate intention to knock down cyclists.

The experimental literature suggests that angry-aggressive reactions to aversive events are more likely if the offending behaviour is attributed to characteristics of the person rather than to the situation or the self (Ferguson and Rule, 1983). Social psychological analyses (Ferguson and Rule, 1983) reveal considerable complexity in the way in which attributions and social judgements are made. When we assess the extent of someone's causal responsibility for an offensive behaviour towards us three separate judgements are made: (1) whether the harm done was 'intentional' or 'unintentional'; (2) whether, if intentional, the harm is motivated by acceptable or unacceptable goals; and (3) whether unintentional harm was foreseeable or unforeseeable. Anger is highest when perceived causal responsibility is high. Ferguson and Rule's analysis suggests that anger is higher the greater the 'is–ought' discrepancy, the 'is' referring to what the offending person has done and his responsibility for it, and the 'ought' referring to what the person should have done.

The notion of a violated 'ought' or moral imperative as a feature of anger can also be found in the early speculations of Heider (Benesh and Weiner, 1982). Heider suggests not only that anger is induced by violated 'ought-ideas', but equally that the retaliation to offensive behaviour ('he ought to be punished') also has this moral component.

Such ideas, derived from social psychological experimentations in the main, seem to me to have many implications for the therapeutic management of anger. Firstly they direct us to areas in which the angry person may have deficits. Do clients with anger problems tend, for example, to infer deliberate intent and malevolent motivations for other people's 'bad' behaviour? It would appear that these are precisely the characteristics that are frequently observed in angry clients. Dodge (1985) has provided evidence that aggressive boys show hostile attributional biases of a 'paranoid' nature. The tendency of angry adults to have biased attributional styles has also been suggested in work by Försterling (1984). The thesis that anger-prone people have a biased attributional style has parallels with the theory that depressives show consistent biases in the attribution process (Peterson and Seligman, 1985). The major difference from depression is clearly likely to be on the internal–external dimension. Even if a reliable correlation can be established between anger processes and biased attributions it is likely to be difficult to prove that the relationship is a linear causal one (cf. Brewin, 1985).

Secondly, such work appears to point to the potential importance of assessing moral imperatives, 'ought' judgements and personal rules in client groups. If the notion that situations are more likely to produce anger when they violate personal moral rules is valid, we should be able to use instances of 'angry' and non-angry situations in a person's life to generate the personal rules that have been violated. A contrast procedure akin to a repertory grid (Fransella and Bannister, 1977) has been used by the present author to generate moral rules in this way.

The elements in such a procedure are aversive/frustrating interpersonal behaviours recorded by the client using a diary over a period of some weeks. The client is then asked to compare and contrast anger-inducing incidents with non-anger-inducing incidents, or to compare strong anger with weak anger situations. Comparing a strong and weak anger situation the client might indicate, for example, that in an angry situation the other person 'had no regard for other people's feelings' while this was not present in the non-angry situation. The client can then be asked to recast this construct as a rule: for example, that 'you should not act in such a way as to disregard the feelings of others'. Laddering procedures from repertory grid techniques (Fransella and Bannister, 1977) can then be used to generate superordinate rules. Thus 'you should not disregard the feelings of others' may be subordinate to a more general rule: for example, that 'you should not act in ways that would lead to social rejection by others'.

This emphasis on the cognitive mediation of anger is shared by rational–emotive theorists and therapists (Ellis, 1977; Grieger, 1982). Grieger (1982) makes a useful distinction between cognitive *dispositional* traits (values or philosophies) which people carry with them across situations, and *situational* appraisals. RET theorists also draw attention to the transformation of values into *must* rules. Grieger summarizes the RET view as being that 'people prone to anger take the philosophic position that they can Jehovistically impose absolute demands on others for certain behaviours, and that it is legitimate for them to condemn the other if he or she violates the standards' (1982: 52).

Grieger, reflecting the theorizing of Ellis, also distinguishes *autistic anger* from *interpersonal anger*. In the former the individual fails to distinguish finding events unpleasant from believing that they *should* or *must* not happen, and he/she also concludes that the events are *terrible* and that the world is to be *condemned* for allowing them to happen. In interpersonal anger the person becomes angry because a consensual explicit code of rules has been violated and the angry person 'punishes' 'as an avenging representative of the collective mass' (1982: 51). This appears to be a useful distinction between personal and public, socially shared rules.

There have been relatively few empirical studies of the relationship between irrational beliefs (of an RET nature) and anger-proneness, though two recent studies with student samples lend some support to the thesis. Hazaleus and Deffenbacher (1985) looked at the correlations between subscales of the Irrational Beliefs Test and the Novaco Anger Inventory (Novaco, 1975). The two beliefs most related to anger were those of 'anxious overconcern' (the belief that negative events should be worried over constantly) and 'blame proneness' (the belief that people should be blamed and punished when they do wrong). There were a number of differences between men and women subjects. Lopez and Thurman (1986) found, again, that high and low trait anger subjects differed with some consistency in their endorsement of irrational beliefs.

The Self and Anger

The clinical literature on anger is replete with suggestions that there is a relationship between self-evaluation and anger. Grieger (1982) identifies 'self-worth anger' whose main characteristic is that the triggering event is responded to intensely because it threatens self-esteem. This theme also recurs in Toch's (1969) early study of violent men. What appears to be suggested is that for some people negative social behaviours, for example an insult, have wider implications for the self-system which is undermined in a general way. In personal construct terms, an insult, for some, may invalidate core self-constructs, whereas for others only peripheral constructs are affected. This would suggest the need to assess and change, in therapy, the personal meanings and implications of provocations for the angry person. Blackburn (1987) similarly suggests that the arousal of anger entails 'the detection of an event which has threatening implications for our self-schemata'.

So far we have discussed the cognitive processes and structures that may be features of anger. Novaco (1978) has also stressed cognitive events themselves, that is the phenomenological self-statements or private speech that accompany anger experiences. The identification of habitual thoughts for anger is akin to the identification of habitual thoughts for depression (Beck et al., 1979).

Clinically, automatic anger-inducing thoughts often seem to focus on rehearsal of the specific provoking situation (what the other person did) on thoughts of inequity and bad treatment and on anticipations of 'revenge' or 'settling' of the conflict. It is my experience that one particular cognitive theme often underlies angry experience for the individual. This can be illustrated by a client, Jane. Jane had a long history of institutionalization from childhood. The main reasons for her confinement were the antisocial ways she responded to frustration including overt violence to relatives, psychiatric staff and psychiatric patients, arson, self-mutilation and generally 'difficult' behaviour. An analysis of the triggers for these behaviours suggested that the important elicitors of anger were personal comments about her appearance, minor rejections, and criticism of any sort. A variety of methods were used to reveal typical self-statements including diary recording in real life, speaking thoughts aloud in role plays and reporting of thoughts while visualizing stressful situations (Novaco, 1975, 1978). These revealed that particular self-statements were present, namely, thoughts that 'nobody loves me', 'they are all against me' and 'it's hopeless'. These thoughts were often followed by secondary action-oriented thoughts to the effect that 'they' deserved to be punished and also that they needed to be made aware of her suffering. It was in this cognitive state that intense anger occurred and acting out behaviour followed.

Arousal
Physiological arousal is an important feature of emotion (Plutchik, 1980) and is widely assumed to be an element in the experience of anger. Physiological activation seems to accompany state anger, though there is not always a clear correlation between subjective and physiological changes (Sebej, Mullner and Farkas, 1984). There are indications that different emotional states are associated with different reported physiological symptoms. Shields (1984) compared symptoms reported as associated with anxiety, sadness and anger and found that perceived somatic activation was less for anger than for anxiety and that the pattern of symptoms for anger was discriminable from both anxiety and sadness. In clinical work extreme physiological activation in response to provocation is commonly reported in people with severe anger problems and may include heart rate change, muscle tension, trembling and sweating.

Behaviour
In the management of angry aggression the therapeutic objective is often to prevent undesirable behavioural expression of anger in the form of personal violence. The violent act itself may occur not as an immediate reaction to the first frustration met, but following an escalating sequence

of social exchanges (Toch, 1969; Patterson, 1985). This raises the question whether changing immediate behavioural reactions themselves might have some therapeutic value. If so, what kinds of behavioural reactions might be targeted because they are violence-provoking, and what methods are available for changing them?

One useful criterion in identifying problem behavioural reactions relates to whether or not the habitual reaction to an initial provocation has the effect of increasing the aversiveness of the subsequent environment. Novaco's (1978) model allows for the possibility that particular behavioural reactions may intensify frustration. Excessively angry and abrasive behaviour, for example, may produce counter-aggression, social rejection and ostracism and even, in extreme cases, legal sanctions. The effects of excessive aggression can be to intensify the very conditions which produced the angry reaction in the first place. This can be illustrated by the case of Jane, who was discussed earlier.

The analysis of Jane's anger can be summarized by Figure 6.1. Such patterns reveal the escalation process frequently observed in violence (Toch, 1969; Patterson, 1985). Patterson's (1985) work has identified some of the features of more complex 'coercive chains' in potentially violent families and suggests that micro-analyses of social interactions are needed to tease out the important reactions and counter-reactions. Toch (1985) has a similar transactional model of violence causation in other settings.

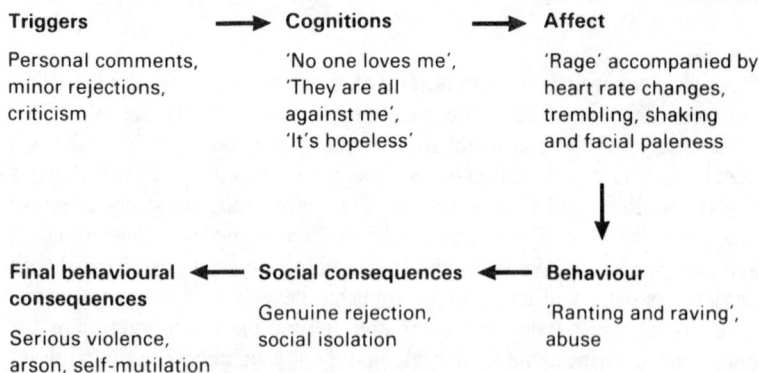

Triggers ➡	Cognitions ➡	Affect
Personal comments, minor rejections, criticism	'No one loves me', 'They are all against me', 'It's hopeless'	'Rage' accompanied by heart rate changes, trembling, shaking and facial paleness

$$\downarrow$$

Final behavioural consequences ⬅	Social consequences ⬅	Behaviour
Serious violence, arson, self-mutilation	Genuine rejection, social isolation	'Ranting and raving', abuse

Figure 6.1 *The anger sequence for Jane*

Transactional theories of this type require that attention be paid in therapy to the behaviour of other people in the environment of the angry person, and to the particular social behaviour of the client that might initiate and maintain transactions which will escalate to violence. In clinical settings the problem arises of distinguishing aggressive behavioural expressions of anger which will escalate the situation from appropriate assertive expression. A number of researchers have attempted to distinguish aggression and assertion (Hollandsworth, 1977; Hollandsworth and Cooley, 1978; Hull and Schroeder, 1979; Kirchner, Kennedy and Draguns, 1979; Hedlund and Lindquist, 1984).

Aggressive people may be prone to the use of social punishments such as ridicule, disparagement and negative evaluations (Hollandsworth, 1977). Threats and verbal 'put-down's may also be important (Hollandsworth and Cooley, 1978; Hedlund and Lindquist, 1984). The emphasis here, as in the early description of aggressive social styles by Toch (1969), is on the verbal content of interactions. Many of the important social behaviours, however, are likely to be of a non-verbal or paralinguistic nature (Trower, Bryant and Argyle, 1978). There is a clear need for further social psychological experimentation to investigate which non-verbal behaviours have 'provocational' effects in interactions with others. Intuitively, facial expression, threatening body postures and gesture are important behaviours. There has been some investigation of the role of proximity (Curran, Blatchley and Hanlon, 1978; Gilmour and Walkey, 1981) and of the prosodic features of speech, such as pitch and volume (Frick, 1985, 1986).

It is likely that anger-expression problems are heterogeneous. So far we have discussed 'undercontrolled' problems, where the person engages too readily in aggressive responses. There is some evidence that violent populations have a high incidence of persons who are excessively inhibited about anger expression. The 'overcontrolled' violent offender was initially identified by Megargee (1966, 1971, 1984) and is characterized by high inhibition and is at risk for excessive acts of violence in the long term (Blackburn, 1968, 1971; Arnold and Quinsey, 1977; Howells, 1983). The overcontrolled aggressor can also be construed as an example of inappropriate behavioural expression (the total absence of assertion) creating a more aversive environment (the person is constantly re-exposed to the provoking situation because it is not resolved).

The Therapeutic Management of Angry Aggression

A comprehensive strategy for helping clients deal more effectively with angry aggression can be derived from the theoretical work which I have reviewed. Any anger-management programme would need to deal with the triggering events, cognitive processes, physiological arousal and behaviour itself, as stressed by Novaco (1978).

Dealing with Triggers

Whatever the nature of the triggers of anger for people in general, any therapeutic enterprise requires a systematic assessment of the triggering events for the particular client. There are a number of sources for such information – a detailed interview covering angry episodes in the present and past, case-records, day-to-day diaries completed by the client, and observation charts completed by other people in the client's environment (nursing staff, relatives, etc.). There also exist inventories of common anger-inducing situations which may have a useful screening function (Novaco, 1975).

The assessment of triggers needs to be conducted in the light of two interrelated psychological facts. Firstly, people may not have complete conscious access to the relationship between events and their affective state (Bowers and Meichenbaum, 1984). Secondly, the immediate trigger for an angry episode may occur in the context of more general background stressors which clearly contribute to the unpleasant affective state of the person at the time the immediate trigger is met but which are not necessarily identified by the person as a 'cause' of their anger. Social, financial, familial and occupational stress are all relevant background factors and need to be investigated. It is my clinical impression that many explosive and damaging expressions of anger occur in response to the final trigger (for example, with violence) while carrying the residual excitatory effects of previous stressors (Zillmann, 1979).

The identification of immediate and background triggering events leads to the question of whether this knowledge can be used in a therapeutic way. It is easy to overlook the power of directly changing the probability of aversive events occurring in the environment so as to make inappropriate anger less likely. There are two strategies available to the therapist. The first is to directly modify the environment itself by removing the person from the aversive environment, or the aversive environment from the person. Where the aversive trigger is 'abnormal', in the sense that it is not a common feature of everyday life for most people, the arguments for trying to remove the trigger are more powerful. Davies (1982), for example, studied violent incidents in a Birmingham prison and discovered that common triggers for violence were 'odd' behaviours or 'stealing, borrowing or scrounging' on the part of cell-mates. One 'therapeutic' solution to these incidents would be to ensure that prisoners at risk for angry violence were not required to share a cell with 'aversive' cell-mates. Clearly the changing of aversive environments is often outside the control of the therapist or the client. In Davies's (1982) case, a reorganization of the entire prison may have been required. Given the importance of background stressors of a financial and occupational nature (for example, unemployment) there would ultimately be a political dimension to attempts to reduce the aversiveness of the experienced environment.

The second therapeutic strategy would stem from acknowledgement of the fact that the individual him/herself determines to some degree the aversiveness of the environment that is met. Deficits in educational, vocational or social skills (Trower, Bryant and Argyle, 1978; Hollin and Trower, 1986) may create frustration and contribute to inappropriate aggression. A sex offender, for example, who is entirely inept in sexual relationships to the extent that he develops angry feelings towards women, is more appropriately treated by being helped to acquire the relevant skills than to control the angry feelings themselves. Training in social and other skills, then, is an appropriate part of a broad-based treatment approach to anger reduction.

The identification of the major triggers and the decision to attempt to modify or eliminate the triggering situations typically create options as to whether the triggers will be tackled directly or in terms of the conditions which maintain them. This can be illustrated by a client, 'Christopher'. Christopher referred himself to an anger-management clinic because of his fears that he would so lose his temper in marital disputes that he would seriously harm his wife. A history of the problem revealed that he was not generally an aggressive man and had lost his temper to the point of becoming violent on only a handful of occasions. The identification of the trigger for these episodes proved straightforward and is illustrated in Figure 6.2.

Antecedents   **Immediate trigger**

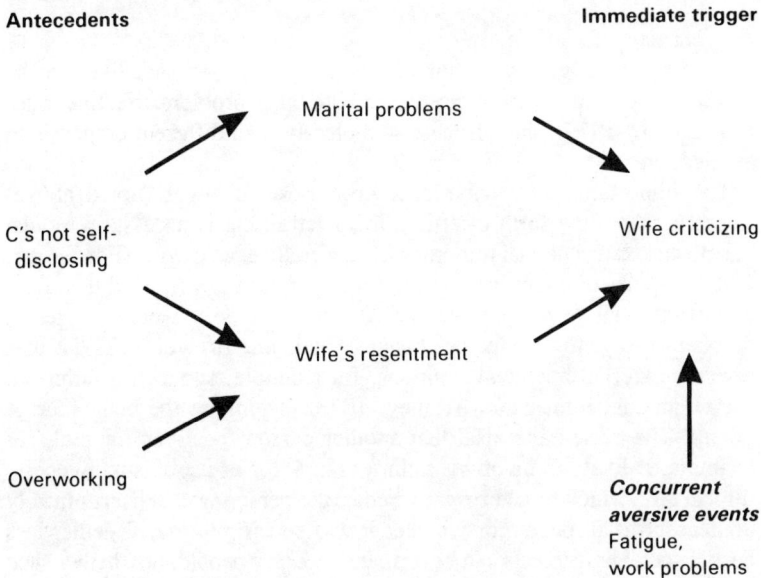

Marital problems

C's not self-disclosing

Wife criticizing

Wife's resentment

Overworking

Concurrent aversive events
Fatigue, work problems

Figure 6.2 *The triggers for Christopher's aggression*

Angry violence had always occurred in response to arguments following critical comments from his wife. The content of these comments was varied. Analysis of the marital relationship generally, however, revealed that the critical comments were an expression of the wife's more general resentment of her husband and of particular problems in the relationship. Both the resentment and the marital problems were, in turn, a product of Christopher's behaviour and his difficulties in talking about his feelings and his overcommitment to work.

In addition, it became clear that the critical comments to which he was likely to respond always occurred at a particular time of the day, namely when he had just returned, feeling fatigued and stressed, from work. This analysis reveals a number of options, then, for removing the trigger: (1) an attempt might be made to work with the wife (if she were available), to change her critical behaviour in the 'risky' situations; (2) Christopher's behaviour at work might become the focus so that he was less likely to return home in a tired and stressed state; (3) the marital problems and his wife's resentments might be worked with through some form of marital therapy; (4) Christopher's general failure to self-disclose and his long-term overcommitment to work might be treated. These options would have various advantages and disadvantages, and some might not be practicable at all, but all have a potential role in reducing exposure to the triggering situation in the future.

Dealing with Cognition

The particular cognitive techniques used for anger are not likely to be substantially different from those used with other problem affective states (Beck et al., 1979), though there will clearly be a different emphasis in application.

The importance of attributional processes for anger (noted above) suggests that some form of attributional retraining is necessary. Whilst the effects of attributional retraining are generally encouraging (Försterling, 1985), reports of cognitive therapy for anger have not isolated the effect of attributional retraining *per se*. Attribution theory would suggest a number of ways for producing change (Antaki and Brewin, 1982). A bias towards external hostile attributions, for example, suggests a failure to use contextual information (Kelley, 1973) in judging the behaviour of others. The biased appraisal that another person 'has it in for me', for example, is likely to involve a failure to look for or use 'distinctiveness' information which would reveal whether the person was indiscriminately unpleasant to all people or whether it was specific to me. Whether less hostile social judgements can be 'trained' in angry people, or whether such biases are resistant to rational analysis, is an important issue for future research.

Novaco (1978) has outlined a programme for controlling anger which has a cognitive basis, based on Meichenbaum's 'stress inoculation training'. This programme has three phases:

(1) *Cognitive preparation*   In this phase a manual is used and diaries are kept to help clients identify triggers and to understand the role of

anger and its interaction with behaviour. The phase would appear to be an educational one intended to produce insight into the nature of anger.

(2) *Skill acquisition*   In this phase an attempt is made to control anger by challenging hostile appraisals, suggesting alternative appraisals, modifying self-statements and teaching a variety of behavioural skills (see below).

(3) *Application practice*   In this phase skills are progressively applied to real anger situations, initially using imagined and role-play methods. Novaco (1975, 1976b, 1978) has reported a study of the effectiveness of this therapy with 34 persons with serious anger-control problems, comparing cognitive treatment, relaxation treatment, combined treatment and control conditions. Overall cognitive therapy produced greater change than the relaxation method and than controls, but was marginally less effective than combined treatment. Novaco (1977a) has also reported a single-case study of a hospitalized patient with anger problems who improved with the programme and maintained improvement one year after discharge.

Cognitive Treatment Studies

A number of outcome studies have suggested improvements with cognitive methods. Moon and Eisler (1983) have reported a comparison of stress-inoculation training, social skills training, problem-solving and a nominal attention control condition. The subjects in this study were high anger students. All the treatments showed significant effects in anger reduction, though on different components of the anger response.

Hazaleus and Deffenbacher (1986) allocated 'angry' students to cognitive, relaxation or control conditions. Both treatment conditions showed therapeutic effects in reducing anger which were maintained at one year follow-up.

Denicola and Sandler (1980) looked at the effects of cognitive behavioural methods (including stress inoculation) and parent training on the behaviour of child-abusing parents. Although it was not possible to isolate the effects of the two treatments there were some indications of a reduction in aversive behaviours in the families as a whole. Therapeutic gains with a similar group have been reported by Novellini and Katz (1983).

A number of papers have reported cognitive anger-reduction methods with child and adolescent groups (Snyder and White, 1979; Feindler, Marriott and Iwata, 1984; Garrison and Stolberg, 1983; Henshaw, Henker and Whalen, 1984). Feindler and his colleagues (Feindler and Ecton, 1986; Feindler et al., 1986) have described and evaluated a comprehensive anger-control programme for institutionalized psychopathic adolescents. In one study (Feindler et al., 1986) group anger-management was given over eight weeks and included a self-instruction component as well as behavioural components. A wide variety of therapeutic changes were observed, with evidence that some were maintained over a long-term (3 year) follow-up. Benson, Rice and Miranti (1986) have reported the effect of an anger-management programme with mentally handicapped adults. A self-instruction treatment was effective in producing change, but no more effective than other anger-management methods such as problem-solving or relaxation training.

These initial studies are encouraging as to the effectiveness of cognitive methods for anger problems (for a more extensive review of outcome studies see Novaco, 1985). Future work will clearly need to separate out the cognitive from the behavioural and other aspects of treatment programmes to determine the relative effectiveness of cognitive methods. Given that the literature reviewed above reveals that a range of cognitive variables (expectancies, attributions, irrational beliefs, etc.) are important for anger, it is to be expected that a range of cognitive therapies are feasible, ranging from stress-inoculation to rational–emotive therapy and attribution therapy. Which emphasis in cognitive therapy is most effective has yet to be established.

Dealing with Arousal

Where strong physiological arousal is an important feature of an anger problem there is a case for the use of relaxation training. As with anxiety problems, the relaxation response has a number of potential functions: (1) to reduce general, longer-term activation so that when new stressors are encountered the person is at a lower baseline and will respond less; (2) as a self-control technique to 'cool off' when high arousal has been produced by a provocation; (3) as a method to enable clients to increase their awareness of body cues so that the escalation of anger in the course of an argument, for example, can be detected and prevented; (4) as an antagonistic response to anger in formal desensitization (Hearn and Evans, 1972; Evans and Hearn, 1973; O'Donnell and Worrell, 1973). Hazaleus and Deffenbacher (1986) used relaxation as a coping skill, in relation to anger-arousing imagery and *in vivo* angry situations, and found improvements comparable to those brought about by cognitive therapy. My own experience is that relaxation as a coping strategy is useful only if the client can detect signs of anger early on in the escalation process. Once a state of very high physiological activation is reached the person feels unable or unwilling to establish control and relaxation is rejected as a useful strategy.

The literature on the effect of relaxation is relatively thin, though sufficiently encouraging to suggest that further studies are needed. Although beyond the scope of the present chapter, the feasibility of using psychopharmacological methods to reduce physiological arousal in people with temper problems has recently begun to be explored (Mattes, 1986).

Dealing with Behaviour

The methods relevant to producing change in behavioural expression itself will be little different from those used in other areas of clinical psychology. Anger-management therapy is based on a skills model and can be construed as a variant of social skills training (Trower et al., 1978; Hollin and Trower, 1986).

Problems of anger expression of an undercontrolled and overcontrolled type appear to be amenable to social skills training (SST). Training procedures have been described by Howells (1976) and Goldstein (1981). Individual case studies involving SST have been reported by Kaufman and Wagner (1972), Foy, Eisler and Pinkston (1975), Frederiksen et al. (1976) and Rahaim, Le Febvre and Jenkins (1980). Group comparison studies by Rimm et al. (1974), Fehrenbach and Thelen (1981) and Moon and Eisler (1983) have all reported some success using SST methods. The aim in SST is to extend the social repertoire of the angry individual so that new strategies for creating less aversive and more rewarding environments are available. The increasing cognitive emphasis in SST (Trower, 1984) suggests that the distinction between the behavioural approach of SST and the cognitive therapies may be difficult to maintain in future.

The task of generating alternative, more constructive ways of expressing anger raises the question of by what criteria an existing behaviour is to be judged inadequate and a new behaviour judged preferable. The criterion of increasing the aversiveness of the environment for the person has already been discussed. The criterion of social unacceptability of the behaviour is not a useful one in a therapeutic context. A person who becomes loud, belligerent and threatening when provoked may behave in a way which is disapproved of by the therapist, and even by society at large, but which may be functional for the person within their particular environment. This same problem of how behaviour is to be judged inappropriate arises within SST and it is proposed here that the solution suggested by McFall (1982), in an SST context, is also applicable to anger-management training. McFall's central argument is that inadequacy needs to be judged in relation to personal goals. Behaviour requires changing when it impedes the achievement of the person's goals. The implication of this point of view is that anger-management needs to be preceded by an analysis of the person's goal structure. Such a viewpoint also suggests a problem-solving orientation to anger-management in which the consequences of alternative behavioural strategies are delineated and compared (D'Zurilla and Goldfried, 1971; Platt, Prout and Metzger, 1986).

In clinical practice the elicitation of short- and long-term goals needs to precede the attempt to generate alternative ways of behaving in angry situations. Jane's 'ranting and raving' and abuse in response to personal comments, minor rejections and criticism (described above) occurred in the context of the short-term goals of 'getting on well with others' and 'being liked by people I live with'. Her major long-term goal was 'to get out of the hospital and live a normal life outside'. Her reactions to provoking situations were thus unambiguously unskilled, from her own perspective.

Alternative behaviours need to be generated at both a molar and molecular level. Thus Jane needs to identify other *strategies* for responding to personal comments and also their molecular behavioural components. She spontaneously identified three alternative strategies: (1) to ignore comments entirely; (2) to respond to comments in a way which let the others concerned know she was angry but which did not escalate the situation; (3) to leave the situation. Jane rejected strategies 1 and 3 because of her expectation and belief that these reactions would be construed as 'weak' and would lead to further provocation by other people. It was clearly a therapeutic option to explore and perhaps challenge this belief, but Jane's preference for strategy 2 led to this being identified as a target.

The identification of the molecular components of showing anger without escalation requires a detailed social skills analysis of Jane's verbal, para-linguistic and non-verbal behaviour in provoking situations, and some knowledge of what behaviours, in general, might have provoking effects (see above). The methods of micro-analysis used in the social skills context (Trower, Bryant and Argyle, 1978) are relevant in this particular problem area. Direct observation of behaviour by staff and video-recording of typical behaviour are usually necessary.

In Jane's case, observation of this sort identified several critical verbal behaviours (reacting to comments with swearing and reciprocal verbal abuse), paralinguistic behaviours (high voice volume, 'contemptuous' voice tone, high pitch) and non-verbal behaviours ('threatening' facial muscula-ture, excessive proximity to the person with whom she is having a dispute, aggressive gesticulation). Once such behaviours are identified and the client enabled to see the relationship between them and particular undesirable social outcomes, the full range of social skills techniques, such as instruc-tion, modelling, rehearsal with video-feedback, role-plays and homework assignments (Trower, Bryant and Argyle, 1978) have some usefulness in producing change. In my own experience, producing change in just a few critical verbal and non-verbal behaviours can have a quick and marked impact on how excessively angry people are viewed by others.

The attempt to elicit personal goals and to identify 'successful' behavioural strategies in clinical work often reveals a generally impoverished reper-toire of social skills. The excessively angry person, who, for example, wishes to obtain the respect and affection of others but habitually fails to do so, may have a limited or non-existent repertoire of positive social behaviour. Not only is the client unskilled in dealing with aversive social behaviour but he or she fails to interact in ways which will promote liking and friendship. Where this is the case there is a need to use social skills methods to encourage the skills involved in behaviours such as listening, giving praise, apologizing and expressing affection.

It can be seen that the anger-management perspective suggests a comprehensive and broad-based approach to the prevention of aggression and violence. There are some aggressive people not suited to anger-management methods, but, where aggression can be construed as a product of unskilled anger regulation, a wide range of therapeutic interventions are suggested by the analyses of Novaco (1975, 1978, 1985) and others. Within this framework, environmental stressors need to be identified, managed and prevented, habitual cognitions need to be elicited and re-evaluated, excessive physical arousal needs to be monitored and controlled, and the details of social behaviour itself and its effects on others need to be understood and changed. Anger-management methods stand to gain from developments in the many other fields of clinical psychology with which it clearly overlaps. Anger-management therapy, perhaps, represents the extension to aggression of the broader psychological models which inform clinical psychology in general.

Conclusions

The aim of this chapter has been to sketch a cognitive-behavioural approach to understanding anger and to managing anger in clients who have problems in this area. The discussion has depended heavily on Novaco's (1978) model of anger and anger-management. Novaco's analysis draws attention to triggering events, cognition, affective/physiological arousal and behaviour itself. An important feature of this analysis is that these components are reciprocally related. Cognition and affective arousal, for example, have a mutual, bidirectional relationship (Zajonc, 1984; Lazarus, 1984).

The therapeutic approach described is comprehensive and multimodal. Environmental, cognitive, physiological and behavioural variables need to be assessed in the individual case, and the formulation of an individual's problems in these terms usually requires a correspondingly broad range of interventions. Therapeutic work in the area of anger is greatly facilitated by the fact that angry aggression has been the subject of considerable theoretical and empirical work within non-clinical experimental psychology. This can be contrasted with depression, for example, where clinical work and analysis generally preceded and stimulated experimental research.

The evaluation of the effectiveness of anger-management methods is at an early stage but initial results are encouraging. Given the social importance of anger-related behaviours, this is likely to become a major area for cognitive-behavioural analysis and intervention in the future.

Note

I would like to thank the Leverhulme Trust for supporting work at Birmingham University on anger problems.

References

Adams, D. (1986) The role of anger in the consciousness development of peace activists: where physiology and history intersect. *International Journal of Psychophysiology*, 4: 158–64.

Antaki, C. and Brewin, C. (eds) (1982) *Attributions and psychological change*. London: Academic Press.

Arnold, L. S. and Quinsey, V. L. (1977) Overcontrolled hostility among men found not guilty by reason of insanity. *Canadian Journal of Behavioral Science*, 9: 330–40.

Averill, J. R. (1982) *Anger and aggression: an essay on emotion*. New York: Springer-Verlag.

Averill, J. R. (1983) Studies on anger and aggression. *American Psychologist*, 38: 1145–60.

Bandura, A. (1973) *Aggression: a social learning analysis*. Englewood Cliffs, NJ: Prentice-Hall.

Beck, A. T., Rush, A. J., Shaw, B. F. and Emery, G. (1979) *Cognitive therapy of depression*. New York: Guilford Press.

Beck, A. T., Emery, G. and Greenberg, R. (1985) *Anxiety disorders and phobias: a cognitive perspective*. New York: Basic Books.

Benesh, M. and Weiner, B. (1982) On emotion and motivation: from the notebooks of Fritz Heider. *American Psychologist*, 37: 887–95.

Benson, B. A., Rice, C. J. and Miranti, S. V. (1986) Effects of anger management training with mentally retarded adults in group treatment. *Journal of Consulting and Clinical Psychology*, 54: 728–9.

Berkowitz, L. (1982) Aversive conditions as stimuli to aggression. In L. Berkowitz (ed.), *Advances in experimental social psychology, vol. 15*. New York: Academic Press.

Berkowitz, L. (1983) Aversively stimulated aggression. *American Psychologist*, 38: 1135–44.

Blackburn, R. (1968) Personality in relation to extreme aggression in psychiatric offenders. *British Journal of Psychiatry*, 114: 821–8.

Blackburn, R. (1971) Personality types among abnormal homicides. *British Journal of Criminology*, 11: 14–31.

Blackburn, R. (1987) Cognitive-behavioural approaches to understanding and treating aggression. In K. Howells and C. R. Hollin (eds), *Clinical approaches to aggression and violence*. Issues in Criminological and Legal Psychology. Leicester: British Psychological Society.

Blanchard, D. C. and Blanchard, R. J. (1984) Affect and aggression: an animal model applied to human behavior. In R. J. Blanchard and D. C. Blanchard (eds), *Advances in the study of aggression, vol. 1*. London: Academic Press.

Bowers, K. S. and Meichenbaum, D. (eds) (1984) *The unconscious reconsidered*. New York: Wiley.

Brewin, C. R. (1985) Depression and causal attributions: what is their relation? *Psychological Bulletin*, 98: 297–309.

Buss, A. H. (1961) *The psychology of aggression*. New York: Wiley.

Clark, D. M. (1986) Cognitive therapy for anxiety. *Behavioural Psychotherapy*, 14: 283–94.

Cottington, E. M., Matthews, K. A., Talbot, E. and Kuller, L. H. (1986) Occupational stress, suppressed anger and hypertension. *Psychosomatic Medicine*, 48: 249–60.

Curran, S. F., Blatchley, R. J. and Hanlon, T. E. (1978) Body buffer zone and violence as assessed by subjective and objective techniques. *Criminal Justice and Behavior*, 5: 53–62.

Davies, W. (1982). Violence in prisons. In M. P. Feldman (ed.), *Developments in the study of criminal behaviour, vol. 2: Violence*. Chichester: Wiley.

Denicola, J. and Sandler, J. (1980) Training abusive parents in cognitive-behavioral techniques. *Behavior Therapy*, 11: 263–70.

Dobash, R. E. and Dobash, R. P. (1984) The nature and antecedents of violent events. *British Journal of Criminology*, 24: 269–88.

Dodge, K. A. (1985) Attributional bias in aggressive children. In P. C. Kendall (ed.), *Advances in cognitive-behavioral research and therapy, vol. 4*. New York: Academic Press.

Dyck, R. J. and Rule, B. G. (1978) Effect on retaliation of causal attributions concerning attack. *Journal of Personality and Social Psychology*, 36: 521–9.

D'Zurilla, T. and Goldfried, M. (1971) Problem solving and behavior modification. *Journal of Abnormal Psychology*, 8: 107–26.

Ellis, A. (1977) *How to live with and without anger*. New York: Readers' Digest.

Evans, D. R. and Hearn, M. T. (1973) Anger and systematic desensitization: a follow up. *Psychological Reports*, 32: 569–70.

Fehrenbach, P. A. and Thelen, M. H. (1981) Assertive-skills training for inappropriately aggressive college males: effects on assertive and aggressive behaviors. *Journal of Behavior Therapy and Experimental Psychiatry*, 12: 213–17.

Feindler, E. L., Marriott, S. A. and Iwata, M. (1984) Group anger control training for junior high school delinquents. *Cognitive Therapy and Research*, 8: 299–317.

Feindler, E. L., Ecton, R. B., Kingsley, D. and Dubey, D. (1986) Group anger control training for institutionalized psychiatric male adolescents. *Behavior Therapy*, 17: 109–23.

Feindler, E. L. and Ecton, R. B. (1986) *Adolescent anger control: cognitive-behavioural techniques*. New York: Pergamon.

Feldman, M. P. (1982) Overview. In M. P. Feldman (ed.), *Developments in the study of criminal behavior, vol. 2: Violence*. Chichester: Wiley.

Ferguson, T. J. and Rule, B. G. (1983) An attributional perspective on anger and aggression. In R. G. Geen and E. L. Donnerstein (eds), *Aggression: theoretical and empirical reviews, vol. 1*. New York: Academic Press.

Försterling, F. (1984) Importance, attributions and the emotion of anger. *Zeitschrift für Psychologie*, 192: 425–32.

Försterling, F. (1985) Attributional retraining: a review. *Psychological Bulletin*, 98: 495–512.

Foy, D. W., Eisler, R. M. and Pinkston, S. G. (1975) Modeled assertion in a case of explosive rage. *Journal of Behavior Therapy and Experimental Psychiatry*, 6: 135–7.

Fransella, F. and Bannister, D. (1977) *A manual of repertory grid technique*. London: Academic Press.

Frederiksen, L. W., Jenkins, J. O., Foy, D. W., and Eisler, R. M. (1976) Social skills training to modify abusive verbal outbursts in adults. *Journal of Applied Behavior Analysis*, 9: 117–25.

Frick, R. W. (1985) Communicating emotion: the role of prosodic features. *Psychological Bulletin*, 97: 412–29.

Frick, R. W. (1986) The prosodic expression of anger. *Aggressive Behavior*, 12, 121–128.

Frude, N. (1987) The physical abuse of children. In K. Howells and C. R. Hollin (eds), *Clinical approaches to aggression and violence*. Issues in Criminological and Legal Psychology, Leicester: British Psychological Society.

Gardner, J. and Gray, M. (1982). Violence towards children. In M. P. Feldman (ed.), *Developments in the study of criminal behavior, vol. 2: Violence*. Chichester: Wiley.

Garrison, S. R. and Stolberg, A. L. (1983) Modification of anger in children by affective imagery training. *Journal of Abnormal Child Psychology*, 11: 115–29.

Gentry, W. D. (1985) Relationship of anger-coping styles and blood pressure among Black Americans. In M. A. Chesney and R. H. Rosenman (eds), *Anger and hostility in cardiovascular and behavioral disorders*. Washington: Hemisphere Publishing Co.

Gilmour, D. R. and Walkey, F. H. (1981) Identifying violent offenders using a video measure of interpersonal distance. *Journal of Consulting and Clinical Psychology*, 49: 287–91.

Goldstein, A. P. (1981) Social skills training. In A. P. Goldstein, E. G. Carr, W. S. Davison II, and P. Wehr (eds), *In response to aggression*. Oxford: Pergamon.

Grieger, R. (1982) Anger problems. In R. Grieger and I. Z. Grieger (eds), *Cognition and emotional disturbance*. New York: Human Sciences Press.

Groth, A. N. (1979) *Men who rape*. New York: Plenum.

Hall, G. S. (1899) A study of anger. *American Journal of Psychology*, 10: 516–91.

Hazaleus, S. L. and Deffenbacher, J. L. (1985) Irrational beliefs and anger arousal. *Journal of College Student Personnel*, Jan.: 47–52.

Hazaleus, S. L. and Deffenbacher, J. L. (1986) Relaxation and cognitive treatments of anger. *Journal of Consulting and Clinical Psychology*, 54: 222–6.

Hearn, M. and Evans, D. (1972) Anger and reciprocal inhibition therapy. *Psychological Reports*, 30: 943–8.

Hedlund, B. L. and Lindquist, C. V. (1984) The development of an inventory for distinguishing among passive, aggressive and assertive behavior. *Behavioral Assessment*, 6: 379–90.

Henshaw, S. P., Henker, B. and Whalen, C. K. (1984) Self-control in hyperactive boys in anger-inducing situations: effects of cognitive-behavioral training and amethylphenidate. *Journal of Abnormal Child Psychology*, 13: 55–77.

Hollandsworth, J. G. (1977) Differentiating assertion and aggression: some behavioral guidelines. *Behavior Therapy*, 8: 347–52.

Hollandsworth, J. G. and Cooley, M. L. (1978) Provoking anger and gaining compliance with assertive versus aggressive responses. *Behavior Therapy*, 9: 640–6.

Hollin, C. R. and Trower, P. T. (eds) (1986) *Handbook of social skills training, vols. I and II*. Oxford: Pergamon.

Howells, K. (1976) Interpersonal aggression. *International Journal of Criminology and Penology*, 4: 319–30.

Howells, K. (1983) Social construing and violent behaviour in mentally abnormal offenders. In J. Hinton (ed.), *Dangerousness, problems of assessment and prediction*. London: Allen and Unwin.

Hull, D. B. and Schroeder, H. E. (1979) Some interpersonal effects of assertion, non-assertion and aggression. *Behavior Therapy*, 10: 20–8.

Julius, S., Schneider, R. and Egan, B. (1985) Suppressed anger in hypertension: facts and problems. In M. A. Chesney and R. H. Rosenman (eds), *Anger and hostility in cardiovascular and behavioral disorders*. Washington: Hemisphere Publishing Co.

Kaufman, L. M. and Wagner, B. R. (1972) Barb: a systematic treatment technology for temper control disorders. *Behavior Therapy*, 3: 84–90.

Kelley, H. H. (1973) The processes of causal attribution. *American Psychologist*, 28: 107–28.

Kirchner, E. P., Kennedy, R. E. and Draguns, J. G. (1979) Assertion and aggression in adult offenders. *Behavior Therapy*, 10: 452–71.

Kremer, J. F. and Stephens, L. (1983) Attribution and arousal as mediators of mitigation's effect on retaliation. *Journal of Personality and Social Psychology*, 45: 335–43.

Lazarus, R. S. (1984) On the primacy of cognition. *American Psychologist*, 39: 124–9.

Lopez, F. G. and Thurman, C. E. (1986) A cognitive-behavioral investigation of anger among college students. *Cognitive Therapy and Research*, 10: 245–56.

McFall, R. M. (1982) A review and reformulation of the concept of social skills. *Behavioral Assessment*, 4: 1–33.

McKellar, P. (1950) Provocation to anger and the development of attitudes of hostility. *British Journal of Psychology*, 40: 104–14.

Manuck, S. B., Morrison, R. L., Bellack, A. S. and Polefrone, J. M. (1985) Behavioral factors in hypertension: cardiovascular responsivity, anger and social competence. In M. A. Chesney and R. H. Rosenman (eds), *Anger and hostility in cardiovascular and behavioral disorders*. Washington: Hemisphere Publishing Co.

Mattes, J. A. (1986) Psychopharmacology of temper outbursts. *Journal of Nervous and Mental Disease*, 174: 464–70.

Matthews, K. A., Glass, D. C., Rosenman, R. H. and Bortner, R. W. (1977) Competitive drive, pattern A and coronary heart disease: a further analysis of some data from the Western Collaborative Group Study. *Journal of Chronic Diseases*, 30: 489–98.

Megargee, E. I. (1966) Undercontrolled and overcontrolled personality types in extreme antisocial aggression. *Psychological Monographs*, 80.

Megargee, E. I. (1971) The role of inhibition in the assessment and understanding of violence. In J. E. Singer (ed.), *The control of aggression and violence: cognitive and physiological factors*. London: Academic Press.

Megargee, E. I. (1984) Recent research on overcontrolled and undercontrolled personality patterns among violent offenders. In I. Jacks and S. G. Cox (eds), *Psychological approaches to crime and its correction*. Chicago: Nelson-Hall.

Moon, J. R. and Eisler, R. M. (1983) Anger control: an experimental comparison of three behavioral treatments. *Behavior Therapy*, 14: 493–505.

Nasby, W., Hayden, B. and De Paulo, B. M. (1980) Attributional bias among aggressive boys to interpret unambiguous social stimuli as displays of hostility. *Journal of Abnormal Psychology*, 89: 459–68.

Novaco, R. W. (1975) *Anger control: the development and evaluation of an experimental treatment*. Lexington, DC: Heath Sand Co.

Novaco, R. W. (1976a) The function and regulation of the arousal of anger. *American Journal of Psychiatry*, 133: 1124–8.

Novaco, R. W. (1976b) Treatment of chronic anger through cognitive and relaxation controls. *Journal of Consulting and Clinical Psychology*, 44: 681.

Novaco, R. W. (1977a) Stress inoculation: a cognitive therapy for anger and its application to a case of depression. *Journal of Consulting and Clinical Psychology*, 45: 600–8.

Novaco, R. W. (1977b) A stress inoculation approach to anger management in the training of law enforcement officers. *Journal of Community Psychology*, 5: 327–46.

Novaco, R. W. (1978) Anger and coping with stress. In J. P. Foreyt and D. P. Rathjen (eds), *Cognitive behavior therapy*. New York: Plenum.

Novaco, R. W. (1979) The cognitive regulation of anger and stress. In P. Kendall and S. Hollon (eds), *Cognitive behavioral interventions: theory, research and procedures*. New York: Academic Press.

Novaco, R. W. (1985) Anger and its therapeutic regulation. In M. A. Chesney and R. H. Rosenman (eds), *Anger and hostility in cardiovascular and behavioral disorders*. New York: Hemisphere Publishing Co.

Novellini, S. and Katz, R. (1983) Effects of anger control training on abusive parents. *Cognitive Therapy and Research*, 7: 57–68.

O'Donnell, C. R. and Worrell, L. (1973) Motor and cognitive relaxation in the desensitization of anger. *Behavior Research and Therapy*, 11: 473–81.

Patterson, G. R. (1985) A microsocial analysis of anger and irritable behavior. In M. A. Chesney and R. H. Rosenman (eds), *Anger and hostility in cardiovascular and behavioral disorders*. Washington: Hemisphere Publishing Co.

Peterson, C. and Seligman, M. E. P. (1985) Causal explanations as a risk factor for depression: theory and evidence. *Psychological Review*, 91: 495–512.

Platt, J. J., Prout, M. F. and Metzger, D. S. (1986) Interpersonal cognitive problem-solving therapy (ICPS). In W. Dryden and W. Golden (eds), *Cognitive-behavioural approaches to psychotherapy*. London: Harper & Row.

Plutchik, R. (1980) *Emotion: a psychoevolutionary synthesis*. New York: Harper & Row.

Rahaim, S., Le Febvre, C. and Jenkins, J. O. (1980) The effects of social skills training on behavioral and cognitive components of anger management. *Journal of Behavior Therapy and Experimental Psychiatry*, 11: 3–8.

Reid, J. B. and Kavanagh, K. (1985) A social interactional approach to child abuse: risk, prevention and treatment. In M. A. Chesney and R. H. Rosenman (eds), *Anger and hostility in cardiovascular and behavioral disorders*. Washington: Hemisphere Publishing Co.

Rimm, D. C., Hill, G. A., Brown, N. N., Stuart, J. E. (1974) Group assertive training in treatment of experience of inappropriate anger. *Psychological Reports*, 34: 791–8.

Rosenman, R. H. and Chesney, M. A. (1982) Stress, type A behavior and coronary heart disease. In L. Goldberger and S. Breznitz (eds), *The handbook of stress: theoretical and clinical aspects*. New York: Macmillan.

Salkovskis, P. M. (1986) The cognitive revolution: new way forward, backward somersault or full circle. *Behavioural Psychotherapy*, 14: 278–82.

Schneider, R. H., Egan, B. M., Johnson, E. H., Drobny, H. and Julius, S. (1986) Anger and anxiety in borderline hypertension. *Psychosomatic Medicine*, 48: 202–48.

Sebej, F., Mullner, J. and Farkas, G. (1984) The relation of subjective and physiological correlates of anger to some cognitive and personality traits. *Studia Psychologica*, 25: 99–103.

Shields, S. A. (1984) Reports of bodily change in anxiety, sadness and anger. *Motivation and Emotion*, 8: 1–21.

Snyder, J. and White, M. (1979) The use of cognitive self-instruction in the treatment of behaviorally disturbed adolescents. *Behavior Therapy*, 10: 227–35.

Stuart, R. B. (ed.) (1981) *Violent behavior: social learning approaches to prediction, management and treatment*. New York: Brunner-Mazel.

Toch, H. (1969) *Violent men*. Harmondsworth, Middx.: Penguin.

Toch, H. (1985) The catalytic situation in the violence equation. *Journal of Applied Social Psychology*, 15: 105–23.

Trower, P., Bryant, B. and Argyle, M. (1978) *Social skills and mental health*. London: Methuen.

Trower, P. (ed.) (1984) *Radical approaches to social skills training*. London: Croom Helm.

Zajonc, R. B. (1984) On the primacy of affect. *American Psychologist*, 39: 117–23.

Zillmann, D. (1979) *Hostility and aggression*. Hillsdale, NJ: Lawrence Erlbaum.

7

An Integrated Cognitive-Behavioural Approach to Withdrawal from Tranquillizers

Moira Hamlin

Tranquillizers, particularly the benzodiazepines, have been used increasingly in the medical treatment for anxiety during the 1970s and 1980s. 40 billion doses per day were consumed worldwide with sales exceeding $1,000 million (Tyrer, 1980). In the USA, for example, 12.9 per cent of the population reported the use of an anti-anxiety/sedative drug (mainly benzodiazepines) in 1981. In the UK one and a half million people take benzodiazepines for more than one year (Balter, Levine and Manheimer, 1974). The long-term effectiveness of tranquillizers has not been established and the Committee on the Review of Medicines stated in 1980 that 'there was little convincing evidence that benzodiazepines were efficacious in the treatment of anxiety after 4 months continuous treatment'. The Committee's guidelines suggested that prescription for benzodiazepines be limited to short-term use. However, about 1.5 per cent of the adult population in the UK take these drugs chronically throughout the year and 0.7 per cent have taken benzodiazepines for over 7 years (Balter, Levine and Manheimer, 1974). Numerous studies have shown a ratio of 2:1 female to male users (Parish, 1971; Cooperstock, 1978) with 80 per cent of long-term users aged over 40 (Woodcock, 1970; Parish, 1971).

The popularity of benzodiazepines and the steep rise in prescribing in the 1970s was partly due to their increased efficacy and safety. Barbiturates were the main alternative before Chlordiazepoxide (Librium) was first produced in 1960. Unlike barbiturates, benzodiazepines appeared to have few side effects, were safe in overdose and did not produce dependency.

First reports of withdrawal problems were dismissed because it was considered that this was an occurrence of the original anxiety (Owen and Tyrer, 1983). Recent studies have shown that symptoms cannot always be attributed to a recurrence of anxiety (Covi et al., 1973), although clinically it may be difficult to make this distinction. Of most concern is the finding that potential for physical as well as psychological dependence exists even at a normal therapeutic dose, for example 20–40 mg Diazepam per day (Petursson and Lader, 1981; Owen and Tyrer, 1983). The dependence is characterized mainly by a withdrawal syndrome following termination of medication. Withdrawal symptoms can be experienced even after brief treatments of 4–6 weeks (Fontaine, Chouinard and Annable, 1984; Murphy, Owen and Tyrer, 1984). Main features of the withdrawal syndrome include anxiety, insomnia, hypersensitivity to sensory stimuli (particularly light and sound), gastro-intestinal disturbances, headaches, muscle spasms, vertigo, unease and depression, metallic taste, perceptual disturbances (Tyrer and Seivewright, 1984), and in extreme cases paranoid symptoms, hallucinations and convulsions (MacKinnon and Parker, 1982).

Between 15 per cent and 45 per cent of long-time benzodiazepine users are likely to experience the syndrome (Hallstrom and Lader, 1982; Tyrer et al., 1983). Typically, benzodiazepine withdrawal symptoms develop slowly, reach a peak and then decline. There is a time lag between the onset of symptoms with long-acting benzodiazepines such as Diazepam, Chlordiazepoxide (Valium, Librium) of 3 to 7 days. Shorter-acting benzodiazepines such as Lorazepam, Oxazepam and Triazolam (Ativan, Serenid, Halcion) produce withdrawal symptoms after 24 hours. It is also becoming clear that shorter-acting benzodiazepines, particularly Lorazepam, are likely to lead to more serious withdrawal problems (Tyrer and Seivewright, 1984). Five to 10 per cent of patients may experience some withdrawal symptoms after 6 months of tranquillizer therapy. After 6–8 years the proportion likely to develop withdrawal symptoms rises to 75 per cent (Petursson and Lader, 1984a).

Long-Term Problems of Tranquillizer Use

One could argue that stress and anxiety have always been present in life. Tranquillizers are merely the latest addition to the search for external sources of relief. Gin, opium and tobacco have played a similar role throughout history. However, underlying the widespread use of tranquillizers lies a tacit acceptance of medication as a valid solution for dealing with stress and anxiety. But where does individual responsibility for health lie in a society where pills are often used as a first line of defence against 'feeling bad'? In their study of doctors and their patients, Gabe and Lipshitz-Phillips (1984) highlighted the ambivalence towards tranquillizers experienced by both groups. The limitations of the drugs were acknowledged, but tranquillizers were still prescribed and still taken. Given the short-term medical effectiveness of tranquillizers (Committee on the Review of Medicines, 1980) it is perhaps surprising that the current problem facing treatment services is the group of people who have been taking tranquillizers for up to 25 years. In a review of the evidence for benzodiazepine dependence Owen and Tyrer (1983) concluded that if the drugs are prescribed regularly for more than 4 months dependence is likely to be produced. They argue that there has been too much complacency in relation to long-term prescriptions for tranquillizers. In addition, Lader and Petursson (1983) have found possible morphological changes in the brain following long-term use of psychotropic drugs. It was 50 years before the dangers of barbiturates were realized and 25 years before the hazards of amphetamines as appetite suppressants were known. Tranquillizers with a life span of 25 years still have a question mark hanging over their long-term effects. The causes for concern which have been expressed over efficacy, dependence potential and long-term effects, sit uneasily with the current level of prescribing and long-term use of tranquillizers. The findings of Murray (1981) are not unusual in this field. In his study 58 per cent of patients taking long-term tranquillizers said that they would find it difficult to manage without their drugs, and 33 per cent claimed they would not manage at all, yet only 1 in 5 of their general practitioners had tried to get them off their tablets. Whether it is the doctor's responsibility or the patient's to initiate withdrawal is an interesting question which will be explored later. What is now apparent is that many people continue to take tranquillizers long after the initial problem has passed.

Two main issues must therefore be addressed in practical terms: (1) what is appropriate treatment/help for people who have been taking tranquillizers for longer than 4 months? (2) what steps should be taken to prevent inappropriate use of tranquillizers in the future?

Psychological Alternatives to Tranquillizers

The main reasons tranquillizers are first prescribed is to alleviate some form of anxiety or stress. Psychological methods, rather than medication, have the potential to produce more effective coping strategies both for prevention of stress and in withdrawal from tranquillizers. For the group of people who are already long-term users an integration of medical and psychological approaches offers the best form of management.

The first problem to be faced is to determine the extent of the interaction between the pharmacology of tranquillizers and the psychological effects. Unfortunately there are no clear-cut formulas which can be applied to particular individuals. The symptoms of tranquillizer withdrawal are similar to the symptoms of anxiety and the two can easily be confused. Not everyone will experience withdrawal symtoms, but the likelihood increases with higher doses and length of time taken. Many people find the hardest part of withdrawal to be the last few milligrams, yet the amount of chemical in the blood is at its lowest. The type of medication is also important. There is increasing clinical evidence that shorter-acting compounds such as Temezepam and Lorazepam produce more severe withdrawal symptoms (Tyrer, Rutherford and Higgett, 1981; Stopforth, 1986).

Withdrawal Schedules
The research attention given to the medical management of withdrawal is fairly extensive in comparison to the relatively neglected area of psychological treatments. Several attempts have been made to compare abrupt or

gradual withdrawal (Tyrer, 1982; Rickels et al., 1984). Higher drop-out rates, more withdrawal reactions and 'further intervention necessary' was the general conclusion for abrupt withdrawal programmes. An interesting finding by Cappell et al. (1987) confirms anecdotal evidence. Patients in the placebo condition in this study used their own tranquillizers to supplement the supplies given by the researchers. This confirms the existence of a pharmacological need for the drug. Gradual withdrawal is generally recommended although the size of the dose reduction and the time period for reduction differ between studies. A range of 4 to 16 week programmes have been recommended (Salkind, 1982; Hopkins, Sethi and Mucklow, 1982; Petursson and Lader, 1984b). In a handbook for physicians (Devenyi and Saunders, 1986), guidelines are given for a faster withdrawal. Firstly patients' drugs are always switched to a Diazepam equivalent dose. For a patient on a daily dose of Diazepam of 100 mg, withdrawal would take only 7 days. On day 1 the dose would be cut by half to 50 mg and tapered on the following daily schedule: 50, 40, 30, 20, 15, 10, 5 mg.

While practical guidelines for the management of withdrawal are necessary and helpful it is also important to consider underlying issues which could militate against successful withdrawal. For many people, taking tranquillizers is an external way of boosting confidence in themselves, the 'magic' pill allows them to do things they feel beyond them without recourse to medication. Passive-dependent personality traits have been found in tranquillizer users (Tyrer, Owen and Dawling, 1983), and a higher external health locus of control than in non-users (Crockett, 1986). A danger in prescribing medication for stress-related problems lies in reinforcing the person's belief that they are not in control of themselves and that they have no influence over events around them. Similarly, during the withdrawal period, if a withdrawal schedule is determined by someone else this belief can lie untouched. The person remains vulnerable to future stress as they have not learned any new coping skills or significantly altered their self-image. Even on pragmatic grounds a predetermined schedule of withdrawal which does not involve the patient sufficiently in the process probably has limitations. Drop-out rates from abrupt withdrawal schedules are high (Tyrer, Rutherford and Higgett, 1981). Even on gradual withdrawal schedules only about one-third of patients are problem-free at the end of treatment (Rickels et al., 1984; Petursson and Lader, 1984a). Follow-up periods in most studies are not of sufficient length to enable a reliable estimate to be made of how many people resume taking their tranquillizers. However, clinical evidence suggests that for long-term users a common pattern of use is one of several periods of withdrawal and abstinence accompanied by resumption of tranquillizers following additional stress.

Withdrawal from tranquillizers should only be seen as the first and easiest step. The real problem is *maintenance*: that is, staying off. This period offers the most scope for psychological intervention.

Psychological Treatments
In the UK many professional health workers and voluntary groups are involved with tranquillizer withdrawal. The Benzodiazepine Interest Group (BIG) has a growing national membership with a newsletter which publishes up-to-date clinical work and research on tranquillizers (BIG Newsletter, 1987). There are numerous articles (for example, Colvin, 1983; Stopforth, 1986; Edwards, 1986) and popular books (for example, Melville, 1984; Curran and Golombok, 1985) which give advice on methods of withdrawal. But there has been a tendency for clinical practice to forge ahead without the benefit of any sound theoretical base. An assumption has been made that cognitive and behavioural techniques can be successfully applied to tranquillizers, but there are few outcome studies to support this view.

Table 7.1 summarizes the most up-to-date work in the field. Ashton (1984) gives a detailed description of a withdrawal programme for 12 patients. Nine patients received inpatient withdrawal over 2 weeks, and 3 outpatient treatment. Treatment was individually based and included the following elements: (1) substituting Diazepam for Lorazepam, (2) gradually tapering the dose on a schedule predetermined by the doctor, (3) substitution of alternative medication where appropriate for depression, pain, panic attacks, etc., (4) daily visits by the doctor for inpatients and on average 18 visits for outpatients. Few details are given on non-medical interventions except for 'listening sympathetically to their complaints and giving simple reassurance'. The major outcome measure used in the study was a checklist of symptoms before and after withdrawal. These were rated mild, moderate or severe by the patient. Of the twelve patients, two were symptom-free and nine showed moderate or definite improvement after 6 months. One patient made no improvement.

The study gives a comprehensive description of the course of withdrawal in 12 patients but it is difficult to generalize from the results for a number of reasons. The size of the sample is small (12 patients), only one out-come measure – self-reported withdrawal symptoms – is used, and the follow-up period is too short (average 3 months) to allow adequate assessment of abstinence. The author reports that only 2 patients had a previous psychiatric history, which is perhaps surprising in view of the severity of the psychological symptoms reported in withdrawal. Prior to the study relatives were asked about patients' psychological functioning, but no formal assessment was reported. The lack of detailed psychological assessment beforehand makes the suggestion 'that the symptoms resulted from benzodiazepine use and not from an underlying anxiety neurosis' less tenable.

Table 7.1　*Results of studies using psychological methods for withdrawal from benzodiazepines*

Study	Number of subjects	Drugs	Dose	Duration of Use	Intervention	Results	Outcome measures	Control group	Follow-up
Cormack and Sinnott, 1983	From 50 initial contacts, 11 Subjects completed group treatment	No details given	No details	6 Subjects 1–7 years, 5 Subjects 7+ years	Group treatment anxiety management, 11–13 weeks	5 patients in group reduced, 12 not in group reduced	Diary of pills and symptoms	Individuals not receiving psychological treatment	5–10 weeks post-treatment
Ashton, 1984	12	8 Diazepam, 7 Lorazepam, Nitrazepam	No details	Mean = 10.4 years	Individual treatment 9 inpatients, 3 outpatients alternative short-term medication	At 6 month follow-up: 2 patients symptom-free, 9 moderate or definite improvement, 1 no improvement	Withdrawal symptoms	None	6 months
Skinner, 1984	35	5 abstinent, 1 Largactil, remainder benzo-diazepines (not specified)	No details	Mean = 2.9 years	Group treatment, 6 lessons on management	24 abstinent, 5 reduced, 6 same	1 self-report symptom of anxiety	None	3 months, 1 year post-treatment

Study	N	Drug	Dose	Duration	Treatment	Outcome	Measures	Control	Follow-up
Tyrer et al., 1985	3	Lorazepam	1.5 mg daily	3.5 years, 5.5 years, 7 years	2 anxiety modulation	Significant reductions in 2 patients	(CPRS) rating scale for psychopathology	1 Subject relaxation therapy – dropped out	1 month progress maintained
Sanchez-Craig et al., 1986	20 (12 M, 8 F)	Diazepam (60%), Lorazepam (25%)	14 mg daily (range 5–35 mg)	7.7 years	Cognitive-behavioural treatment for problem drinkers (5 sessions), 11 Subjects treatment	Placebo group more symptoms, no significant difference in outcome, over 50% improved or abstinent at 1 year	STAI measures, plasma benzodiazepine levels	9 Subjects placebo group	1, 3, 6, 12 months
Cappell et al., (1987)	42	27 Diazepam, 11 Lorazepam, other benzodiazepines	14–16 mg, daily dose	Mean = 6.1 years	Individual treatment, behaviour therapy both groups. Random assignment to placebo or drug group	84% of placebo group used additional non-prescribed benzodiazepines compared to 33% of drug group	Self-monitoring behavioural/physical assessments, blood/urine samples	Yes: placebo group	No details

A study by Cormack and Sinnott (1983) is frequently cited as evidence that psychological alternatives to tranquillizers have limited effectiveness (Tyrer and Seivewright, 1984; Lader and Higgitt, 1986; *Lancet*, 1987). However, the study has serious weaknesses which should limit the conclusions that can be drawn from the results.

Fifty patients from a GP practice were contacted by letter inviting them to reduce their medication. Only 11 joined the group treatment programme of 11–13 weeks. It consisted of training in anxiety management which combined physical relaxation with cognitive approaches such as self-monitoring and the substitution of positive for negative statements. Weekly diaries of pills taken and symptoms experienced were kept by the patients. Using a success criteria of reduction, not abstinence, the authors concluded that 5 patients in the treatment groups and 12 patients not receiving psychological treatment were successful in cutting down their medication.

The original 50 patients were selected on the basis of no psychological or psychiatric involvement in the previous 2 years. This biases the sample in favour of people with less severe problems than might be routinely seen in clinical practice. Some patients have been found to be able to stop taking tranquillizers without experiencing any withdrawal effects (Tyrer et al., 1983) and there is evidence from studies (for example, Ashton, 1984) that patients with fewer psychological problems can withdraw more easily. The Cormack and Sinnott study does not necessarily reflect the ineffectiveness of anxiety management groups in tranquillizer withdrawal, but suggests there may be a group of patients who need minimal intervention in order to reduce. Further research is needed to identify the characteristics of such patients. Eleven patients is a small number completing treatment, but no details are given of those who declined or were not invited to join groups. Nor is it known what medication patients were taking and if this was equivalent between those who joined groups and those who did not. This is particularly important given the reported difficulties in withdrawal from Lorazepam (Owen and Tyrer, 1983). The degree of reduction in tranquillizers is not reported and it is unclear whether anyone was completely abstinent, which makes it difficult to compare with other studies where abstinence was the success criteria or percentage reductions from baseline are reported. Little information is given about the group treatment itself, and it would have been useful to have known patients' and therapists' evaluations of the intervention, the level of experience of the therapists, etc. Finally, of the 12 patients who were considered successful in reducing their medication, 8 had attended an assessment interview which in itself constitutes an intervention, if only a minimal one. This further confounds a true comparison of group treatment with those not receiving psychological treatment.

In a study which was carried out as part of a normal clinical service, Skinner (1984) reports the results of 6 anxiety management 'lessons' for

35 tranquillizer users. Unlike many studies, descriptions are given of the content and format of lessons, and a year follow-up was incorporated in the design. The lessons were a combination of information about stress and anxiety, and skills teaching. The cognitive element emphasized thought-distraction techniques and the development of a problem-solving thinking style along the lines proposed by Meichenbaum (1977). With 24 abstinent at the end of the year, results were encouraging. However, there were 5 patients abstinent at the start of the study, and duration of tranquillizer use for the group was only 2 years 9 months, which is considerably less than in most studies. In addition Colvin (1983) reports that from a sample of 75 patients the ones who had most difficulty withdrawing had been taking medication for 4–14 years.

In one of the better controlled studies to date Cappell et al. (1987) looked at the role of Diazepam as a reinforcer for chronic users of tranquillizers. Forty-two subjects were randomly assigned to either a placebo or drug group. Both groups received individual behaviour therapy of up to 8 sessions by two qualified psychologists. The therapy was adapted from that used for early stage problem drinking (Sanchez-Craig, 1984). It emphasized a functional analysis of reasons for benzodiazepine use and the development of coping strategies which did not rely on tranquillizers. Subjects were informed that complete withdrawal from tranquillizers was expected by the fourth or fifth session. Multiple outcome measures were employed in the design and included self-monitoring, behavioural/physical assessment and screening of blood and urine.

The researchers found that subjects in the placebo group supplemented the non-active tablets they were given with their own tranquillizers significantly more than the drug group. This was taken as additional evidence for a pharmacological effect of tranquillizers even at low doses. The study provides interesting insights into the ways tranquillizers are used, but is less helpful on clinical aspects. No information is given on the number of chronic tranquillizer users who did not meet the criteria for inclusion in the study. Exclusion criteria included significant psychiatric history, use of tranquillizers in conjunction with alcohol or other substances, and a range of medical conditions. Subjects were also on low doses of tranquillizers, on average only 14–16 mg per day (range 5–45 mg). It is not clear whether the subjects in this research study are representative of the general population of tranquillizer users.

The recent letters in the *Lancet* (Tyrer et al., 1985; Sanchez-Craig et al., 1986) give further support to the use of cognitive-behavioural treatment for dependence on tranquillizers. Tyrer et al. report the use of a new treatment, anxiety modulation, which has been developed from Beck et al.'s (1979) work with cognitive therapy of depression. This concentrates on redefining pathological symptoms of anxiety by altering attitudes and perceptions. It also includes strategies such as role-play.

Results were reported on 3 patients taking Lorazepam who had been previously unable to withdraw. Two were allocated to anxiety modulation and one to relaxation therapy. Both patients in the new treatment made significant reductions in medication and had maintained their progress at one month follow-up. The patient on relaxation therapy dropped out of the study after week 6. Obviously, success at one month follow-up with two patients cannot be taken as evidence for the efficacy of the treatment. However, it is a good attempt to move away from emphasis on pharmacological factors to the development of a psychological alternative.

Sanchez-Craig et al. (1986) had a sample of 20 patients in their study. Patients were randomly assigned either to a drug condition or a placebo condition. The aim of the study was to investigate the efficacy of a cognitive-behavioural treatment which had been found successful in problem drinkers (Sanchez-Craig et al., 1984). Two patients dropped out of treatment and the remaining 18 received on average 5 individual counselling sessions. At the end of treatment there was little difference in abstinence between the two conditions, although the placebo group experienced more withdrawal symptoms. At one year follow-up the 5 abstinent patients in the placebo condition maintained their abstinence, but only 3 treatment patients remained abstinent although 2 had made over 50 per cent reductions from baseline. The study included 12 men and 8 women, which is unusual as the ratio of men to women taking tranquillizers is 2:1 (Cooperstock, 1978). The doses of diazepam (or equivalent) were relatively low (14 mg), which makes comparison with other studies difficult.

Overview
The limited amount of work on benzodiazepine withdrawal provides few guidelines for the practitioner in developing effective alternative methods. The psychological methods used to date have either been adjuncts to withdrawal schedules or anxiety management programmes with less cognitive emphasis. Tranquillizer users have been considered a homogeneous group, but there is every indication from the literature that they comprise two distinct sub-groups. One group may require a minimum intervention or none at all in order to withdraw. The remainder, with higher dose, longer duration of use, etc., are likely to have other psychological problems in addition to their tranquillizer use. The task ahead lies in identifying the characteristics of patients who fall into these sub-groups and to determine the interventions required in relation to long-term outcome.

The Withdraw Project

Description
The Withdraw Project was set up within a District Health Authority to deal specifically with the problem of tranquillizers. It offers a clinical

psychology service to both men and women who wish to withdraw from tranquillizers. A research study is run in parallel with the clinical service which has the following aims: (1) to identify characteristics of patients which predict successful withdrawal from tranquillizers, (2) to assess the severity of psychological problems before and after treatment, (3) to evaluate the effectiveness of the Project's psychological intervention, (4) to include a minimum intervention control group. The model of intervention used is a three-tier one.

Information only	*first tier*
Information and education	*second tier*
In-depth intervention	*third tier*

The first tier is the provision of information only. For a large section of the population, information in the form of written material, television, radio, etc., is sufficient to enable them to withdraw. It is assumed that this group can process the information content and apply it to themselves without significant contamination by irrational beliefs or inappropriate feelings. A parallel is drawn with smoking research where this applies to a proportion of smokers (Warner, 1977; OPCS, 1981, 1983). This level of intervention is aimed at the general public and health professionals in an attempt to raise the level of awareness about the subject and to help prevent the problems of long-term tranquillizer users.

This method of work requires a change from the traditional health care model which involves waiting for people to present with problems. It requires a more 'active' role of identifying high-risk groups and attempting to intervene before problems worsen. For the ultimate goal of prevention, it means attempting to prevent problems arising in the first place. In practice, this has meant the following: producing posters and leaflets advertising services which are widely available in the community, and displaying them in shops, libraries, voluntary organizations, health centres; giving talks and running workshops for schoolchildren, self-help groups, health professionals, voluntary organizations; building up contacts with local press, radio and television to ensure regular items on tranquillizers; mounting exhibitions on tranquillizers in libraries, health fayres and public buildings. It is beyond the scope of this chapter to examine this mode of work in detail. However, interesting questions are raised, such as the skills and abilities needed by counsellors for this type of work, whether current training equips them for the change of role, and what are the changes in job satisfaction which must arise.

If information alone is insufficient the second tier, the information and educational component, is the next level of intervention to be employed. This takes the form of short-term groups led by a psychologist or counsellor. The aim of the groups is not only to help people stop taking tranquillizers, but to help them learn alternative ways of coping. A significant proportion of clients in this category have attempted to stop several times and some have had periods of abstinence. Unfortunately, as soon as they are subjected to additional stress they restart medication. The main problem, therefore, is not so much coming off tranquillizers, but the problem of *maintenance – staying off* tranquillizers. Short-term groups are discussed in detail below.

The third tier, in-depth intervention, is reserved for those who need more than the above two levels. Clients may have all the facts and information they need on how to withdraw. They may understand what they can do instead of taking tranquillizers; they may even have the skills and yet still fail to give up tranquillizers. At this stage more intensive therapy is needed which looks at fundamental beliefs.

A longer term group of 6 months is offered which includes the educational component on tranquillizers featured in the short-term groups but allows more time to explore problems in greater depth (see Table 7.2). Long-term groups usually include clients who are on higher doses of tranquillizers, particularly Lorazepam. Their duration of tranquillizer use tends to be longer and combined with other medication. A previous psychiatric history, often with inpatient treatment, is present, as well as other psychological problems. Treatment goals in the group would include work on related problems as well as tranquillizer withdrawal.

Short-term groups
The majority of clients are seen in groups of 8–12 led by a psychologist or counsellor. Groups meet for one and a half hours weekly for 8 sessions, with the last 2 sessions at fortnightly intervals. A booster session is held 3 months after the eighth session. Although withdrawal from tranquillizers is the main aim of people attending groups, the approach adopted is to focus on issues underlying and maintaining tranquillizer use. Each session is devoted to a separate topic and by the end of the course it is hoped clients will have acquired new skills, attitudes and beliefs which will help them to continue withdrawing from medication and resist relapse in the future. Guidelines are offered on actual withdrawal but the pace of withdrawal is determined by the client. This may be accomplished quite quickly or take up to a year in some cases. It is not expected that all clients will have withdrawn by the end of the course.

Table 7.2 *Example of patient characteristics in a long-term group*

Client	Length of time on tranquillizers	Daily dose	Other medication	Previous psychiatric history	Other problems
1	7 years	Valium 40 mg	Anti-depressants	4 inpatient admissions	Mother on tranquillizers, repeated admissions to hospital. Threatened suicide. Patient copes by complete withdrawal to bed
2	5 years	Lorazepam 24 mg	Anti-depressants, pain killers	Post-natal depression, attempted suicide, inpatient treatment	Husband committed suicide
3	16 years	Lorazepam 7 mg	Anti-depressants	Post-natal depression, inpatient treatment	Obsession with razor blades and harming others
4	5 years	Lorazepam 7.5 mg	Anti-depressants	'Breakdown', inpatient treatment	Phobia about cancer; cannot be on her own
5	10 years	Diazepam 20 mg	Anti-depressants	Outpatient psychiatric treatment	Depression, agoraphobia
6	11 years	Lorazepam 4 mg	Anti-depressants	Overdose and inpatient treatment	Marital and relationship problems
7	5 years	Diazepam 15 mg	Anti-depressants	Inpatient treatment	Agoraphobia
8	6 years	Lorazepam 10 mg, Temazepam 20 mg	Anti-depressants, Beta blockers	Inpatient treatment	Depression, sexual problems

Problem Areas
Clinical assessments revealed patterns of dysfunction which were fairly common across tranquillizer users.

Depression   Data on the first 50 clients entering withdrawal groups revealed a significant level of clinical depression. (Mean = 16.32 as measured by the Beck Depression Inventory, range 0–37). According to Beck et al. (1979) negatively biased thinking is a core process in depression. Typical cognitive distortions for people using tranquillizers include some of the following:

1 *Overgeneralization*   After one past experience of failure to withdraw from tranquillizers years before, 'I'll *never* manage to give up these tablets'.
2 *Arbitrary inference*   'If people knew I took tranquillizers they wouldn't have anything to do with me.'
3 *Magnification (catastrophizing)*   'I can't cope without tranquillizers. I'll have to stay on them forever.'
4 *Absolutistic thinking*   'I must be a hopeless failure or I wouldn't need to take tranquillizers.'
5 *Selective abstraction*   'Cutting down doesn't count, I've still got a long way to go.'

Anxiety   The same group of clients demonstrated high levels of anxiety. (State, mean = 44.5 (range 22–70); Trait, mean = 52.6 (range 26–68), using the State–Trait Anxiety Inventory, Spielberger, 1983). Clients reported panic attacks, inability to relax, constant worrying and sleep problems.

Low self-esteem   On repertory grid measures using given constructs clients rated themselves on the negative ends of bipolar adjectives. For example, on a 6-point scale of confident to lacking confidence there was a difference between how clients rated themselves taking tranquillizers now and how they thought they would be without tranquillizers. (T = −2.69, df = 48, p<0.003). In general, clients saw themselves on the unconfident end and thought being without tranquillizers would considerably increase their confidence.

Isolation   Clients usually had few social outlets and intimate contacts. Even married clients felt they had no-one to talk to who really understood their problems with tranquillizers. The length of time on tranquillizers was on average more than 7 years, with a range of 5 months to 25 years. Many people felt really guilty about taking tranquillizers and considered it a sign of failure on their part. It was not uncommon for them to conceal their tranquillizer use, which in turn, increased their feelings of isolation.

An Integrated Approach
In devising the framework for groups the aim was to incorporate the following general principles:

1 to provide an opportunity for clients to experience rather than intellectualize their problems,
2 to give people a feeling of being listened to,
3 to provide clients with a framework to make sense of their experiences,
4 to provide information and the chance to discuss it,
5 to provide an opportunity to share experiences with others,
6 to help build confidence and self-esteem,
7 to teach useful skills for the future.

Clients with tranquillizer problems present with a wide range of dysfunctions. Deficits in cognitions, emotions and behaviour suggested that a successful approach must address each aspect. The therapy should ideally have a broad base and the therapist should be flexible in approach, drawing on different strategies to meet a variety of client needs. The therapeutic approach adopted for groups was a cognitive-behavioural one with transactional analysis methods added. This marriage is based largely on clinical experience: that clients respond best to a flexible approach which takes account of different needs throughout the process of therapy. This requires a therapist to be willing to revise tactics as necessary and to avoid being too firmly wedded to one 'right' approach. An interdependence between thoughts, feeling and behaviour is assumed which should be explicitly addressed in therapy. This approach is in line with that advocated by Lazarus's (1981) multimodal therapy, and shares a belief in the importance of working in several modalities for lasting therapeutic change. The base cognitive approach adopted was to work directly on clients' maladaptive cognitions using the model presented by Beck et al. (1979). Uniting cognitive methods with behavioural techniques is now a well established way to facilitate change. Advantages can be seen in using, first, cognitive methods to identify and challenge problematic cognitions, then behavioural techniques, for example, to train skills or create specific homework tasks.

Experiential techniques such as gestalt or transactional analysis can be a useful addition in therapy, particularly at points where the therapist and client are blocked and the way forward seems unclear. Enabling clients to directly experience a situation or emotion may intensify the affect, and help uncover complex beliefs and assumptions less accessible through a direct cognitive route. Illustrations of cognitive therapy in conjunction with Gestalt techniques are described by Arnkoff (1981). In a similar way the present tranquillizer withdrawal groups added transactional analysis to

Objectives
(1) To introduce group members to each other
(2) To set the pattern of group sessions
(3) To reassure that no-one will be forced to withdraw from tranquillizers
(4) To explain how tranquillizers work, side-effects, withdrawal symptoms
(5) To stabilize tablet taking
(6) To examine tension and relaxation

Resources
(1) Relaxation recording sheet for each group member
(2) 'Trouble with Tranx' for each (group member
(3) Suggested titles of relaxation tapes
(4) Sticky labels – one for each person, including leader

Procedure
(1) *Introduction* by Leader
Welcome group members. Give aims and purpose of the group with a focus on tranquillizer withdrawal. Establish 'rules': punctuality in starting and finishing, commitment to attend all the sessions and why, need for confidentiality. Reassure that withdrawal is done at the pace decided by the user.

(2) *Exercise*
Give each person a sticky label, to write name in large letters across top. Fold in half, on one side write one hope about the group and on the other side one worry about the group. Find a partner and tell them about your hope and worry and hear theirs. Return to group and introduce partner telling of their hope and worry. (30 mins)

(3) *Input on tranquillizers* by Leader
Use the themes emerging from the group exercise to explain how tranquillizers work, and focus on how people see themselves as tranquillizer users. Emphasize support for that self-image as well as the desire for change.

(4) *Diaries*
Collect tablet-taking diaries for previous week. Notice chaotic use and ask them to stabilize. Talk about side-effects and how they are similar to withdrawal symptoms. Explain how alcohol, cigarettes and analgesics interact with tranquillizers. (30 mins)

(5) *Relaxation and tension*
Look at tense posture in the group. Ask people to recall their arrival in the group. Give examples and get group to give examples. Start to get people to relax jaws, face, neck, shoulders, stomach, bottom, thighs, toes and learn to breathe out. Hand out relaxation record sheet, explain how it will help people identify anxious times, and compare with times tablets are taken.

(6) *Support*
Give out 'Trouble with Tranx' (Release Publications). Ask members to read the leaflet and get family and friends to read it too. It is important that the family understand about tranquillizers and withdrawal so that they can offer support. Allow time for questions and reactions from group members.

Homework
(1) To record times in the week when a member feels anxious

(2) To notice body tension and practise relaxing muscles

(3) To read 'Trouble with Tranx'   (30 mins)

Figure 7.1 *Group leaders' guidelines for session 1*

cognitive-behavioural methods. This was restricted to a part of transactional analysis called structural analysis which deals with communication. The advantage of this approach is that it provides clients with a structure which enables them to make better sense of their own internal and external experience. At its simplest level thoughts, feelings and behaviour are seen as falling into three distinct patterns or ego states. The three ego states – Parent, Adult and Child – are classified according to their differing behaviour characteristics. (For a fuller description of transactional analysis readers are referred to Woollams and Brown, 1979; Pitman, 1984.) In groups clients are introduced to these concepts with the aim of understanding their own and other people's responses in order to facilitate more effective communication. It is an approach which uses familiar everyday words, and people seem to grasp the concepts very quickly and are able to use it to identify with their own experience.

Content of Sessions
The content of sessions could vary with the needs of a particular group, to include specific topics of interest, such as assertion or positive imagery. It is, however, important to follow the structured framework and use the general principles given above in devising content.

The eight basic sessions cover the following topics: information on tranquillizers and withdrawal methods, relaxation and stress management, building a positive self-image, leisure and social activities, negative thinking. Each session includes didactic input from the group leader, an experiential exercise, discussion time and homework. Within that framework the clients have an opportunity to work on issues of current concern. A set of guidelines for group leaders (session 1) are presented in Figure 7.1 to illustrate therapeutic objectives and procedures.

Although each session deals with a separate topic the content from previous sessions is always referred to and linked with the new material. As each new skill is introduced it continues to be practised throughout the course, with new homework being added per session. Weekly diaries of pills taken are completed and each session begins with a progress check on withdrawal. Adjustments/suggestions to withdrawal schedules are made at that time. Discussions of homework are also included at the beginning of each session.

Reductions in Tranquillizer Use
Preliminary results from the Withdraw Project research reveal that the short-term groups are effective in helping people to reduce and withdraw from tranquillizers. Clients in the treatment group significantly reduced the sedative value of their tranquillizers and this reduction was maintained up to 6 months after the groups finished. The minimum intervention provided sufficient incentive for clients to begin withdrawal from tranquillizers.

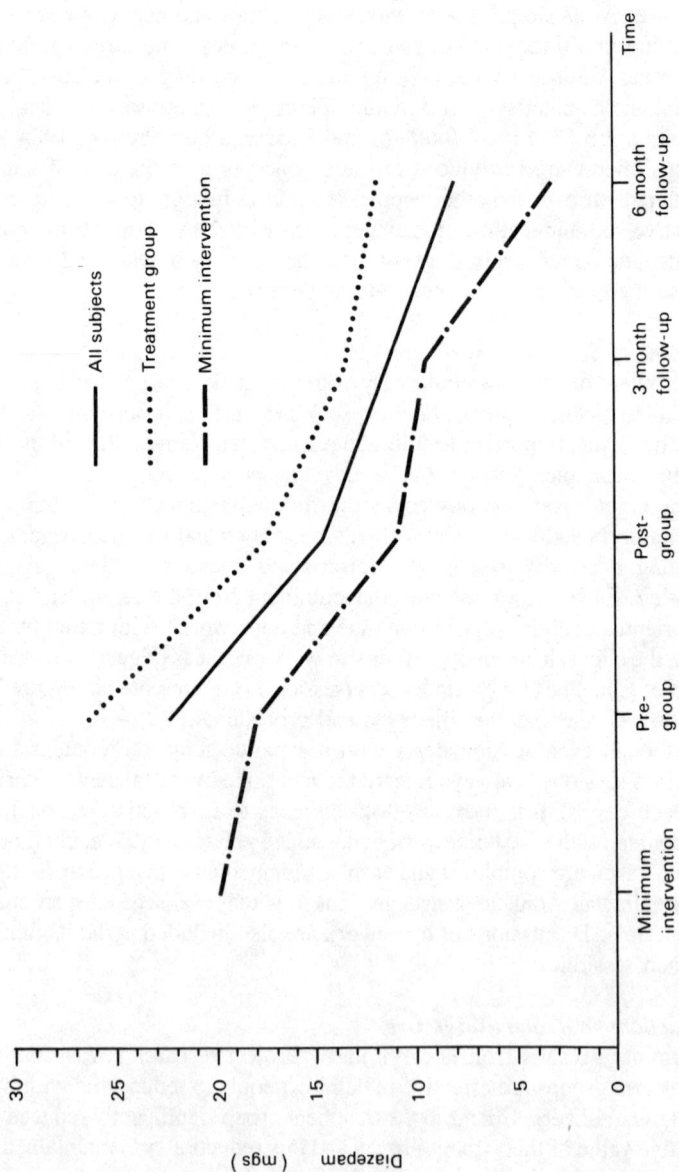

Figure 7.2 *Mean sedative value (see Table 7.3) during withdrawal*

Table 7.3   *Results of* t *tests performed on sedative value[a] data for all subjects*

Research group	Pre-control Post-control	Pre-group Post-group	Pre-group 3-month follow-up	Pre-group 6-month follow-up
All subjects		$t = 4.45$ df = 52 $p<0.0001$	$t = 5.00$ df = 39 $p<0.00001$	$t = 4.66$ df = 26 $p<0.0001$
Treatment group		$t = 5.37$ df = 29 $p<0.00001$	$t = 5.21$ df = 20 $p<0.0001$	$t = 3.39$ df = 14 $p<0.01$
Minimum intervention control group[b]	$t = 2.17$ df = 35 $p<0.05$	$t = 1.87$ df = 22 $p<0.05$	$t = 2.72$ df = 18 $p<0.01$	$t = 3.26$ df = 11 $p<0.01$

[a] Since some tranquillizers are stronger than others it is useful to compare them using their 'sedative value'. This is achieved by using an index of drugs sedative strength and converting it to its equivalent dose in mgs Diazepam (e.g. 1.5 mg Lorazepam = 15 mg Diazepam).
[b] The minimum intervention acts as a control group. People receive an individual assessment, a research home visit, and basic information about tranquillizers and withdrawal. In addition there is a waiting list period of at least 10 weeks.

However, this intervention alone did not have the same impact on withdrawal as the treatment intervention. Following entry into the group treatment programme the minimum intervention group made further reductions which were also maintained at 6 month follow-up.

A Case Example

Jane was a 45-year-old married woman with two teenage children, working part-time as a shop assistant, and who had been prescribed a variety of tranquillizers for 12 years. At the time of referral she was taking 30 mg Diazepam daily. She was originally prescribed tranquillizers following the death of both parents within a year. Over the following years Jane was able to reduce her dose of Diazepam intermittently and withdraw completely for several months on two occasions. She usually felt stressed and barely able to cope and any additional stress such as problems at work or illness in the family resulted in a relapse. Jane thought tranquillizers had helped her initially but that they no longer had any effect.

Despite any lack of received benefit Jane used her tranquillizers as a coping mechanism in difficult situations and could not see herself as managing without them. Tranquillizers in this case performed the following functions: they provided an external source of confidence, and they enabled negative feelings to be suppressed.

Jane had a low opinion of herself, believing that she was boring and of no interest to people. Taking tranquillizers enabled her to face social situations with neighbours and people at work. Her main irrational beliefs (iBs) included 'I *must* take a tranquillizer or I won't be able to talk to people and they will see how boring I am. I *should* be able to interest people and I'm pretty useless if I can't.'

Allied to a poor self-image was a low level of assertive skills. Jane described herself as being 'walked all over' by her children and particularly by her mother-in-law. Taking tranquillizers enabled her to deny any feelings of annoyance at unreasonable demands. Although her children were 12 and 15 she continued to do all their washing, cooking, cleaning, and drove them around, at the expense of her own needs for rest and help with the chores. Jane's mother-in-law stayed with the family every weekend and 'interfered' with Jane's handling of domestic situations. She found this very difficult but felt unable to change the situation. Her main irrational beliefs (iBs) were 'I must not say no to people or tell them what I really feel. I should not hurt their feelings. If I assert myself people will hate me and I would feel devastated. I should be a perfect mother and perfect mothers should cater to their children's every demand.'

Initial individual assessment suggested several areas where change would be beneficial, and treatment goals were devised. As Jane had successfully withdrawn herself from tranquillizers in the past the main issues were seen as acquiring new beliefs and skills in order to maintain abstinence. The objectives were:

1 stabilize daily dose of Diazepam, and gradual withdrawal,
2 teach relaxation methods as an alternative coping mechanism,
3 identify main irrational beliefs maintaining tranquillizer use and actively dispute them,
4 work on giving client 'permission' to say no to people,
5 practise assertion skills,
6 build a more confident and positive self-image.

Jane joined a time-limited tranquillizer withdrawal group of 8 sessions led by a psychologist. The group consisted of 3 men and 5 women, average age 42, who had been taking tranquillizers for a mean of 5 years (range 0.8–17 years). In the initial sessions Jane was quite withdrawn although would contribute if someone spoke directly to her. She complied with all homework requests and did not challenge any of the material in group sessions. This was in contrast to a few members of the group who were initially resistant to challenging their irrational beliefs.

Session 2 focuses on stress and relaxation with a homework exercise of monitoring stressful situations. On a scale of 0–10, where 10 is very tense, one of Jane's most stressful times (rated 7) was in the morning getting the children ready for school and in the evening when they returned.

Another (rated 8) was having her mother-in-law around at the weekend. She responded well to progressive relaxation teaching and by the end of the course was using relaxation as an alternative to medication in situations she found difficult.

Session 3 concentrates on identifying negative thoughts and the ways individuals sabotage their efforts to give up tranquillizers. By this time Jane had cut her medication in half but was still a fairly passive member of the group. From her occasional comments to people it became clear that she was actively listening and learning in the group. She realized that she put up with demands most people would consider unreasonable, but felt guilty if she experienced resentment. She acknowledged that she often felt she 'hated people' but could not accept this 'nasty' side of her at this stage. She blamed tranquillizers for making her have these negative feelings.

By session 4 Jane was starting to acquire sufficient confidence to speak more openly in the group. She had begun to question whether she had a right to say 'no' to unreasonable demands, and was becoming increasingly aware when she acquiesced on a daily basis. During role-play she practised interactions which involved her saying no to her children and her mother-in-law. The group members were used as an additional check and support for her right to say 'no' to unreasonable demands. Homework tasks included telling her mother-in-law the family were going out for the day on the following Sunday and making the children's pocket-money contingent on helping with the washing up. To her surprise she was able to complete these tasks relatively easily although she had to continually challenge her guilty feelings afterwards. In the later sessions Jane disclosed how nervous she had been when the groups had started and embarrassed when she had to speak. She now began to appreciate the feeling of support she had of being in a group where everyone was working towards similar goals and able to share experiences. Jane was able to use the transactional analysis material on parent, adult, and child ego states from session 5 to monitor *how* she behaved in interactions with her children and to identify how to improve their communications. A combination of challenging her belief that she should accede to all their demands and recognizing she made requests to them from her child ego state, with accompanying gestures and tones of voice, helped Jane to change the way she related to her children. Jane was still somewhat reserved in later sessions but it appeared she used the group to listen and learn and did considerable work herself outside the sessions.

By the end of the course Jane had withdrawn from her medication and was still abstinent at a one year follow-up. She had increased in confidence and had persuaded her husband to participate in reducing the demands of his mother. In a post-treatment self-report Jane answered the question 'What did you actually get out of the course?': 'I came off tranquillizers and I look at life in a different way now.'

References

Arnkoff, D. B. (1981) Flexibility in practicing cognitive therapy. In G. Emery, S. D. Hollon, and R. C. Bedrosian (eds), *New directions in cognitive therapy*. New York: Guilford Press.

Ashton, H. (1984) Benzodiazepine withdrawal: an unfinished story. *British Medical Journal* 288 (6424): 1135–40.

Balter, M. B., Levine, J. and Manheimer, D. I. (1974) Cross-national study of the extent of anti-anxiety/sedative drug use. *New England Journal of Medicine*, 290: 769–74.

Beck, A. T., Rush, A. J., Shaw, B. F. and Emery, G. (1979) Cognitive therapy of depression. New York: Guilford Press.

Benzodiazepine Interest Group Newsletter (1987, Jan.) available from WITHDRAW Project, Community Centre for Addiction, Slade Road Centre, Erdington, Birmingham B23 7LA.

Cappell, H., Busto, U., Kay, G., Naranjo, C., Sellers, E. M., Sanchez-Craig, M. (in press). Drug deprivation and reinforcement by diazepam in a dependent population. *Psychopharmacology*, 91: 154–60.

Colvin, M. (1983) A counselling approach to out-patient benzodiazepine detoxification. *Journal of Psychoactive Drugs*, 15: 105–8.

Committee on the Review of Medicines (1980) Systematic review of the benzodiazepines: guidelines for data sheets on diazepam, chlordiazepoxide, medazepam, chlorazepate. *British Medical Journal*, March, 910–12.

Cooperstock, R. (1978) Sex differences in psychotropic drug use. *Social Science and Medicine*, 12B: 179–86.

Cormack, M. A. and Sinnott, A. (1983) Psychological alternatives to long-term benzodiazepine use. *Journal of the Royal College of General Practitioners*, 33: 279–81.

Covi, L., Lipman, R. S., Pattison, J. H., Derogatis, L. R. and Uhlenhuth, E. H. (1973) Length of treatment with anxiolytic sedatives and response to their sudden withdrawal. *Acta Psychiatry Scandinavica*, 49: 51–64.

Crockett, S. A., (1986) The use of over-the-counter analgesics by chronic benzodiazepine users – a pilot study. MSc clinical psychology thesis, University of Birmingham.

Curran, V. and Golombok, S. (1985) *Bottling it up*. London: Faber & Faber.

Devenyi, P. and Saunders, S. J. (1986) *Physicians' handbook for medical management of alcohol and drug-related problems*. Toronto: Addiction Research Foundation.

Edwards, J. (1986) Tranquillizers: are you hooked? *Living* (IPC Magazines, London), May.

Fontaine, R., Chouinard, G. and Annable, L. (1984) Rebound anxiety in anxious patients after abrupt withdrawal of benzodiazepine treatment. *American Journal of Psychiatry*, 1141: 848–52.

Gabe, J. and Lipshitz-Phillips, S. (1984) Tranquillizers as social control. *Social Review*, 32 (3): 524–46.

Hallstrom, C. and Lader, M. (1982) The incidence of benzodiazepine dependence in long-term users. *Journal of Psychiatric Treatment and Evaluation*, 4: 293–6.

Hopkins, D. R., Sethi, K. B. S. and Mucklow, J. C. (1982) Benzodiazepine withdrawal in general practice. *Journal of the Royal College of General Practitioners*, 32: 758.

Lader, M. and Petursson, H. (1983) Long-term effects of benzodiazepines. *Neuropharmacology*, 22: 527–33.

Lader, M. H. and Higgitt, A. C. (1986) Editorial: Management of benzodiazepine dependence. *Update*, 81: 7–10.

Lancet editorial (1987) Treatment of benzodiazepine dependence. *Lancet*, January, 78–9.

Lazarus, A. A. (1981) *The practice of multimodal therapy*. New York: McGraw-Hill.

MacKinnon, G. L. and Parker, W. A. (1982) Benzodiazepine withdrawal syndrome: a literature review and evaluation. *American Journal of Drug and Alcohol Abuse*, 9 (1): 19–33.

Meichenbaum, D. (1977) *Cognitive behavior modification: an integrative approach*. New York: Plenum.

Melville, J. (1984) *The tranquilliser trap*. Glasgow: Fontana Paperbacks.

Murphy, S. M., Owen, R. T. and Tyrer, P. J. (1984) Withdrawal symptoms after 6 weeks treatment with diazepam. *Lancet*, ii: 1389.

Murray, J. (1981) Long-term psychotropic drug taking and the process of withdrawal. *Psychological Medicine*, 11: 853–8.

Office of Population Censuses and Surveys (1981) *Random omnibus survey carried out for the Office of Population Censuses and Surveys on smoking habits*. London: NOP Market Research Limited.

Office of Population Censuses and Surveys (1983) General household survey: cigarette smoking 1972 to 1982. *Government Statistical Service*. GHC, 83 (2).

Owen, R. T. and Tyrer, P. (1983) Benzodiazepine dependence: review of the evidence. *Drugs*, 25: 385–98.

Parish, P. A. (1971) The prescribing of psychotropic drugs in general practice. *Journal of the Royal College of General Practitioners*, 21 (Suppl. 14): 1–77.

Petursson, H. and Lader, M. H. (1981) Benzodiazepine dependence. *British Journal of Addiction*, 76: 133–45.

Petursson, H. and Lader, M. H. (1984a) *Dependence on tranquillizers*. Institute of Psychiatry. Maudsley Monographs no. 28, Oxford: Oxford University Press.

Petursson, H. and Lader, M. (1984b) Benzodiazepine tolerance and withdrawal syndrome. In G. D. Burrows and J. S. Werry (eds), *Advances in human psychopharmacology*. Greenwich, Connecticut: JAI Press.

Pitman, E. (1984) *Transactional analysis for social workers and counsellors: an introduction*. London: Routledge & Kegan Paul.

Rickels, K., Case, G. W., Winokur, A. and Svenson, C. (1984) Long-term benzodiazepine therapy: benefits and risks. *Psychopharmacology Bulletin*, 20 (4): 608–15.

Salkind, M. (1982) *Topics in drug therapy*. Milton Keynes: Open University Press.

Sanchez-Craig, M. (1984) *A therapist's manual for secondary prevention of alcohol problems*. Toronto: Addiction Research Foundation.

Sanchez-Craig, M., Annis, H. M., Bornet, A. R. and MacDonald, K. (1984) Random assignment to abstinence and controlled drinking: evaluation of a cognitive-behavioral program for problem drinkers. *Journal of Consulting and Clinical Psychology*, 52: 390–403.

Sanchez-Craig, M., Kay, G., Busto, U. and Cappell, H. (1986) Cognitive-behavioural treatment for benzodiazepine dependence. *Lancet*, February, 388.

Skinner, P. T. (1984) Skills not pills: learning to cope with anxiety symptoms. *Journal of the Royal College of General Practitioners*, 34: 258–60.

Spielberger, C. D. (1983) *Manual for the state–trait anxiety inventory*. Palo Alto, Calif.: Consulting Psychologists Press, Inc.

Stopforth, B. (1986) Out-patient benzodiazepine withdrawal and the occupational therapist. *British Journal of Occupational Therapy*, October: 318–21.

Tyrer, P. (1980) Dependence on benzodiazepines. *British Journal of Psychiatry*, 137: 576–7.

Tyrer, P. (1982) Clinical and pharmacological evidence of dependence on benzodiazepine hypnotics. In A. Nicolson (ed.), *Hypnotics in Clinical Practice*, 7. Oxford: Pembroke.

Tyrer, P., Owen, R. and Dawling, S. (1983) Gradual withdrawal of diazepam after long-term therapy. *Lancet*, i: 1402–6.

Tyrer, P., Rutherford, D., and Higgett, T. (1981) Benzodiazepine withdrawal symptoms and propranalol. *Lancet*, i: 520–2.

Tyrer, P. and Seivewright, N. (1984) Identification and management of benzodiazepine dependence. *Postgraduate Medical Journal*, 60 (Suppl. 2): 41–6.

Tyrer, P., Murphy, S., Oates, G. and Kingdon, D. (1985) Psychological treatment for benzodiazepine dependence. *Lancet*, i: 1042–3.

Warner, K. E. (1977) The effects of the anti-smoking campaign on cigarette consumption. *American Journal of Public Health*, 67: 645–50.

Woodcock, J. (1970) Long-term consumers of psychotropic drugs. In M. Balint, J. Hunt, D. Joyce, M. Marinker and J. Woodcock (eds), *Treatment or diagnosis*. London: Tavistock.

Woollams, S. J. and Brown, M. (1979). *Transactional analysis: the total handbook*. New York: Prentice Hall.

8

Cognitive Therapy with Depressed Inpatients

Jan Scott

The use and efficacy of Beck's cognitive therapy (CT) in the treatment of depression in the primary care and hospital outpatient setting is now well established on both sides of the Atlantic (for example, Rush et al., 1977; Blackburn et al., 1981; Teasdale et al, 1984; Murphy et al., 1984). However, its use with inpatients is less well documented. Only brief reference is made to it in Beck et al.'s (1979) book on CT of depression, and whilst they suggest that improvement can be achieved they do not give a detailed description of the application of CT to this population. In fact, there is only one more extensive report published in the literature (Shaw, 1981). Shaw's work focused on the importance of the multi-disciplinary model of treatment and the need for a problem-orientated conceptual base for therapy, but he again used the same model of CT as was used in the outpatient setting

Our work in a district general hospital psychiatric unit and in a smaller day and inpatient psychotherapeutically orientated unit has allowed us to assess some of the advantages and disadvantages of using CT in this setting. In our earlier attempts at inpatient CT we used the 'standard' approach of about fifteen individual therapy sessions (initially twice weekly reducing to one weekly). Whilst this treatment 'package' is highly effective for moderately severe, unipolar outpatient depressives we faced a number of difficulties in transferring CT to an inpatient unit. The problems encountered can be classified into four broad categories: (1) the patient population, (2) the treatment setting, (3) the family, (4) the multi-disciplinary team.

The Patient Population

Obviously, many factors dictate why a depressed patient may be admitted to hospital. Most of the patients we worked with suffered from a more severe illness than seen in the outpatient setting; this often impeded their ability to engage in a collaborative treatment and some were unable to tolerate sessions of forty-five minutes. Thus, more intensive treatment had a negative rather than a positive effect, leading to demoralization in both patient and therapist. Shaw (1981) suggests that, with the non-functioning patient, physical treatments may be used initially to create a 'milieu' in which the patient can then take a full role in the psychological therapy. We found surprisingly few problems in getting patients to accept this combined treatment approach, although some felt confused by the 'mixed messages' they were being given about the nature of their difficulties.

Some depressed inpatients exhibit psychotic features and CT is not an acceptable approach in the acute phase of such an illness (Beck et al., 1979; Scott, 1984). For other patients it was not the intensity but the chronicity of their symptoms that had led to admission. These individuals were often very difficult to engage in CT: the standard treatment package was often too brief to allow any significant impact on symptoms, and a much longer course of therapy seemed to be indicated.

Lastly, most patients had their own views on the aetiology of their illness. Their beliefs significantly affected their motivation to engage in CT. Some believed only physical treatments would help, whilst others wished to be the passive recipient of a 'cure' and found difficulty in taking an active, collaborative role. The characteristics of the patients made us rethink our assessment critieria for, and the system of 'delivery' of, inpatient CT.

The Treatment Setting

The unit we worked in treated patients with a wide variety of psychiatric problems. Within the ward setting several different illness models were being followed by the different multidisciplinary teams. Consequently, the patients sometimes felt confused by the conflicting approaches around them. Even where patients shared a common diagnosis their own theories about the causation of their disorder varied enormously. Not surprisingly, we had difficulty socializing some patients into the cognitive model and getting their collaboration in therapy. In addition, other patients felt jealous of those receiving CT viewing them as getting 'special' treatment.

Most units have some form of 'routine', often specific programmes for the patients or group sessions for them to attend. In our early attempts at inpatient CT we found that between-session homework tasks did not easily fit into these programmes. Also, the inpatient setting does reduce the availability of some potentially enjoyable activities or restricts the issues that may be tackled. Patients often showed some deterioration after going home as they had to deal with problems they had been sheltered from during their admission. The fact that they had been distanced from these difficulties meant that cognitions related to these areas had not been explored and further work was obviously needed after discharge. Even where problem-solving skills had been developed some individuals found it difficult to transfer these techniques to their home environment.

The Family

It has been suggested that the attitude of a patient's family towards CT may affect individual outcome more than any other factor (Shaw, 1981; Teasdale et al., 1984). The spouse of a depressed patient is rarely 'neutral': they may be angry, frustrated or overly solicitous and can reinforce the individual's negative view of him/herself. Primary or secondary marital or family problems are frequent in such situations and thus individual therapy is not always sufficient. Also, the family's understanding or lack of it obviously affects the patient's opportunities or their motivation to collaborate in CT. Shaw (1981) highlights the importance of family-related cognitions in working with inpatients, but we again felt the standard CT approach needed modification to take account of these problems.

The Multi-Disciplinary Team

Despite the difficulties listed above, we felt that, more than anything else, for CT in the inpatient setting to be effective required frequent, clear communication between members of the multi-disciplinary team (MDT). Essentially, the problem can be viewed as 'communication versus confusion'. Although the inpatients received individual CT, their treatment in the unit did not just involve the cognitive therapist. Even with regular MDT meetings, many problems arose: staff were sometimes unaware of the aims of particular tasks and not all of them understood the cognitive theory or therapy of depression. Staff changes were frequent and attitudes fluctuated among the different personnel. The staff themselves often harboured negative cognitions toward the patients, perceiving them as manipulative or not trying. Again, the patients often ended up with conflicting views of their problems.

One particular problem was the approach to the hopeless-helpless patient. Such individuals receive a great deal of staff input, but not all staff approached it from the CT viewpoint. Whilst staff support is obviously vital to such patients, there was a need to try to avoid dependency or removing all personal responsibility from the individual (which would undermine the therapy in progress). For some staff an attitudinal shift was required so that they structured their input with these patients, changing the content of the interactions to produce a collaborative, problem-solving relationship.

In our earliest attempts at inpatient CT, we did not spend enough time developing a consistent approach with the entire MDT. Over time we have gradually given more prominence to staff training through seminars and workshops, etc. These not only improve the CT skills of all members of the team, but also provide a useful forum for interdisciplinary discussion of all aspects of the approach and allow the correction of any misconceptions.

Considering the many problems listed above, it is perhaps surprising that eight chronically depressed patients (mean length of illness four years) who had failed to respond to any other standard anti-depressant regimes, showed a modest response to a combination of pharmacotherapy and CT (Scott, 1986). All received fifteen sessions of treatment over a period of twelve weeks and their mean Beck Depression Inventory (BDI) scores fell by fifty per cent. However, its was obvious to those involved that, whilst the cognitive approach could play an important role in the treatment of depressed inpatients, considerable modification was needed to overcome the hurdles identified and produce more effective results.

A New Model of CT

Over the last eighteen months we have gradually evolved a new model of CT. We have retained the essential elements of this approach and no new cognitive or behavioural techniques have been introduced. The importance of a psychotherapeutic approach in CT has been emphasized with all the staff involved. However, the system of delivery of the treatment and the emphasis on involving other members of the MDT in the ward setting is a new development.

The System of Delivery

The first problem we tackled was that of the non-functioning patient who could not tolerate twice weekly sessions of forty-five minutes. We decided initially to reduce the length of the sessions (to about twenty or thirty minutes), whilst increasing the frequency of the sessions to three times a week. Patients seemed able to maintain their involvement in the sessions for this length of time and the increased frequency allowed us to retain the intensity of the therapy. A key therapist (any member of the MDT trained in CT) was appointed and they continued to see the patient after discharge from hospital. Most individuals eventually received twenty to thirty therapy sessions, the later ones in the outpatient setting being longer and less frequent. We felt this was a more realistic course of CT in view of the severity of the problems being tackled and it took into account the additional difficulties that needed to be dealt with after discharge.

The early stages of therapy with the inpatients were dominated by behavioural interventions (Activity Scheduling, Mastery and Pleasure Ratings, Graded Task Assignments and Task Assignments). The work done in the CT sessions was then supplemented by additional input from other members of the MDT carried out in the ward environment. The shortened sessions ultimately became a place where previous 'homeworks' were reviewed and new hypotheses were generated. CT techniques were discussed and taught but it was outside the sessions (with the other staff) that most of the hypothesis testing and problem-solving took place. The advantage of this system was fourfold:

1 patients were not disadvantaged by the shorter sessions: the rate of progress was, if anything, increased by the constant reinforcement of the CT model in the ward setting;
2 patients realized that all members of the MDT had an active and important role to play in their treatment;
3 staff who were not key cognitive therapists were provided with a valuable experience of explaining and working with CT and developing their own skills in this area;
4 the CT approach merges well with the problem-orientated nursing process and many members of the MDT already have experience in behaviour therapy or running specific programmes (such as anxiety management, social skills) for inpatients.

Although CT was carried out outside of the therapy setting, the amount of time the staff spent with the patient did not have to be significantly increased. The input was more structured and the problems being worked on in the CT had to be communicated efficiently, but as the following example demonstrates, this approach can be very effective:

Case 1 JB was a 56 year-old male with a severe depression (BDI 39). He felt unable to engage in any daily activities and felt he had lost all interest and pleasure. Prior to admission, he was off work and was becoming increasingly withdrawn socially. He procrastinated over simple tasks which he failed to complete and this made him feel even worse at the end of the day. He had received outpatient treatment with anti-depressants, but had failed to make much progress and was reluctant to 'keep taking tablets'. His key therapist explained the principle of 'Activity Scheduling' and 'Mastery and Pleasure Ratings' and he was asked to plan a daily schedule. Three other staff were involved in the exercise: a nurse from the day staff, one from the night staff and an occupational therapist. Using these techniques alone his BDI score fell to 23 after a fortnight. Each member of staff had a slightly differing role.

The day nurse (i) Activator (5–10 minutes) – the nurse met briefly with the patient first thing in the morning. Together they went through the activity schedule that JB had devised (if he had not managed this the nurse collaborated on producing a plan). Both tried to identify 'major' activities or potential difficulties that might arise and he was asked to predict his likely achievement. The nurse then left JB to go about the planned activities.

(ii) Reinforcer (5–10 minutes) – the nurse joined the patient at specified points during the day after a 'major' or potentially difficult activity (for example, in this case the patient found it hard to cope with going out of the unit alone). They gave immediate feedback for achievements and reinforced the cognitive model, accelerating JB's socialization into this approach. The patient could also give immediate mastery and pleasure ratings, rather than record them later in the day (when they may be less accurate).

(iii) Motivator (10–15 minutes) – Shaw (1981) points out that many patients are convinced that corrective actions are not available or are doomed to failure. This logically leads to a decision not to try. There is an opportunity with inpatients for staff to overcome this problem using CT strategies. Again referring to the schedule devised by JB, the nurse arranged to be available immediately prior to specific activities (such as going to a ward community meeting) to motivate him to carry them out and also to monitor his predictions about success or failure immediately before the 'attempt'.

(iv) Collaborator (15+ minutes) – the nurse was involved in specific activities with the patient. In this capacity they were able to help the individual arrange 'on the spot' experiments to test out hypotheses, or help generate alternative problem-solving strategies. As the programme continued, JB took responsibility for arranging for the nurse to collaborate in particular activities (such as a nurse and some other patients to accompany him in a trip to the ten-pin bowling alley).

(v) Observer – throughout the day, the nurse had many opportunities to objectively monitor the patient's performance. This was discussed with the patient and provided valuable additional data for MDT meetings.

The night nurse Benatov (1981) describes the technique of 'Evening Therapy'. The aim is to redress the negative bias of a depressed individual which influences what they select from everyday events to pass into their long-term memory. In essence, it shares the same aim as 'reality testing' in CT (Williams, 1984). In our version of this technique, JB met with one member of staff (for about 15 minutes) to review the day's events. This also involved reviewing predictions made that morning and mastery and pleasure ratings given to different activities during the day. The night staff 'debriefed' the patient and were able to act as an objectifier, neutralizer or decatastrophizer as needed. Initially, our inpatients were prone to selective abstraction of unpleasant events and overgeneralization (despite ratings made at the time!). The 'Evening Therapy' approach served the purpose of redressing that imbalance and also allowed the patient to discuss the proposed schedule for the next day. In addition, it helped to keep the night staff aware of the patient's progress and gave them an important role in the individual's therapy. Again, the nurse was not spending an excessive amount of time with the patient, but the input was more structured than previously.

The occupational therapist The occupational therapist (OT) can play a vital role in inpatient CT, particularly where the individual is functioning at a below-normal level. In JB's case they played a prominent part as he was off work, was unable to engage in even simple tasks around the home and got little pleasure from hobbies he had previously enjoyed. In the early part of his admission, it was difficult to get him to attend OT at all as he felt he would 'fail' at any activity he tried there. The OT was engaged in setting up graded task assignments in both daily living skills and in seeking pleasurable activities. Again, the patient can be encouraged to collaborate directly with the OT in deciding on the tasks or hypotheses to be tackled and how to go about it.

The approach described above has a greater behavioural emphasis than a standard CT approach with outpatients and can be more directive. However, within a few weeks this patient was able to work cognitively with the same staff. The day nurse was able to help him record automatic thoughts at the start of the day or prior to engaging in (or avoiding) planned activities. Likewise, the OT was able to work on cognitive distortions that presented in the occupational therapy setting. The staff could also help the patient in identifying and recording dysfunctional thoughts, constantly reinforcing the techniques learnt in the briefer CT sessions and the links between events, thoughts and feelings. The 'evening therapist' was also able to help the patient review the dysfunctional thought records and collaborate in completing unfinished ones through examining the evidence or generating alternative interpretations of events.

Within five weeks, JB was having weekly sessions which continued with his key therapist after discharge. During the latter half of his admission, he was encouraged to rely on the 'co-therapists' less and to try to use the cognitive techniques on his own. Initially the day staff took a less active role until their main input was as the 'Activator'. The OT then gradually withdrew. Thus, the patient was left with two brief ten-minute sessions at the beginning and end of the day. Lastly, the nursing staff allowed the patient to function more autonomously, leaving JB to relate mainly to his key therapist on a one-to-one basis.

The new CT sessions
With the reduced time available, the therapist and patient changed the content but not the structure of the CT sessions. They were now used to review the previous few days and detail the next problem the patient had identified to work on. For some patients the day nurse acted as a co-therapist in the CT sessions. The use of two therapists has been described previously (Moorey and Burns, 1983). In this setting it has a number of advantages: (1) therapists can demonstrate coping strategies through role plays or model activities for the patient to observe; (2) communication of 'goals' between the key therapist and the nurse is clear because both are present at the discussions with the patient; and (3) the less experienced therapist can acquire additional CT skills on an 'apprenticeship' basis.

After about three weeks the sessions are reduced from thrice to twice weekly and gradually the length of the session is extended. At discharge, the patient is usually receiving only once weekly sessions similar to the 'standard' CT approach used with depressed outpatients. The work on assumptions is usually carried out in the latter stages of therapy and so tends to be addressed after discharge from hospital.

Transfer of Learning

Shaw (1981) highlights the problems of generalizing skills learned in hospital to the 'natural' environment. Our solution was to institute weekend leave as soon as possible. This helps in several ways: (1) it promotes the transfer of 'hospital learnt' skills to the home environment; (2) it allows collection of data about situations or problems that exacerbate the patient's symptoms, but that are not encountered in the hospital setting; (3) the patient is allowed to function independently of staff and to see if they can use CT without reinforcement; (4) the individual is faced with additional stresses and gets some idea of progress; (5) setbacks can be dealt with quickly within the CT sessions on return to hospital; and (6) patients can rehearse tasks or engage in role plays within the unit to practise coping with problems they might encounter whilst on leave.

The weekend leaves are particularly helpful in allowing the patient to gather and challenge dysfunctional thoughts related to his/her home environment and interpersonal relationships. However, even with these attempts to create links between the hospital and the home setting virtually all patients suffer mild relapse on discharge. The key therapist discusses this with the patient as discharge draws nearer and an attempt is made to identify new stresses or problems the individual will encounter. Alternative coping strategies and cognitive rehearsal can then be used to try to minimize these difficulties.

Involving the Family

At least three joint sessions of about an hour each are held with the patient and their family (or significant others) during the course of CT. The aims of these sessions are: (1) to socialize the family into the CT model and answer their questions about this approach; (2) to involve family members where appropriate as reinforcers or collaborators in the therapy; (3) to examine the family's cognitions and where necessary alter their thinking style; (4) to try to reverse any potentially negative input from them by observing the interactions within the family sessions; and (5) to help re-integrate the depressed individual into the family and (particularly with the chronic depressive) to 're-negotiate' their role as a healthy member of the family unit.

Time is required for the family to understand CT and to accept the changes the patient tries to make in their thinking style. Some families are quite resistant to attempts to modify their interactions, and tact is obviously required to ensure they see these sessions as collaborative rather than punitive. The sessions can be very helpful in engaging the help of family members in reinforcing and monitoring the patient's behaviour outside the hospital sessions. The problems encountered can be tackled using alternative therapy or other CT techniques and maladaptive views can be challenged, as demonstrated in the following case:

Case 2 EW was a 43-year-old former nursery nurse who was married with three teenage children. She was admitted following an overdose of anti-depressants. EW had suffered from a chronic depression of fluctuating severity for over four years, but was making good progress with CT alone in the inpatient unit. Unfortunately, there were a number of difficulties during the course of her weekend leaves and she repeatedly returned to the unit feeling demoralized. It seemed that during the course of her illness her eldest teenage daughter had become a 'surrogate' mother to the two younger children and EW's husband had also incorporated many household 'chores', such as shopping and cooking, into his daily routine. EW had tried to negotiate with the family to be allowed to do more at home with limited success and so this issue was used as a focus for one of the family sessions.

The session highlighted a number of problems. The children were anxious not to let EW 'overdo it' during her time at home as they feared this might precipitate a further overdose. The eldest daughter also expressed some difficulties in relinquishing her role as 'mother' which EW had failed to fulfil for much of the past four years. EW's husband was reluctant to allow her to do household tasks as he felt her improvement might simply be temporary; her illness had fluctuated in the past and he felt it unwise to get out of his routine until he was certain the improvement would be sustained. Discussion allowed misconceptions about protecting EW from activity to be resolved. Further problem-solving, through the assessment of the advantages and disadvantages of persisting in the existing pattern and using alternative therapy, allowed significant attitudinal shifts to occur. In alternative therapy, the family are initially encouraged to generate as many potential solutions as possible to a specified problem. Everyone is encouraged to come up with alternatives. The list of suggestions is then re-examined and the family are encouraged to decide collectively on the most viable solution to their problem. Through negotiation, the eldest daughter allowed her mother to take a more active role in looking after the two younger children. The advantage to the daughter was that this gave her more time to engage in pleasurable activities of her own, and the advantage to EW was that it improved her self-image and her mood, leading to a further increase in her level of activity. Although EW's husband proved more reluctant initially to give up his 'chores', he did allow his wife to take over certain household activities. The emphasis was put on a gradual rather than a sudden change and only if EW coped with each new task did the couple negotiate any further 'chores' for her to take over. She coped with these well and he gradually allowed her to take on more and more. Consequently, EW was allowed an increased role within the family. This improved her self-esteem and led to further improvement which was reinforced by their positive response to her.

Staff Training and Communication

In order to improve the understanding and co-operation of all members of the MDT with the inpatient CT approach, we invite staff to attend regular lectures, seminars and workshops. These need to be repeated frequently to take into account staff turnover, particularly amongst nursing staff. In addition, both day and night staff are invited to attend: an acknowledgement that inpatient care is a twenty-four-hour-a-day process and that all staff need to be aware of the essential elements of CT. Within the unit, regular 'teach-ins' and seminars with time allocated to feedback from the staff allow us to discuss specific problems that arise and to examine their own cognitions about the patients and the difficulties they are having.

Shaw (1981) emphasizes the use of joint patient assessments and regular MDT meetings to ensure a common conceptualization of the patients' problems. This is obviously important to ensure a consistent approach and communication of goals and priorities. Briefer meetings are also held by the two or three staff working with any particular patient and this also allows more individual supervision to take place.

Improving the Setting

Our early inpatient CT was carried out in a fifty-bed district general hospital unit. Although all the patients receiving CT were treated by one MDT, three other MDT's were sited there. We have recently worked at a smaller unit with a more psychotherapeutic orientation. This unit has only twelve inpatient beds, but has day patient facilities as well. The more psychological orientation of the unit and the smaller number of staff and patients appears to be an advantage. The patient has fewer conflicting illness models to cope with and communication between the staff is easier. As the patient improves he/she can move from inpatient to day patient status and then finally to outpatient status, giving a more gradual progression. Whilst CT is quite feasible in a large unit, the advantages of the smaller unit are important considerations for those contemplating using CT in the inpatient setting.

Outcome

So far, twelve patients have been treated by this regime. The interpretation of our outcome data is complicated by the fact that some patients received a combined treatment involving drugs and CT, and others were being treated for severe chronic illnesses. However, nine patients showed a statistically and clinically significant improvement on the Hamilton Rating Scale for Depression (HRSD) and the BDI over a three month period. The mean HRSD score fell from 24.5 to 9.6 and the mean BDI score fell from 28.2 to 7.5. Three patients made very little progress, two were suffering from a chronic depressive illness and one was a manic depressive. Previous research suggests that these problems are difficult to treat with CT (Beck et al., 1979; Fennell and Teasdale, 1982). Whilst no definite predictors of outcome were identified, we found that the length of illness and lack of adaptation to change by the patient's family seemed to have a negative effect on prognosis. Paradoxically, we noted that those patients who had developed secondary psychiatric complications of their depressive illness (such as alcohol or drug abuse), responded well to CT. Our sample is too small to know if this is a significant factor, but we postulate that these secondary problems represent maladaptive coping strategies and that the CT helps the individual substitute more effective adaptive techniques.

The Future

At present, we have not carried out enough work to be dogmatic about the efficacy of inpatient CT. However, the approach seems to be valuable even in cases where the patient is also receiving physical treatments. One problem in using a combined approach is that it is difficult to apportion the effect of each component on outcome. When CT is used alone it might be suggested that any improvement is due to non-specific factors, such as the patient's belief that he/she is getting 'special' treatment. This criticism cannot be totally dismissed and only further research can counter such arguments, but these patients do not receive more attention from the MDT. It is the structure of the input rather than the length of time spent with the patient that is altered. Lastly, it has been claimed that CT merely systematizes 'good clinical practice'. I think this is unlikely (Scott, Barker and Williams, 1985), but even if this were the case, if it ensures that the skills of all the members of an inpatient MDT are used effectively, then this in itself is worthwhile.

In the long term, I feel that the model of inpatient CT used here could eventually be incorporated into the nursing process without the need to include individual therapy sessions. Obviously, an alternative approach would be the use of group CT in the inpatient setting. This would have the advantage of efficient use of staff time and incorporates vicarious learning within the patient group (Eidelson, 1984–85). CT could also be modified to address the problems of inpatients suffering from almost any non-psychotic illness by adaptation of the CT models already being used to treat these disorders in the outpatient setting. A whole unit could be run along cognitive-behavioural lines, even when the patients are receiving physical treatments. The CT would enhance practical, problem-solving skills and could be used to improve compliance with treatment (for example, by examining cognitions related to the treatment being given). Attempts at increasing compliance with prophylactic lithium treatment by cognitive interventions have already yielded promising results (Cochran, 1984). In addition, the work of Reda (1983) suggests that, even when a patient has made a good response to tricyclic anti-depressant treatment, some 'drug-resistant' maladaptive beliefs persisted which left the patient vulnerable to relapse. Thus, a combined approach might tackle these cognitions more effectively than either treatment alone.

Whilst the use of CT with psychotic patients is unrealistic in the acute phase of the illness, there is an obvious role for this approach in the rehabilitation of these individuals. In addition, the secondary handicaps suffered by the chronically depressed can be helped by CT. There is surprisingly little written on the rehabilitation of patients suffering from affective disorders and few workers have approached this problem systematically. Our work with chronic depressives in Newcastle (Scott, 1986) has left me convinced that inpatient CT will have a vital role to play in the attempts to rehabilitate these individuals and that this area of research needs to be expanded in the future. Finally, CT with inpatients should not only be viewed as beneficial to the patients; the staff also gain from the opportunity to learn essential psychotherapeutic skills within the framework of a structured approach to the individual's problems.

References

Beck, A. T., Rush, A. J., Shaw, B. F. and Emery, G. (1979) *Cognitive therapy of depression.* New York: Guilford.

Benatov, R. (1981) Evening therapy: psychotherapy of short-term memory. Paper presented at First SPR European Conference on Psychotherapy Research, Trier FRG, Sept. 1981.

Blackburn, I. M., Bishop, S., Glen, I. M., Whalley, L. J. and Christie J. E. (1981) The efficacy of cognitive therapy in depression: a treatment trial using cognitive therapy and pharmacotherapy, each alone and in combination. *British Journal of Psychiatry*, 139: 181–9.

Cochran, S. D. (1984) Preventing medical non-compliance in the outpatient treatment of affective disorders. *Journal of Consulting and Clinical Psychology*, 52: 873–8.

Eidelson, J. (1984–85) Cognitive group therapy for depression. *International Journal of Mental Health*, 13: 54–60.

Fennell, M. J. V. and Teasdale, J. D. (1982) Cognitive therapy with chronic, drug-refractory outpatients: a note of caution. *Cognitive Therapy and Research*, 6: 455–60.

Moorey, S. and Burns, D. D. (1983) The apprenticeship model: training in cognitive therapy by participation. In A. Freeman (ed.), *Cognitive therapy with couples and groups.* New York: Plenum Press.

Murphy, G. E., Simons K. D., Wetzel, R. D. and Lustman, P. J. (1984) Cognitive therapy and pharmacotherapy: singly and together in the treatment of depression. *Archives of General Psychiatry*, 41: 33–41.

Reda M. (1983) Cognitive organisation and antidepressants. In M. Reda and M. J. Mahoney (eds), *Cognitive psychotherapies*. Cambridge, Mass.: Ballinger.

Rush, A. J., Beck, A. T., Kovacs, M. and Hollon, S. (1977) Comparative efficacy of cognitive therapy and pharmacotherapy in the treatment of depressed outpatients. *Cognitive Therapy and Research* 1: 17–37.

Scott, J. (1984) Cognitive behaviour therapy of depressive illness. *Psychiatry in Practice*, 3: 9–15.

Scott, J. (1986) Cognitive therapy with treatment-resistant depressives. Paper presented at BABP Meeting. Warneford Hospital, Oxford, April 1986.

Scott, J., Barker, W. A. and Williams, J. M. G. (1985) The teaching of cognitive therapy in Newcastle. *The Bulletin of the Royal College of Psychiatrists*, 9: 33–4.

Shaw, B. F. (1981) Cognitive therapy with an inpatient population. In G. Emery, S. D. Hollon and R. C. Bedrosian (eds), *New directions in cognitive therapy*, New York: Guilford Press.

Teasdale, J. D., Fennell, M. J. V., Hibbert, G. A. and Amies, P. L. (1984) Cognitive therapy for major depressive disorder in primary care. *British Journal of Psychiatry*, 144: 400–6.

Williams, J. M. G. (1984) *The psychological treatment of depression: a guide to the theory and practice of cognitive behaviour therapy*. London: Croom Helm.

9

Cognitive Psychotherapy through the Career Cycle

Diana R. Richman

People spend much of their waking hours working (Neff, 1977; Weinrach, 1980). Whether for an income or to accomplish tasks around the house, the expenditure of energy to achieve a goal is an integral part of the process of living. Clinicians will attest to the fact that relationship issues and work are the two major themes discussed in therapy (Criddle and Tracy, 1977; Ellis, 1972). Unfortunately, society tends to think in absolutistic all-or-nothing terms, making the personal and working life of human beings into two distinct entities. Media, corporate training programs, and educational institutions reinforce this extremely dichotomous thinking. We can see the results in the specialization of professionals who lose sight of the whole person or project. Many organizations believe that job titles define an individual's total worth and identity. In fact, the personal lives of employees are often considered to be completely unrelated to job performance. These attitudes could be no further from the truth. Individuals bring their total selves to the work situation. At home, work or in a social environment the cognitions, emotions, behaviours, and physical sensations are experienced by that same individual. The premise of cognitive psychotherapy, that our perceptions and evaluations of events and situations determine to a large extent how we feel emotionally and behave (Beck, 1976; Ellis, 1962) fully recognizes the significant influence of the discrepancy between individual and organizational attitudes.

The public became familiar with the application of cognitive psychology to problems of daily living largely through the work of Albert Ellis (1962). By developing a systematic procedure for identifying, disputing, and modifying irrational beliefs individuals experienced a reduction in negative emotions and an increase in appropriate goal directed behaviours (Di Giuseppe, Miller and Trexler, 1977). Ellis (1962) explains that he originally treated people for marital and sexual problems. He soon became dissatisfied with using traditional psychotherapy as he found that problem relationships are caused by disturbed individuals. While his motivation to develop rational–emotive therapy (RET) came from his experience of treating interpersonal problems, Ellis found that RET could be effectively applied to a variety of issues. However, most of the literature on the application of RET and allied cognitive-behavioural techniques has focused on the area of interpersonal relationships and social skills (Ellis and Bernard, 1985; Hauck, 1977; Kendall and Hollon, 1979; Wolfe and Brand, 1977) without much reference to interpersonal issues that occur in the workplace (Neff, 1977; Pierre, 1986). Professionals and laymen often associate cognitive psychotherapy solely with the treatment of personal relationship issues and emotional disturbance. Advice giving, information dissemination, job finding skills training, and aptitude testing have been traditionally used for helping individuals with career and job related problems (Zaccaria, 1970). The irrational attitudes reinforced to a great extend by society, that work is simply what we must do to earn a living and that individuals should follow all rules and regulations, hinder progress in identifying and eliminating barriers to the individual/organizational attitudinal conflicts.

While cognitive psychotherapists are well aware that personal problems are interwoven with work issues, the cognitive psychotherapeutic literature has neglected to keep up with the direct application of cognitive techniques to the work setting. Theoretical approaches to career counselling recognize the importance of considering values and attitudes of individuals in making satisfactory career choices (Schein, 1978; Super, 1957). As early as 1909, Parsons put forward a trait-factor approach to counselling which assumed that human beings think rationally, and if given accurate information about themselves and the world of work they could make reasonable career choices. Recently many career, guidance, and rehabilitation counsellors have become familiar with RET and allied cognitive-behavioural techniques. The counselling literature has reflected this increased interest in applying cognitive-behavioural techniques to work related problems brought up in counselling sessions (Mallary and Conner, 1975; Richman, 1979, 1982; Thompson, 1976; Weinrach, 1980). Research has been done with a variety of populations that are accessible to experimental control such as the hardcore unemployed, inmates, students, and physically disabled individuals (Block, 1978; Gandy, 1985; Manzi, 1986; Richman, 1979, 1982; Smith et al., 1979).

Although Ellis and Blum recommended 'Rational Training' as a method of facilitating management and labour relations as early as 1967, it has been only recently that attempts to apply RET within a corporate setting have been made (Klarreich, Di Giuseppe and Di Mattia, 1987a) or directed to corporate clientele (Criddle and Tracy, 1977; Richman and Nardi, 1985). This is surprising since much of the industrial/organizational research on job satisfaction and job performance reflects the significant influence of a cognitive component (Korman, 1970; McGregor, 1960; Porter and Lawler, 1968; Vroom, 1964). Corporations are becoming increasingly aware of the relationship between the mental and social well-being of the workforce and performance on the job (Brodey, 1983; Kram, 1985; Pierre, 1986). So perhaps the 1980s is the time that RET and allied cognitive-behavioural techniques will be more directly applied to problems in the workplace.

My own background as a career counsellor, prior to obtaining my Ph.D. in clinical psychology, and a strong interest in cognitive-behaviour therapy placed me in a unique position to apply these techniques to counsel my clients. In working with the hardcore unemployed, I found that several central cognitive themes interfered with their obtaining or keeping jobs. Beliefs such as 'I *should* be given a job immediately and easily because of what I suffered in the past'. or 'I *should* only work when it is convenient for me', reflect two of Ellis's eleven irrational beliefs, and Beck's faulty thinking styles (Beck, 1976; Ellis, 1962). Helping my clients to actively take the appropriate steps for obtaining employment was a difficult task with those who thought in a demanding style. They seemed to put up many barriers to changing their behaviours and irrational beliefs. In fact, those individuals on welfare for a long period of time tended to have more irrational beliefs, as based on a self-report belief inventory, than those more recently on welfare (Richman, 1981).

While helping clients with their career problems, I always wondered why job related issues were considered to be superficial and not warranting the assistance of mental health professionals. So often, those with the more intractable personal and work problems are counselled by the least trained counsellors (Siassi and Messer, 1976). Employee assistance programs (EAPs) are now realizing that their highly vulnerable clients certainly deserve to be counselled by competent, skilled, and knowledgeable providers (Nye, 1986). Klarreich, Di Giuseppe, and Di Mattia (1987b) point out that the intervention strategies utilized by even the best-trained counsellors need to be considered. RET provides a framework within which counsellors can work when assigned to more difficult clients. As a psychologist, I encounter individuals from all levels of the workforce who maintain demanding, unrealistic, self-defeating beliefs which result in extremely negative disruptive emotions and ineffective work behaviours. Certain events may never change in the work world, but as individuals experience control over their beliefs about work related events, they begin to feel better and get better at home and on the job.

Historically, the needs of the organization versus the needs of the individual have been an issue (Gibson, 1980; Landy and Trumbo, 1980). Typically organizational attitudes, such as 'people *should not* bring their problems to work', have reinforced the neglect of corporations in providing mental health services for employees. But as the detrimental effects of high turnover, lateness, absenteeism, and alcoholism (Myers, 1984) have been felt among corporations, the need for organizations to consider playing a role in helping employees has become stronger. Corporations may not use the terms like 'therapy' or 'counselling,' but programmes are now being developed to help employees because of an increasing recognition that the mental health of individuals can affect their performance in any situation, including the many hours spent at work. In a nine-year study, the Canadian Mental Health Association (1984) found that the workplace serves as a significant setting for promoting mental health by strengthening the employee's pride in his/her work and increasing his/her interpersonal skills, sense of self, and sense of belonging.

The recent plethora of self-help books on topics of job burnout, stress-management, and dual-career conflicts more than acknowledges the existence of problems in the work world. However, American corporations tend to seek quick solutions without eliminating the cause of problems. In a study of United States and Japanese college students (Iida et al., 1986), American students placed more emphasis on actual outcome while Japanese students emphasized effort. Since actual outcome is not always evidenced by workers, the perception that employers do not value effort may lead to work problems. As Ellis (1972) emphasizes, all the seminars, workshops, and courses designed to combat work issues make the faulty assumption that employees are mentally healthy and can directly benefit from their company's recommendations and suggestions. Those employers and employees with faulty belief systems will continue to have longstanding work related problems. Superficial changes may be exhibited through intermittent outcome improvement, but the same problems are likely to recur unless the underlying belief systems are identified and changed.

Schein (1978) points out that work and developing a career are integral to all of human living, but at the same time are separable from the biological–social ageing and family cycles. Society's definition of needs, to a large extent, controls the opportunities and constraints which create the work career cycle. Many daily work encounters are uncontrollable and unchangeable. Cognitive psychotherapy teaches individuals to accept external conditions, even when not liking or disagreeing with the circumstances, and to focus on changing internal attitudes about those undesirable conditions (Ellis, 1985). The work setting repeatedly presents individuals with externally controlled, undesirable conditions such as a fixed salary level, a demanding boss, and an inconvenient work location. Since the career cycle to a large extent is determined by our external educational and occupational structures, as well as the ageing process, it is likely that attitudinal changes can make a difference in how successfully one makes the passage through the career cycle.

Much research has been done on the stages of human development from birth through old age biologically, sexually, and socially (Erikson, 1980; Freud, 1905/1962; Levinson, 1978; Sheehy, 1974). Schein (1978) has identified the natural life cycle of career in relation to the other cycles. It is time that we addressed work and interpersonal issues as an integral part of the total individual's life. This chapter will conceptualize the application of cognitive psychotherapy, which consists of RET and allied cognitive-behavioural techniques (Beck, 1976; Ellis, 1962; Kelly, 1955; Lazarus, 1976) to work related issues within Schein's (1978) dynamic career cycle. No matter where in the career cycle individuals may find themselves, they have control of their thoughts. Schein's dynamic career cycle serves as a realistic, workable model and combats the traditional unrealistic belief which is still reinforced in some career counselling settings that we must take the perfect steps to achieve a permanent and singular career goal (Thompson, 1976). Cognitive psychotherapy provides a systematic, practical, replicable approach to deal with the natural transitions in the life cycle of human beings, and the career cycle in particular.

Entry into the Work World

Obtaining a first job is considered to fall into Schein's (1978) entry stage in the career cycle. While this early stage in the career cycle usually occurs between the ages of sixteen and twenty-five, it is important to keep in mind that many women first enter the labour market in their thirties and forties after raising their children. Much of the research relevant to over-coming the issues and tasks at this stage have focused on behavioural techniques for the decisions to be made and steps to be taken in finding a job. Interview skills, résumé (CV) writing, assertiveness training, and making job contacts are several behavioural techniques that are taught to job candidates (Azrin, Flores and Kaplan, 1975; Keil and Barbee, 1973; Lazarus, 1976; McGovern et al., 1975; Richman, 1979, 1982). The populations usually studied at this early stage of the career cycle have been students, clients of State employment agencies, and displaced homemakers (Hurst and Shepard, 1985; Miller and Walter, 1977; Richman, 1979). In order to reduce mismatches so often made during the recruiting process, corporations are seeking the expertise of mental health professionals and career development specialists at an increasing rate (Lewis and Lewis, 1986; Myers, 1984). Behavioural techniques teach appropriate interview behaviours to job candidates. Cognitive interventions provide a framework for individuals and organizations to maintain flexible, productive attitudes necessary for dealing with the uncontrollable external changes which occur throughout the career cycle and for increasing the likelihood that appropriate work behaviours will be maintained.

Schein (1978) describes the task at this entry stage as making a realistic and valid first job choice. The issue involved in accomplishing the task is to obtain the first job which can then be the basis of a career. While learning the specific skills and practising the behaviours required to obtain the first job are essential, the attitudinal component must be considered in actually accomplishing the task of making a realistic and valid job choice. Omitting the cognitive component may result in a highly unrealistic first job choice and misery in the long term.

Throughout the career cycle there exists the individual perspective and the organizational perspective (Schein, 1978). At the entry stage, this is of particular importance to understand since numerous mismatches are made due to a lack of clarity as to what these perspectives are and how they interact. A company may have certain expectations for new recruits that are in contrast to the goals of the new employee. Both the individual's and organization's needs must be identified and examined in order to make a suitable person–job match. Much research has shown the significant effect of human needs and expectations on motivating individuals to perform their work (Herzberg, 1966; McGregor, 1960; Maslow, 1943). The organization and the job candidate would benefit from insight into their own and each other's belief systems. Cognitive psychotherapy is certainly appropriate for bringing about rational, productive, realistic views which will increase the probability that the new recruit has made a realistic and valid first job choice, and that the organization has made a suitable selection based on a rational perspective. Schein's (1978) 'psychological contract' describes so well the interrelationship between the potential employee and the organization: 'A matching of what the individual will give with what the organization expects to receive, and what the organization will give relative to what the organization expects to receive' (1978: 80–2). The delicate balance of this relationship can be maintained and strengthened if the attitudes of both the individual and organization are identified, understood, and modified. The significant effect of one's expectations cannot be overlooked and lends further credence to the applicability of cognitive techniques at the entry stage of the career cycle.

As Ellis explains, his eleven irrational beliefs can be subsumed into three basic beliefs: (1) 'I *must* do well at the tasks I perform and be approved of by the others for doing well'; (2) 'You *must* treat me fairly, kindly and justly'; (3) 'The conditions under which I live *must* be easy, unfrustrating, and enjoyable' (1982: 17). Respectively, these statements represent unrealistic, absolutistic demands made on oneself, others and the world. For purposes of this chapter, 'others' will refer to people and situations within the organization as viewed by individuals going through the career cycle. The vocational irrational beliefs (VIBS) that will be listed and described for various stages of the dynamic career cycle exemplify an attitude of demandingness towards self and others. In addition to the basic irrational demands made by both the individual and the organization, several job related themes can be found. I originally found these themes to be central to irrational thoughts of people suffering the symptoms of burnout: expectation, commitment, and competence. The significance of the themes may vary at different stages in the career cycle and more than one theme may be central to each VIB. Each theme may be directed towards oneself or the organization. The job candidate's expectations seem to be a salient theme at this beginning stage in the career cycle.

Here are some of the common VIBs of job candidates at the entry stage. These VIBs may shed light on the effect cognitions have on helping or hindering individuals in their search for employment. Society reinforces these unrealistic, extreme, demanding styles of vocational thinking:

1 'I *should* know exactly what kind of work I want to do.' (expectation)
2 'I *must* find the perfect job.' (expectation)
3 'Whatever job I choose *must* be permanent and secure.' (expectation, commitment)
4 'If I work hard and make the right decisions, I *should* feel happy for the rest of my life.' (expectation)
5 'I'll *never* get the kind of job I want so why even try?' (competence)

The above listed VIBs about oneself and others may be viewed as myths or distortions many of us have carried around since childhood. As Ellis frequently states, human beings are prone to thinking crookedly and will learn to maintain those irrational beliefs that seemingly result in some kind of payoff.

The belief that 'I *should* know exactly what kind of work I want to do' is certainly reinforced by the numerous times adults in our lives have asked, 'What do you want to be when you grow up?' It would be difficult to avoid the hidden message that 'You *should* know what kind of work you want to do or something must be wrong with you.' The increase in counselling services can be helpful to individuals going through the career development process, but these services often fail to recognize that the way in which they are presented may lead impressionistic, inexperienced job seekers to believe that they should find the vocational solution quickly and easily or else something must be wrong with them. Individuals often go through many career counselling sessions, take all the appropriate vocational tests and inventories, and learn to write the 'perfect' resumé, but they still do not obtain employment because the cognitive factor has been overlooked. Cognitive career counsellors teach their clients that it is to be expected not to know exactly what kind of job they want. Decision making is a process requiring effort and hard work. More information and experience may be needed to make a realistic, valid first job choice. The uncertainty in the job finding process may be uncomfortable, but job candidates can learn to stand it.

It is a myth to believe that 'I *must* find a perfect job.' Media reinforces the image of people who have total control of their work lives. These people move through the career cycle smoothly and easily. From their first perfect job choice it is happiness through to retirement. Recently, career counselling firms, businesses that teach resumé writing, and the numerous vocational tests on the market have further reinforced the myth that there exists a perfect job if you take all the perfect steps – which are very costly to take. I have worked with individuals and conducted many career workshops hearing repeatedly that 'I took all the steps my career counsellor recommended and I still do not know what is stopping me from finding the right job.' Identifying and understanding attitudes, particularly expectations towards oneself and others at this early stage in the career cycle, is an essential and frequently overlooked step in today's career counselling packages.

The common irrational belief that 'the first job chosen *must* be permanent and bring guaranteed security' makes it harder for individuals to act on a decision. Fear of making the wrong decision is increased, and after choosing the job, it becomes more difficult for the individual to face the possibility of having made a mistake. This unrealistic expectation that a job should last a lifetime can lead to procrastination and frustration in taking appropriate action (Knaus, 1979, 1983). Instead of viewing each job experience as part of the career development process, individuals often look for the one job which will result in living happily ever after. Just as marital relationships between people are hard work and may end in divorce, so too can the relationships between people and their jobs.

The Judaeo-Christian ethic reinforces the belief that if we work hard, we must reap the benefits. This belief works wonders for those in powerful positions. Parents and teachers communicate this philosophy to their children and students in order to make discipline easier for themselves, and perhaps because adults do not want to face the unrealistic aspects of this idealistic belief. Throughout the ages there has been no evidence that competence guarantees obtaining a desired goal. It is fortunate when a person is offered a job based solely on his/her competence. However, those who have been in the work world for many years would be the first to state that competence may help but certainly is not the only factor considered in selecting new employees. It may seem unfair, but as in other areas of life, the job finding process is loaded with unfairness. An individual may be the most competent person for the job, but someone else with the right connections or a good personality may be the one who is hired. For all the emphasis on equal opportunity, believing that fair treatment must exist can result in extreme anger, frustration, and giving up in taking the necessary actions for obtaining employment.

The belief that 'I will *never* get the kind of job I want, so why even try' reflects a lack of self-confidence in one's competence. The entry level stage of the career cycle requires a great deal of risk-taking behaviours, and the ability to accept rejection without condemning oneself. Equating personal worth with success on a job interview will drastically interfere with progressing through this early career stage. Several different types of challenges are needed to unlearn this irrational belief. First it is important for counsellors to increase their clients' awareness of job requirements and characteristics. Then the realistic variables and barriers to obtaining these jobs should preferably be discussed. Supply and demand in the job market is an important factor in who will obtain specific jobs. Finding a job is hard work, just like achieving any other life goals. As children we often assume our parents somehow came together, or that people were just made for their jobs. It is not until we begin to perceive and acknowledge the reality of situations that we face the difficulty of accomplishing tasks at each stage in the life cycle. The entry stage of the career cycle can have a profound impact because many individuals give up at this stage and never make an assertive, realistic choice. Job candidates usually have a low frustration tolerance for the hard work and discomfort involved. They often represent those individuals who fall into whatever job is easiest and most convenient at the beginning of their career cycle, and remain in the same job or position until retirement. Effective cognitive career counselling can prevent job stagnation and burnout (Richman and Nardi, 1985) because it helps individuals to understand and accept the transitions in the career cycle, views the process realistically, and teaches this rational thinking to clients at the onset of the career development and planning stage.

Now that I have discussed just a few of the common irrational beliefs of potential job candidates, and how the career counsellor can help job candidates to learn more productive ways of viewing themselves and the organization, the irrational thoughts of the job interviewer, recruiter, and manager also need to be identified and challenged. Schein (1978) points out that from the organization's perspective it is important to avoid the negative outcomes of: (1) turnover of high-potential new hirees, (2) demotivation and the learning of complacency, (3) failure to discover incompetence early in the career, and (4) the learning of values and attitudes which are out of line with what will be needed later in the career. The task for management at the entry stage of the job candidate is to be able to assess, evaluate, and select the most suitable person for the available position and future positions on the career track in that firm.

Often those job interviewers and recruiters who are in the position to hire the best candidate for a job place excessive demands on themselves and the interviewees which result in undesirable outcomes in the recruitment process. Here are just a few of the frequently overlooked irrational perspectives the interviewer, recruiter, or manager may have that can lead to a poor person–job match:

1 'I *have to* make the job sound perfect for the right candidate to accept the position.' (expectation)
2 'Candidates *must* have the exact experience that the job description calls for or else they will not be able to perform the duties well.' (competence)

3 'I *have to* make the job sound as difficult as possible to see if the candidate is willing to work hard.' (commitment)
4 'I *must* find the perfect candidate for the job or I am no good.' (competence)
5 'The candidate I select *must* remain with our firm forever or else I made the wrong choice.' (commitment, competence)

Interviewers who believe they must exaggerate the positives of a job to assure the right candidate accepting the position are almost always doomed to make a poor selection. Unless the rational interviewee sees through the hyped up image of the job duties, unrealistic expectations will result in later job dissatisfaction. Presenting the job in realistic, honest terms will avoid problems later in the career cycle. Interviewers who believe that one has to present a perfect picture experience pressure which can interfere with concentrating on the interviewee's statements and responding accurately to questions. Some interviewers present a perfect image of themselves as representatives of a great company in order to boost their own ego. While it is fortunate to work for a prestigious company, it does not increase the value of the human being who works there. As everyone attempts to present a perfect image, stress is created from the need to maintain the unrealistic image and act against some personal values.

In this world of specialization, people are frequently pigeon-holed. The personnel department is told to select only those individuals who fit exactly into the job specifications. This rigid thinking places pressure on interviewers and leads them to negate other important factors necessary for selecting the most suitable job candidate. It is also nonproductive for companies to demand that once individuals have an area of expertise, these individuals remain in that area forever, or that they are not capable of learning another area of expertise. Basing selections on this rigid, inflexible thinking often results in employees feeling trapped, frustrated, and burned out. Job descriptions and specifications can be used as guides, but when used solely as the selection critieria, they may interfere with making the best person-job match over the long term.

Making the job sound more difficult than it really is presents a stressful type of interview to the job candidate. While some level of tension is known to be helpful in motivating a person to take action if the goal is perceived as acceptable (Locke and Latham, 1984), there is no guarantee that excess tension will lead to improved performance (Gomersall and Myers, 1966). Conscientious individuals will tend to work hard on easy or difficult tasks. Presenting unrealistic images of the job duties once again will lead to job dissatisfaction and a high turnover rate. A direct honest description enables the candidates to base their choice on accurate information. Knowing the facts can result in more logical choices. Presenting an exaggerated picture of job difficulty may also serve to boost the ego of the interviewer and company represented. When image and self-esteem interfere with the interviewer's goal, the objective of choosing the best candidate may be lost. Many recruiters base their self-worth on whether or not they are able to select the perfect job candidate. It is impossible to always make a perfect choice. In fact, there is no one perfect choice, but rather more suitable choices. A job choice may be right for a period of time and then due to personal or organizational changes, the match is no longer suitable. When basing self-worth on job performance, the selection process becomes more anxiety-producing and diverts the interviewer from focusing on the relevant factors to be assessed and evaluated in making a suitable person–job match.

Firms communicate the belief that good workers should be committed for life to their company. Thus, interviewers tend to believe that they must seek out those job candidates who are committed to this unrealistic, extreme organizational expectation. Of course it is appropriate for companies to let go of employees at the organization's own time and discretion. When unrealistic demands are made of job candidates, these highly motivated individuals will learn how to present the desired image in order to obtain the job even if there is no intention to remain with the company for a long period of time. The long-range goals of the firm will therefore not be met. In time, recruiters condemn themselves for not achieving what is in fact an unrealistic goal. The problem is to change the expectation. Nothing stands still. Those candidates with a flexible, adaptable style of thinking are more likely to succeed than those who seek to stay in the same position forever. They are also more likely to adapt to internal changes in the company throughout their career development. It is unrealistic and unwise to expect the interviewer or interviewee to maintain a lifetime commitment to their jobs.

During the early phases of the entry stage, it would be helpful for the job candidate to challenge the above listed irrational beliefs and practise thinking more productive beliefs. In addition, the job interviewer, recruiter, or manager might identify their own irrational beliefs and challenge them, as well as recognize the common misperceptions job candidates may have of the organization. Recognizing and modifying the attitudinal component will increase the probability that both the interviewers and interviewees will make a wise, suitable person–job match. Maybe not forever, but for the present, and that is a good beginning.

Adjusting to Daily Work Routines

The individual completes the tasks of the entry stage by making the decision to accept employment. The task of socialization is central to this next stage and may be viewed as a type of basic training into the world of work (Schein, 1978). The issues involve adjusting to the reality of work and membership in the organization. The degree to which an individual is prepared to develop attitudinal values necessary for succeeding in his/her chosen occupation will enable the socialization stage to be completed successfully. The attitudinal component at this stage very much centres on how realistic one's expectations are about the job tasks. During this stage, behavioural counselling techniques move away from emphasizing job interviewing skills and writing resumés. Socialization and communication skills training now become the focus. The socialization tasks include learning to get along with the boss, other trainees, asking appropriate questions in order to learn a new job, and balancing submissive and assertive behaviours in the new subordinate role. The cognitive component can make a significant difference as to whether or not the new workers can fit into their new positions and still maintain a healthy perspective of their individuality. Job dissatisfaction, and eventual job burnout, can be prevented to a large extent if realistic modifiable expectations are formed and maintained at this early stage in the career cycle.

The tasks which need to be performed during the socialization stage involve specific reality-testing behaviours. New workers who believe that 'It would be awful if I fail', or 'I should not have to perform tasks I do not like', may experience difficulty adjusting to the reality of the daily routine and performing the appropriate behaviours. Schein (1978) describes the rites and rituals associated with being a novice on the job as doing much of the dirty work and 'mickey mouse' type of tasks. It is at this stage that images are often shattered and the nitty-gritty reality of daily work is presented. The theme of commitment becomes an issue. New workers decide how much of a commitment they want to make to this new-found reality of the work world. Equating one's value as a person with the specific tasks assigned can easily result in job dissatisfaction and resistance to completing the tasks during this stage. Frequently an organization is surprised when a new worker quits. This indicates that the organization never understood the discrepancy between the individual's expectations and the reality of the daily job duties.

As with other stages, both the individual's perspective and the organization's perspective should be identified and understood. The individual needs to find a balance between (1) learning and responding to the demands of others, and (2) identifying and acting on opportunities to take the initiative and develop challenging activities of one's own (Schein, 1978). Making first impressions, as with any type of relationship, may be more influenced by faulty perceptions and resistance to accepting reality rather than based on the actual facts about the new work situation.

Here are some examples of new workers' nonproductive beliefs which may serve as barriers to them completing the socialization stage successfully:

1   'I *have to* show my boss I can do an excellent job or I will be a failure.' (competence)
2   'If I do not like the job right away, I will *never* find a job that is for me.' (competence)
3   'I am bright and talented and therefore *should not have to* do the mundane jobs.' (expectation, competence)
4   ' I *have to* fit in right away or they will *never* keep me at this firm.' (competence, commitment)
5   'I *cannot stand* not using my potential.' (competence, expectation)

Expecting oneself to do an excellent job, and rating oneself on performance, reflects a perfectionistic, demanding style of thinking. While adjusting to the new work situation is a task of the socialization stage, it is important for individuals to be patient and recognize that adjustment and acceptance take time. Low frustration-tolerance often occurs during the process of making a transition into a new and unfamiliar situation. Demanding that one consistently do a perfect job will lead to burnout as one begins to lose the delicate balance between personal needs and those of the organization. Unfortunately, managers learn to communicate in a demanding manner believing that this style of communication will make others comply. Those subordinates who base their personal worth on receiving the approval of others will internalize their bosses' demands and experience much anxiety. This will decrease the likelihood of maintaining a high level of performance. Rating oneself on job performance will interfere with maintaining a relaxed positive attitude during this learning period. Focusing on pleasing the boss instead of concentrating on actually learning the task may make it more difficult to master the task successfully. Believing 'I will do the best job I can', and 'How I perform does not reflect my worth as a human being', will increase the likelihood that new employees will successfully learn the job tasks and maintain a good communicative relationship with their bosses.

Concluding that 'I will never find another job if this one does not work out' reflects a common overgeneralization. One bad experience does not mean it will always be that way or that a suitable job match will never be made. It is also unrealistic to expect to like a job right away or to like every aspect of a new job. Perceptions of the messages from the work world, media, and even career counselling lead many individuals to conclude that once they have decided on the job, something must be wrong with them if they do not like the job chosen. This was their one chance and now it is all over. Nothing could be further from the truth. Unrealistic expectations of how a job should be or how one should perform on a job may lead to resentment towards the organization or oneself, even before the individual fully learns the job. It would be productive to believe that 'If I do not like the job right away I will find out what I can do to make it better for myself.' It is important to give oneself and the job a chance before deciding that it would be better to make a job change. One bad experience does not generalize to 'I will never make a successful job match.' Individuals can learn from every job experience about themselves and the work world.

With the numerous highly educated professionals graduating and entering the job market today, many unrealistic expectations centre on the theme that 'Because I am smart, well-educated, competent, and have the right credentials I should not have to start at the bottom.' Such individuals demand that the organization immediately give them more challenging and prestigious positions. However, credentials and competence are not the only factors considered in placement within a company. It is also highly irrational to believe that all aspects of a job will be interesting or meet with one's potential. Accepting and learning from the rites of passage in the workplace can be extremely frustrating for those with this highly unrealistic, demanding belief. Instead of accepting the structure and rules of the system, these individuals make themselves miserable and will either be fired or eventually leave. If they choose to continue seeking corporate positions while maintaining the same unrealistic beliefs, this self-defeating cycle perpetuates itself.

Lack of confidence in oneself may upset the delicate balance between making an appropriate niche for oneself and depending completely on the organization to set the standards. Spending all one's energy trying to fit in with co-workers and employers results in loss of individual initiative and potential. Trying too hard may lead the organization to believe that the individual may need too much structure, direction, and approval from the organization. Adjusting to the new work environment may be done in moderation so that the individual talents of the new worker will be recognized and rewarded gradually. Believing that 'I will learn what the company expects and maintain my own individuality within that framework' will help the individual and company to accept one another.

As a reward for fulfilling the educational and training requirements and acquiring the necessary job credentials, many new workers demand that the organization provide the perfect niche in which they can fulfil their potential. There is no evidence or guarantee that individuals should use their potential on a job or that an organization must find job duties which meet an individual's potential. While it is preferable that a person–job match be based to some extent on the level of the job tasks and the level of a job candidate's skills and abilities, this cannot always be a reality. The belief that 'I cannot stand not using my full potential' will result in anger towards the organization and possible undesirable job performance. Believing 'I can stand not using my full potential', and balancing one's life outside the work situation with other interests, will help reduce resentment towards this reality of the work world. As the potential that people bring to the job is identified more accurately, it becomes very important to accept the reality that no job can provide tasks which fully and constantly utilize and challenge one's potential.

While many of the VIBs held by new workers result in negative emotions and behaviours on the job, organizations continue to maintain their rituals, entrance rights, and gradual acceptance of new employees. I have emphasized the need for new workers to challenge their thoughts which interfere with accomplishing the task of socialization at this early stage in the career cycle, without losing a sense of their identity. Practitioners often describe to their clients the reality of adjusting to a new job but tend to omit teaching their clients methods to modify their nonproductive beliefs. What is even more neglected is the cognitive component in training individuals who do the interviewing, hiring, and initial supervision of new workers. Here are nonproductive beliefs typically held and reinforced by the organization:

1 New workers *must* learn the job slowly, going through every single step. (expectation, competence)
2 People who are new to the firm cannot have anything to contribute and therefore *should not* have their views considered. (competence, commitment)
3 Beginning workers *should* do as we say and not ask questions or expect feedback unless we choose to give it. (expectation)
4 New workers *should* be given the easiest tasks. (expectation, competence)
5 New workers *should* be tested out by being assigned to do the most difficult tasks right away. (competence)

Setting standards for training and observing beginning workers without consideration for their individual career anchors – that is, abilities, work styles, motivation, and values (Schein, 1978) – very often leads to demotivation, complacency, or quitting. Organizations design specific training programmes without teaching trainers how to deal with individual differences. Just as new workers would benefit from gathering information about the firm, talking to fellow workers, and adopting a flexible attitude towards their job, so the organization would do well to maintain a flexible attitude when bringing a new worker into the group. Presenting new workers with many obstacles and hurdles is fine if there is evidence that each of these individuals will benefit and grow from the experience. Some individuals learn faster than others, but organizations often confuse the need to have power over the new worker with a need to help the new worker become a contributing member of the organization. A productive attitude for the firm would be to assess the progress of new workers during the training period and modify the training programme to bring out the best potential possible.

New workers certainly have much to learn in terms of the tasks, interpersonal relationships, and politics of a firm. But the newness does not necessarily mean the person has nothing productive to contribute to the firm. In fact, quite the opposite is often true in those firms where the rules and standards have been inflexible for years. Listening to ideas from a beginning worker may enhance the company in the long run and increase the likelihood that the worker will become a highly motivated member of the firm. Resistance to change on the part of the organization has discouraged many potentially good employees from remaining with a company. It would be more productive to think that individuals are hired because the organization believes that the new workers have potential to perform well for the firm. So it makes more sense to be open to what new workers may have to offer. Validating the views of new members of the organization enables the firm to learn about the needs of these individuals which can then be used to develop and maintain a healthy productive relationship throughout the career development process.

The third VIB is related to the previously discussed belief but demands that new workers be treated as children, in the sense that the company knows best and that new workers have no rights until they prove themselves. Asking questions may reflect a desire to learn and become part of the firm. When this behaviour is not reinforced, the workers may behave complacently or give up on finding a place for themselves and leave. Listening to questions and giving feedback can actually help the new workers to become an integral part of the team sooner and with a more positive attitude which can affect their work habits. In order for a company to challenge the belief that 'beginning workers should do as we say and not ask questions or expect feedback unless we choose to give it', the company would do well to really believe in their own ability to answer questions and to deal effectively with honest disagreement. To avoid giving feedback keeps the new worker in an extremely dependent position. It is false to believe that this will make new workers into better performers. Underlying this belief is the need for companies to maintain power and control over workers so that their staff will comply. Believing that giving feedback is constructive and does not reduce management's power and control will increase the likelihood that the new worker will be socialized more appropriately into the organization.

Constantly assigning new workers the easiest or dirtiest tasks may reinforce poor work habits and result in low motivation and job dissatisfaction. Cognitive psychotherapy frequently teaches the importance of moderation. Setting extreme expectations for employees on either the easy or difficult end of the task continuum will tend to evoke more extreme emotional and behavioural response. It is constructive to teach new workers that the reality of the job consists of a balance between doing challenging and boring tasks. Making new workers prove themselves to an extreme degree may result in having cooperative, complacent workers for the present time, but resentful, demanding staff in the long term. It would be more rational for the organization to act on the belief that new workers would benefit from facing mundane tasks at the very start of their training while simultaneously being introduced to more challenging and rewarding aspects of the job.

The other extreme of the VIB that new workers should be given the easiest tasks is to test them out by assigning the hardest tasks from the beginning and observing which individuals remain with the firm. If so much time and effort go into deciding which individuals to hire, then why not make more of an effort to keep them rather than threaten them and see how the new workers can take it? Presenting this type of anxiety-producing situation at the beginning of one's career gives false information about the actual job. Workers who lack confidence or low frustration-tolerance may be screened out, but might have done well on the job if given a gradual hierarchy of task difficulty. On the other hand, the overly confident workers may demand hard work all the time and expect this to be reciprocated accordingly. More problems will arise in later stages of the career cycle if the firm maintains this extreme view.

Deciding Whether or Not to Remain on the Job

During this next stage, the task of mutual acceptance is accomplished as the individual and organization make adjustments to each other. While there is no perfect match, each partner decides if there is enough to be gained by working at making the match work. On the part of the individual, rational thinking in making the decision to stay becomes very important since remaining on the job based on the thought that 'I will never find another job', will lead that individual to fear losing the seemingly protective, secure atmosphere of the organization. The individual who truly accepts the reality of organizational life will more likely view the various kinds of constraints, delays, or undesirable work conditions as temporary than if he or she demands that improvements occur more quickly and easily than they do. Ellis's (1985) emphasis on the need for self-acceptance and its corollary of other-acceptance in business certainly is relevant to this stage in the career cycle.

Making the decision to remain may in itself reduce some anxiety or discomfort on the part of the individual. The tasks involved continue to centre on developing and maintaining healthy relationships with co-workers and bosses. Knowing one plans to stay makes acceptance of these tasks somewhat easier. Finding a mentor and adjusting to a period of dependence or subordination is part of the early phase of this stage. Thinking rationally will enable the accepted new members of the organization to balance more effectively their own needs for independence with those of the organization. While in this somewhat subordinate role, developing groundwork for future advancement can be accomplished. The common irrational thoughts associated with this stage of mutual acceptance are reflected in themes of impatience, unfairness, expectations of others, and need for approval from higher level staff. These are some of the irrational beliefs:

1 'It would be *awful* if my boss criticizes my work now that I have decided to keep the job.' (competence)
2 'I *could not stand* it if I find out later on that the job is not for me.' (expectation, commitment)
3 'Now that I am staying, the company *should* promote me and give me a better assignment right away.' (expectation)
4 'The company *should* treat me fairly and rationally now that they know I am staying.' (expectation, commitment)
5 'It would be *unfair* and *horrible* if new workers do not have to go through the same boring tasks I had to do.' (expectation)

At this stage of mutual acceptance, when individuals decide to remain with the firm, those who believe that they must always have their bosses' approval will experience anxiety which may negatively affect their work. There is no evidence that these employees must have approval from their bosses. It may be preferable, but the 'must' just leads to nonproductive emotions and less likelihood of initiating tasks and doing creative work. In addition, criticism of a worker's performance at any stage of the career cycle is not a condemnation of the whole person but simply an evaluation of the individual's job performance. Criticism is evaluated as 'awful' when individuals equate their self-worth with the criticism of a particular performance on the job. Rating oneself as the result of criticism at any level on the job will increase anxiety and lead to resentment towards the boss who has the right to criticize performance. Viewing criticism as a constructive learning experience which does not reflect on one's personal worth will enable the employee to benefit from the criticism and remain motivated to do good work.

Hopefully, making the decision to remain on this first job is based on facts, rationale, and logic. This does not therefore mean that a lifetime commitment to the job will be right for the individual. Here we get into perfectionistic thinking and the need for constancy. It is important for workers to remember that career development is dynamic and that changes within the same job position can occur. Resisting change can lead to emotional, behavioural, and physical symptoms which are detrimental to job performance. If, in time, the job is not right for the person problem-solving is the appropriate step. Ruminating over how awful it is or that nothing can be done about the situation will decrease the likelihood of taking the next appropriate steps for continuing to progress throughout the career cycle.

Once the decision is made to stay and the individuals know that the company wants to keep them, these individuals may exhibit low frustration-tolerance and impatience. The expectation that the desired rewards should be given immediately is unrealistic and will evoke anger toward the firm if the demand is not met. This will in turn lead to nonproductive behaviours on the job and negative perceptions on the part of the firm. Acceptance of the organizational requirements and plans to develop oneself within the system will help reduce the negative emotions that do develop, so that passage through this stage will be relatively smooth and productive.

In a similar way to the last irrational belief, workers set up unrealistic demands on the company when they believe themselves to be in a secure position within the organization. There is no evidence that, once a mutual decision is made for the workers to remain, the company will reduce expectations or guarantee that there will always be a position for these employees. Believing the following will help reduce the individual's anger resulting from unrealistic demands made on the company: 'I am glad we made a mutual decision of acceptance, and I will continue to accept the structure of my company. I can work to fulfil my personal needs and potential within their establishment. They do not have to treat me fairly, and I can stand it if they do not.'

Requirements for a job may remain the same, increase in difficulty, or become easier. Instead of focusing on whether other employees have it easier, it is more productive to focus on personal progress and goals. Unfairness will exist, and employees will not always know the basis for a firm's decisions. Even so, employees can fulfil some of their personal needs while accepting and adjusting to the firm's style of functioning. Focusing on the positive aspects of arriving at the next stage of the career cycle, and believing that it does not matter that much what kind of tasks new employees are assigned, will help individuals to perform effectively and continue their personal growth.

Turning to the first supervisors, the following VIBs may interfere with their ability to achieve acceptance of the supervisees:

1 'I *should* know whether the new worker really wants to stay on board, or else I am a failure.' (competence)
2 'I *cannot stand* not knowing what the employee's long-term plans are.' (expectation)
3 'I *have to* give my new employees more privileges to make them stay with the firm.' (competence, commitment)
4 'It would be *awful* if we have disagreements at this early stage.' (expectation)
5 'I *must* be extra careful in my criticisms to make sure my new staff will stay on board now that the decision to stay has been made.' (expectation, commitment, competence)

Schein (1978) talks about lack of communication between supervisor and supervised at this stage, and says that this mutual avoidance causes stagnancy in organizations. While it is important for the supervisor to be open to conflicts that employees may be experiencing in becoming an integral part of the team, it takes two to form a working relationship. Those supervisors who believe that they should know whether the new worker really wants to remain with the firm are unrealistically expecting that they can read the minds of their new staff. Blaming themselves for not fully knowing the career and personal objectives of their staff can result in a poor supervisory style. Believing 'I would like to better understand the plans of my staff, and I will communicate as effectively as I can' would make improved communication more likely. It would help to open up channels of communication for workers experiencing difficulties in deciding whether or not to remain on this first job.

Poor communication from the beginning stages can lead to the problem of the organization not knowing the long range goals of the worker and therefore may result in a clash between the objectives of the organization and individual. Human resource personnel would do well to take demands off themselves to have to know everything, but still strive to communicate effectively to determine whether the organization and individual can come to a more long-range acceptance and understanding of each other's needs.

Just as the individual may unrealistically expect immediate rewards for staying, a human resource person or supervisor may feel pressure to give staff extra privileges so that the chosen employee will be happy and stay. This action may irrationally seem to reflect the competence of the recruiter. In reality it will increase the demands made by the employees and result in extreme negative emotions on the part of the organization. The organization may in turn go to the opposite extreme and hold back some rewards, which would make the situation worse. Believing rationally that 'We will observe and communicate with the employee, and study which incentive plans work best' would decrease this common problem.

Once a mutual decision is made, there is no guarantee it will remain that way. Any future disagreements need not be viewed as awful. It is natural and necessary to have disagreements if effective communication is to occur. Often organizations look for quick clean solutions and avoid the process of problem-solving. The rational thought, 'I can stand disagreements and know this does not mean I made a wrong choice in selecting this individual', will help open a forum for continued communication.

Holding back on criticism is a disservice to the employee who needs to learn and perform the assigned job tasks. Mutual acceptance cannot be achieved if either partner feels inhibited from communicating directly and honestly. Constructive criticism about the employee's job performance can only serve to come closer to meeting the needs of the organization as well as helping the employee to base the decision to stay with the firm on realistic feedback and information. There is also no guarantee that an employee will remain committed to a firm regardless of how much pampering the individual receives.

Mid-Career Crisis

As the large number of baby boomers has been reaching the thirty-five and over group, there has been an increased interest in the crisis of the mid-life years. Many issues are encountered as individuals reach the mid-years of their life cycle. The reality of one's mortality is experienced, and depending on the individual's perceptions, can cause excessive anxiety and depression. Those issues which were not confronted during previous stages now become more difficult to avoid or deny (Sheehy, 1974).

Schein's (1978) description of 'mid-career crisis' substantiates once again that the issues confronted during the development of a career are an integral part of the individual's life cycle. The individual at mid-career has now invested many years into working. Just as the attitudes, values, and needs formed at an early stage in the career development process play a significant role in determining career decisions made throughout the career cycle (Schein, 1978; Super, 1957), the influence of rules set early in our human development govern our present actions and emotions (Beck, 1976; Wessler and Hankin-Wessler, 1986). Assessing whether to make a job change, to seek new challenges within the present position, or level off and emphasize another area of one's life become areas for making decisions. Deciding whether to give up on dreams not yet fulfilled or to forge ahead to unachieved goals is a conflict often faced at this stage. Needs not fulfilled in personal and family areas may lead individuals to level out in their career and focus on balancing their lives. An evaluation of career accomplishments without a self-evaluation enables individuals to decide which direction to proceed within the career cycle. Here are several irrational beliefs pertaining to mid-career issues which act as barriers to successfully completing this stage:

1 'I *should* have achieved a higher status position by this age in my life.' (expectation, competence)
2 '*I cannot stand* that I may never accomplish my career goals.' (expectation)
3 'I am *worthless as a person* because others my age have gone further.' (competence)
4 'I *cannot stand* mentoring younger workers who may move up beyond my position.' (competence)
5 'I *should not* level off in my career or redefine my goals because this will mean I am weak and not ambitious enough.' (competence)

Believing 'I should have achieved a higher status position by this age in my life' often results in anger towards oneself and in a lack of further effort to pursue realistic goals. While mid-career is an appropriate time for reflecting and re-evaluating one's achievements, a crisis occurs when individuals condemn themselves for not having achieved vocational goals which may have been unrealistic in the first place. It is productive to re-evaluate goals so that sensible decisions can be made to prepare for the next career transition. Believing rationally that 'I understand why I have achieved my present position and I accept where I am even though I do not like it' can alleviate a lot of self-directed anger and frustration. Options for further growth are certainly available to the individual. It is the individual's perceptions and evaluations that will determine taking action towards either further growth or stagnation.

Coming to the realization that certain career goals may never be accomplished, or that the trade-offs at this time in life may not be worth the effort, comes hard to many individuals. This stage certainly highlights the relationship between decisions made and actions taken earlier in the career cycle. Facing and accepting goals not yet accomplished is the first step in deciding rationally what to do next. The rational belief that 'I can stand that I may never accomplish my career goals, and that I can still accept myself with my non-accomplishments and redefine more realistic goals' will help the individual to reduce the mid-career crisis issues during this stage.

Rating and berating oneself for not achieving what others have accomplished by the same age and stage results in feelings of depression, anxiety, and resentment. Throughout one's career life there will be others who accomplish more and those who accomplish less. Those individuals who view highly successful co-workers as inspirational models instead of as threatening adversaries are helping themselves to progress realistically and productively in their careers.

At mid-career it is natural for individuals to serve as mentors to newer workers. This role poses a threat to those who believe that: 'I cannot stand others moving ahead of me, and there is no way I will make it easier for them to do it.' In an attempt to keep one's knowledge and ideas from new workers, mid-career workers may alienate themselves from their firm. Helping others to grow is an integral part of many experienced employees' jobs as seen from the organizational viewpoint. By rationally believing 'I can benefit from seeing my influence on what others learn, and I can feel satisfied sharing my knowledge and expertise', the individual will be more likely to go beyond this stage and focus on personal needs and new career goals. Even if levelling off is a career goal, it will be viewed as positive at this stage in the cycle and within the control of the mid-career worker.

Many individuals who are on the fast track reach mid-career and realize that they have neglected their personal and family lives. They experience great conflict at this stage because their priorities throughout their career and life cycle were to progress successfully in their career. These individuals equated their career accomplishments with their personal worth. Now as they begin to focus on personal areas of their lives, they believe that they are weak and not ambitious enough. It would be productive for them to believe 'I am glad for my present career accomplishments, but now I think it would be better for me to concentrate on personal and family goals. Redirecting my goals does not mean I am weaker than those who continue to put everything into their careers.' This type of thinking enables individuals to make decisions based on healthy attitudes, motives, and values. Those individuals who maintain a balance between their personal goals and organizational needs are likely to experience career satisfaction throughout their working lives.

Organizations have traditionally pigeon-holed employees. They have assumed that individuals who were satisfied with their positions would and should remain so. Although recently more companies are accepting the need for mid-career workers to re-evaluate their career and personal priorities, organizations still maintain some irrational views which may interfere with achieving mutual benefits during this stage:

1   If the mid-career individuals do well in their specialization, they *should not* want to make any kind of change. (expectation, commitment)
2   Employees' increased concern about their families means they can no longer be trusted as committed company people. (commitment)
3   The mid-career individuals *should not* suddenly try to make a name for themselves at this stage in their career. (expectation)
4   We *should not* offer mid-career workers any growth opportunities since their time here is limited. (commitment)
5   Mid-career workers seem too conflicted and unmotivated to be given any challenging assignments. (competence)

The organization would do well to understand the need for personal growth among employees, especially at a time when individuals are likely to view their options as narrowing and decreasing. The rational belief that 'It is healthy for the mid-career workers, no matter what their level of competence, to question and re-evaluate their present positions' will enable the organization to get more productivity out of their employees and help them in turn to grow during this difficult stage.

The increase in Employee Assistance Programs (EAPs) reflects the recognition of companies that mid-career workers find it increasingly difficult to negate their personal and family concerns. The company that rationally believes that individuals may be very committed to their jobs while at the same time may need help in dealing with realistic personal and family conflicts will increase the probability that the individuals will do their best to remain productive members of the firm.

With the view that time is running out, many mid-career individuals put pressure on themselves to make a name for themselves as soon as they can. The desire to contribute and be recognized, without basing one's worth on the outcome, is appropriate. Organizations that understand the irrational pressure workers place on themselves can help these employees by accepting the mid-career workers' needs, and by challenging the corporate belief that there is no place for these individuals to grow. Opportunity for growth to a large extent comes from one's cognitions. The company that believes in the growth of the employees as well as that of the organization provides an atmosphere in which mutual growth finds its own place in which to flourish.

The belief that 'organizations should not offer mid-career workers any growth opportunities since their time with the firm is limited' often results in spending time and effort in training new workers who may not do as effective a job in a higher level or new position. Reinforcing employees for jobs well done, and considering opportunities for utilizing employees' potential, can be beneficial to both the individual and the organization.

It is easier to assume that mid-career workers are unmotivated and therefore should not be given any challenging assignments than it is to test out this hypothesis by offering them challenging assignments. Lack of motivation and depression are often symptoms resulting from the perception that 'the company no longer cares about my growth or needs, and no longer values me as an employee'. At the mid-career stage, individuals may give up any attempts to perform productively when perceived positive reinforcers are lacking.

Late Career and Disengagement

During their late career, individuals usually have senior positions with the responsibility for selecting and developing key subordinates. As these individuals progress through this stage, they learn to accept a gradual decline in levels of power and responsibility, and move towards gradual disengagement. The attitudes one maintains throughout the career cycle will help the individual move through these later stages in the cycle. Throughout the career cycle it is important to remember that the family and biosocial cycle influence the individual as well.

While in the late career stage an individual may irrationally believe:

1 'I *have to* take on more responsibility and show the firm that I can still do the job.' (competence)
2 'Younger workers *have no right* to compete with me since I have given so much to the firm.' (expectation, commitment)
3 'I *should not* let go of my power and responsibility because I will be viewed as weak.' (competence)
4 'I *should not* let go of my job ever because I have nothing else.' (competence)

Older workers often fear competition and place pressure on themselves trying to prove that they can take on more responsibility. Although this is often a good time to increase some responsibility, it had better be done based on expertise, experience, knowledge, and on an attitude of confidence and enthusiasm. To take on responsibility in order to prove it can be done when someone else may be better qualified for the particular task is unwise and irrational. As with earlier stages, frantically working to obtain approval leads to pain in the long run. Throughout the career cycle time will continue to move on and people will continue to age. Accepting these realities and taking action in accordance with these realities will reduce feelings of resentment and depression so common during this stage in the career cycle.

The energy, hunger, and drive in youth to 'make it' is obvious. Delegating appropriate responsibility to youth, and teaching them to work as a team with all levels of staff can be beneficial for everyone. Accepting those young workers who are very motivated and ambitious, instead of demanding that they change, will save individuals in their late careers from unnecessary resentment and depression.

Fear of letting go of power and control in effect says that 'I do not really believe that I had the power and control in the first place.' To assertively decide when to let go will help reduce fear and anxiety. Holding the rational belief 'I am glad to give the power and control of my position to someone else so that I can focus on more meaningful tasks and activities for myself' will enable the individual to make the transition to eventual retirement.

Many individuals hold on to jobs and careers they no longer enjoy or are successful at because they believe that they will have nothing else in their lives. Preparation, in terms of balancing career development with other areas in the life cycle, can help to alleviate this irrational fear. Believing 'by letting go of my job and engaging in more enjoyable activities during my retirement I will be doing more for myself than holding on to my job' will help make the transition out of the labour force less painful.

Many types of counselling programmes, both in-house and external to the corporation, have been developed to help employees get through this transition and those issues encountered during earlier stages of the career cycle. Organizations are beginning to acknowledge that job performance is not equated with the human worth or value of their employees, and that a balance between work and personal life is good for the firm as well as for the individuals concerned.

Summary

In this chapter, I have demonstrated the applicability of cognitive psychotherapy (RET and allied cognitive-behavioural techniques) throughout the stages of the dynamic career cycle. Individuals spend much of their lives participating in the labour force. They bring their attitudes, values, emotions, habits, and physical total being to their jobs. The increased recognition of the relationship between mental health and job performance has resulted in an expansion of services and resources for troubled individuals and organizations. Since a lack of understanding of the attitudinal differences between the individual and organization can lead to serious conflicts, cognitive psychotherapy may be the logical component to integrate into present and future programmes for alleviating job related problems.

References

Azrin, N. H., Flores, T. and Kaplan, S. J. (1975) Job-finding club: a group-assisted program for obtaining employment. *Behaviour Research and Therapy*, 13: 17–27.

Beck, A. T. (1976) *Cognitive therapy and the emotional disorders*. New York: International Universities Press.

Block, J. (1978) Effects of a rational–emotive mental health program on poorly achieving disruptive high school students. *Journal of Counseling Psychology*, 25: 61–5.

Brodey, J. L. (1983) *Mid-life careers*. Philadelphia: Westminster Press.

Canadian Mental Health Association (1984) *Work and wellbeing – the changing realities of employment*.

Criddle, W. and Tracy, J. (1977) Rational skills for business people. In J. L. Wolfe and E. Brand (eds), *Twenty years of rational therapy*. New York: Institute for Rational-Emotive Therapy.

Di Giuseppe, R., Miller, N. and Trexler, L. (1977) A review of rational–emotive psychotherapy outcome studies. *The Counseling Psychologist*, 4: 64–72.

Ellis, A. (1962) *Reason and emotion in psychotherapy*. New York: Lyle Stuart.

Ellis, A. (1972) *Executive leadership: a rational approach*. New York: Institute for Rational-Emotive Therapy.

Ellis, A. (1982) The treatment of alcohol and drug abuse: a rational–emotive approach. *Rational Living*, 7: 15–24.

Ellis, A. (1985) A rational–emotive approach to acceptance and its relationship to EAPs. In S. H. Klarreich, J. L. Francek and C. E. Moore (eds), *The human resources management handbook: principles and practice of employees' assistance programs*. New York: Praeger.

Ellis, A. and Bernard, M. (eds) (1985) *Clinical applications of rational–emotive therapy*. New York: Plenum Press.

Ellis, A. and Blum, M. L. (1967) Rational training: a new method of facilitating management and labor relations. *Psychological Reports*, 20: 1267–84.

Erikson, E. (1980) *Identity and the life cycle*. New York: Norton.

Freud, S. (1905/1962) *Three essays on the theory of sexuality* (trans. and rev. by James Strachey). New York: Basic Books.

Gandy, G. L. (1985) Frequent misperceptions of rational–emotive therapy: an overview for the rehabilitation counselor. *Journal of Applied Rehabilitation Counseling*, 16: 31–5.

Gibson, C. F. (1980) *Managing organizational behavior*. Homewood, Ill.: Irwin.

Gomersall, E. R., and Myers, M. S. (1966) Breakthrough in on-the-job training. *Harvard Business Review*, 44: 62–72.

Hauck, P. A. (1977) *Marriage is a loving business*. Philadelphia: The Westminster Press.

Herzberg. R. (1966) *Work and the nature of man*. Cleveland, Ohio: World Pub.

Hurst, J. B. and Shepard, J. W. (1985) Counseling dislocated workers in job training placement act title III programs. *The Vocational Guidance Quarterly*, Sept.: 47–51.

Iida, M., Reeder, G. D., McCabe, S., Miura, K. and Goldstein, M. (1986) Moral evaluation of achievement outcomes in the United States and Japan. Presented at the meeting of the American Psychological Association, Washington, DC.

Keil, E. C. and Barbee, J. R. (1973) Behavior modification and training the disadvantaged job interviewee. *Vocational Guidance Quarterly*, Sept.: 50–6.

Kelly, G. (1955) *The psychology of personal constructs*. New York: Norton.

Kendall, P. C. and Hollon, S. D. (eds) (1979) *Cognitive-behavioral interventions: theory, research, and procedures*. New York: Academic Press.

Klarreich, S. H., Di Giuseppe, R. and Di Mattia, D. (1987a) The cost effectiveness of an employee assistance program using rational–emotive therapy. *Professional Psychology*, 18: 140–4.

Klarreich, S. H., Di Giuseppe, R. and Di Mattia, D. (1987b) EAPs: mind over myth. *Personnel Administrator*, 32(2): 119–21.

Knaus, W. J. (1979) *Do it now: how to stop procrastinating*. Englewood Cliffs, NJ: Prentice-Hall.

Knaus, W. J. (1983) *How to conquer your frustrations*. Englewood Cliffs, NJ: Prentice-Hall.

Korman, A. (1970) Toward an hypothesis of work behavior. *Journal of Applied Psychology*, 54: 32–41.

Kram, K. E. (1985) *Mentoring at work*. New York: Scott Foresman.

Landy, F. J. and Trumbo, D. A. (1980) *Psychology of work behavior* (rev. ed). Homewood, Ill.: Dorsey.

Lazarus, A. A. (1976) *Multi-modal behavior therapy*. New York: Springer.

Levinson, D. J. (1978) *The seasons of a man's life*. New York: Ballantine Books.

Lewis, J. A. and Lewis, M. D. (1986) *Counseling programs for employees in the workplace*. Monterey, Calif.: Brooks/Cole.

Locke, E. A. and Latham, G. P. (1984) *Goal setting: a motivational technique that works*. Englewood Cliffs, NJ: Prentice-Hall.

McGovern, T. V., Tinsley, D. J., Liss-Levinson, N., Laventure, R. O. and Britton, G. (1975) Assertive training for job interviews. *The Counseling Psychologist*, 5: 65–8.

McGregor, D. (1960) *The human side of enterprise*. New York: McGraw-Hill.

Mallary, N. D., Jr. and Conner, B. H. (1975) An example of employment service adjustment counseling. *Journal of Employment Counseling*, 12: 55–8.

Manzi, P. A. (1986) Cognitive appraisal, stress, and coping in teenage employment. *The Vocational Guidance Quarterly*, Sept.: 47–51.

Maslow, A. H. (1943) A theory of motivation. *Psychological Review*, 50: 370–96.

Miller, C. and Walter, T. (1977) A behavioral employment intervention program for reducing juvenile delinquency. *Behavior Therapy*, 8: 270–2.

Myers, D. W. (1984) *Establishing and building employee assistance programs*. Westport, Conn.: Quorum Books.

Neff, W. S. (1977) *Work and human behavior*. Chicago: Aldine.

Nye, S. G. (1986) As EAPs come of age as clinical care providers, what doth the law require? *Employee Assistance Quarterly*, 2: 99–101.

Parsons, F. (1909) *Choosing a vocation*. Boston, Mass.: Houghton Mifflin.

Pierre, K. D. (1986) Enhancing well-being at the workplace: a challenge for EAP's. *Employee Assistance Quarterly*, 1: 19–28.

Porter, L. W. and Lawler, E. E. (1968) *Managerial attitudes and performance*. Homewood, Ill.: Irwin-Dorsey.

Richman, D. R. (1979) A comparison of cognitive and behavioral group counseling techniques for job finding with welfare women. Unpublished doctoral dissertation, Hofstra University.

Richman, D. R. (1981) Delay of gratification in relation to the rational thinking and demographic characteristics of welfare women. Unpublished manuscript, The Institute for Rational–Emotive Therapy.

Richman, D. R. (1982) A comprehensive skills program for job-finding with the hardcore unemployed. In R. M. O'Brien, A. M. Dickinson and M. Rosow (eds), *Industrial behavior modification: a management handbook*. New York: Pergamon Press.

Richman, D. R. and Nardi, T. J. (1985) A rational–emotive approach to understanding and treating burnout. *Journal of Rational–Emotive Therapy*, 3: 55–64.

Schein, E. H. (1978) *Career dynamics: matching individual and organizational needs*. Reading, Mass.: Addison-Wesley.

Sheehy, G. (1974) *Passages*. New York: Bantam.

Siassi, I. and Messer, S. B. (1976) Psychotherapy with patients from lower socioeconomic groups. *American Journal of Psychotherapy*, 30: 29–40.

Smith, R. R., Petko, C. M., Jenkins, W. O. and Warner, R. W., Jr. (1979) An experimental application and evaluation of rational behavior therapy in a work release setting. *Journal of Counseling Psychology*, 26: 519–25.

Super, D. E. (1957) *The psychology of careers*. New York: Harper & Bros.

Thompson, A. P. (1976) Client misconceptions in vocational counseling. *Personnel and Guidance Journal*, 55: 30–3.

Vroom, V. H. (1964) *Work and motivation*. New York: Wiley.

Weinrach, S. G. (1980) A rational–emotive approach to occupational mental health. *The Vocational Guidance Quarterly*, Mar.: 208–17.

Wessler, R. L. and Hankin–Wessler, S. W. R. (1986) Cognitive appraisal therapy (CAT). In W. Dryden and W. Golden (eds), *Cognitive-behavioural approaches to psychotherapy*. London: Harper & Row.

Wolfe, J. L. and Brand. E. (eds) (1977) *Twenty years of rational therapy*. New York: Institute for Rational–Emotive Therapy.

Zaccaria, J. C. (1970) *Theories of occupational choice and vocational development*. Boston, Mass.: Houghton Mifflin.

10

Training Parents to be Effective:
A Cognitive-Behavioural Approach

Elin H. Evans and Elspeth McAdam

Until recently child psychotherapy was conducted on an individual basis. The child would see a psychotherapist alone and parents were left in the dark as to what took place behind the closed door. An hour later the child would return to the parents, who were then left to cope with the child for the rest of the week. There was increasing dissatisfaction amongst professionals with the ineffectiveness of such therapies, but it took clinicians a long time to realize that the most logical candidate for therapist or helper would be the parents themselves (Levitt, 1971). The pioneering work of using mothers as therapists was carried out by Guerney (1964). Guerney's emphasis was on training mothers to develop an understanding relationship with the child. He postulated that since the child's behaviour was a direct result of parental attitudes, the best milieu to learn alternative behaviour would be to change parental attitudes. (Levitt, 1971).

The work of Patterson and his colleagues (Patterson et al., 1975) has been the most extensive in the field of 'parents as therapists'. They worked with parents of highly aggressive boys aged between 3 and 14 years and employed behaviour modification techniques. In Patterson's programmes parents were taught to observe and note the problem behaviour and their own reaction to this behaviour. These authors wrote a training manual for parents which the parents studied before attempting to modify their own and their child's behaviour. These programmes were successful, but Patterson and his colleagues advise that for these children and their parents, periodic retraining or 'top up' sessions are necessary. Moreover, they have argued that failures in parent training can be accounted for by the fact that there are often other problems, not necessarily child-related, within and without the family system (Patterson, Cobb and Ray, 1973). This has been confirmed by Griest and Forehand (1982) who investigated which factors affected failures in parent training programmes. They found that there was a significant relationship between child-related problems and parents' perceptions of their personal adjustment, parents' perceptions of their marital status and parents' perceptions of their extrafamilial interactions (1982). They did not find that parent-training programmes on their own helped parents to generalize to the other problem areas in their lives. De'Ath (1983) supported the argument that effective parenting cannot be isolated from the economic and social constraints on parents' lives and a multi-modal approach was necessary.

Most of the parent-training literature has focused on families with aggressive or overactive children, and more recently on parents who physically abuse their children. Training placed heavy emphasis on behaviour modification techniques and social learning theory. In addition to the behaviour modification training, parent-training programmes in more recent literature have included cognitive-behaviour therapy to cope with anger and assertiveness (Ambrose, Hazzard and Haworth, 1980; Denicola and Sandler, 1980; Wolfe, Sandler and Kaufman, 1981). A number of other programmes have included Parent Enhancement Therapy (PET) which focuses on communication between parent and child. The programmes using PET alone have been found to be less effective in changing children's behaviour than training parents in behaviour modification techniques (Dubey, O'Leary and Kaufman, 1983). These authors also found that the parents who were trained in behaviour modification techniques rated them more helpful and more applicable to their problems than the PET parents and reported less behaviour problems in their children. They also were less likely to drop out of the programme and were more likely to recommend the programme to friends. Another study which compared behaviour modification training programmes for parents with client-centred parent counselling showed, however, that although behaviour modification was more effective, the improvement was not maintained at a 6-month follow-up (Bernal, Klinnert and Schultz, 1980).

Griest et al. (1982) have carried out a comprehensive evaluation study comparing outcome and generalization of parents receiving behaviour modification training only, to those of parents receiving behaviour modification training with parent enhancement therapy. The study also included a non-treatment control group. The results showed that the parents who also received enhancement therapy were more successful in carrying out behavioural procedures and maintaining progress. The authors suggest that the enhancement therapy was necessary, as it enabled the parents to overcome the personal problems which interfered with putting child management skills into practice. The non-treatment control group showed no improvement over the follow-up period, suggesting that maturational growth or life-events do not produce effective change by themselves and that parent training of some sort is necessary. The literature also suggests that training parents in groups rather than using an individual or a family approach is more effective (Johnson and Katz, 1973; Pevsner, 1982).

The 'Bethel' Parent Training Programme

The Bethel Child and Family Centre's parent training group is run for two groups of parents: parents who have physically abused their children, and parents who have severe handling difficulties with their children. We focus on the preschool range, since child development theory indicates that parents as therapists will be most effective with that age range (Levitt, 1971). Our aim is to combine the various needs of parents and children which have been highlighted in the literature. We have taken into consideration the shortcomings of the various training programmes by adding extensive cognitive-behaviour therapy sessions dealing with parents' feelings of hopelessness and depression, as well as including cognitive sessions on anger and assertiveness. In addition, our programme encourages parents and children to use effective and empathic ways of communicating.

Both training groups follow the same curriculum with sessions lasting an hour and a quarter. We have found that the child abusers need a greater number of sessions, which are repeated until parents feel competent in using the techniques. The group is task orientated and follows a curriculum. There are 12 components to the curriculum, which focus on behavioural techniques, communicational skills and cognitive-behaviour therapy.

The training programme starts with the behaviour modification training and communicational skills, before going on to cognitive-behaviour therapy. There are a number of reasons for this. Dubey, O'Leary and Kaufman (1983) have shown that when parents ask for help with behaviour problems with their children, the parents are more likely to attend training sessions and find them more relevant if initial focus is on behaviour management. We have found that parents in both groups score in the moderately depressed range of the Beck Depression Inventory. Williams (1984) has argued that in order to give the depressed patients a sense of positive achievement, it is often necessary to start with behavioural tasks before embarking on the cognitive side of cognitive-behaviour therapy. We would also argue that because the children are initially out of parental control and limits are few and inconsistently applied, the children feel insecure and the parents feel they have failed. By starting the training with behavioural expectations and reasonable limit setting, the parents begin to take control, feel in charge and thereby experience some success, and the children will in turn feel secure. Initially the parents and children are in a very negative relationship. Parents are asked to do baseline measurements in order to observe and get to know their children. This observation helps the parents to become more realistic in their expectations of their children, which enables them to see that all children behave in both positive and negative ways. They will also achieve some 'distance' from the problems they are having and later be able to see positive behaviours to reinforce. In this way, the parents and children start to move out of the negative relationship. Once the parents have achieved some success in coping with their children it is possible to use cognitive techniques to help the parents to understand why they have failed in the past.

Format of the Group
Group leaders must meet with the parents and the children for 15 minutes before the group starts. This time is used to observe parent–child interaction, to reinforce parents for appropriate handling and to model ways of dealing with problem behaviour. The parents and children then separate for one hour. The parents in the training groups are requested to complete homework sheets every week. The homework sheets are a means of asking parents to put into practice, at home, the topic of the previous session. The homework sheets are specific and contain revision notes to remind the parents of the content of the session. Each session starts with a review of the previous week's homework and produces examples with which the group can work. There is no emphasis on group process and there is no opportunity for the parents to discuss personal crises within the sessions. However, it is made explicit at the start of every course that should the need arise, because a parent is going through a difficult personal crisis, one of the therapists will be able to see him/her outside the parent training sessions. This opportunity is rarely used. When the parents have requested extra sessions it has usually been to discuss marital issues, although housing and other economic problems have also required attention.

A children's group is run parallel to the parents' group and is staffed by a nurse-therapist and an occupational therapist who have specialized in working with children. In this group the children play freely but limits are set and socialization is encouraged. In addition, puppets or other toy material are used to demonstrate the reasons behind common behavioural problems (O'Brien and Loudon, 1985). The puppets act out alternative behaviours to allow children to see they have a choice as to how they behave. Throughout the group feedback is given verbally or non-verbally on the children's behaviour to help them understand the reasons why they are behaving the way they are. These reflective techniques are used to help the children understand their feelings and behaviour. We would argue that using reflection lays foundations for good cognitive practices as the children learn to accept and recognize automatic thoughts which make them feel sad or angry.

Description of Curriculum

Introduction and Welcome
In the first group, after introductions, the group leaders stress the fact that they too are parents as well as trained child specialists, and that they

have every confidence that they can pass on their professional skills to the parents. It is emphasized that skills can only be mastered if they are put into practice, so the parents are requested to do homework every week. The analogy of learning to drive a car is used as a way of demonstrating that merely studying the theory of driving is not sufficient to drive competently. Practice is necessary, and confidence grows with practice. It is stressed that some of the homework will initially feel awkward and stilted, like first steps in learning to drive. Each action has to be remembered – look in the mirror, clutch in, change gear – and yet with practice, as confidence grows, this becomes one action, smooth and natural. The same applies to positive interactions with children and other people.

Communication and Observation Skills

We have found that parents referred to our groups often have poor communication skills, both with their children and with adults. In this group the emphasis is put on the skills necessary to enhance communication with children. In her paper on normal families, Hansen (1981) observed that these parents seemed to 'listen' to their children and therefore had realistic expectations of them. These parents did not seem to feel any reluctance about controlling the children when they became too demanding. She also observed that when children felt positively handled by their parents, the children responded reciprocally. In the group, the importance of making a child feel significant and good about him/herself is highlighted. Ways of talking to children and listening to them are discussed. Children are often lectured to and not allowed a say. When adults talk to children they tower above them or shout from another room, a way of communicating to which adults are not usually subjected. The language used is often too complicated for children to understand: their hurts and emotional pain are frequently dismissed, instead of being accepted and an understanding verbalized to the children. Communication and conversational skills are role-played by the leaders and practised by the parents. The parents are asked to feed back how they feel about the different conversational styles – for example, being ignored, bullied or listened to – and how it feels when people try to understand their feelings in an empathic way.

Throughout the group sessions the importance of good and sensitive observation is emphasized as a way of enhancing relationships and improving children's behaviour. Initially, basic behaviour modification techniques are taught and parents are encouraged to become observers of their children, stepping back and just watching. In order to make this task easier for them, parents are asked to assess their children's development levels using simple child development scales. This homework serves a number of functions. It initiates training in observational skills. It helps parents get to know their children, enabling them to respond to their children as they are and making the parents aware of their frequently erroneous developmental expectations. The observation and assessment also allow some positive interaction with the children while they are being assessed.

Positive Behaviour

The second session is spent discussing and identifying positive charac-. teristics and positive behaviour of the children. The group members are asked to say something positive about the referred child. They all have great difficulties with this. The developmental charts are used as a source of positive behaviour. We prompt with ideas of behaviour parents take for granted, such as putting on shoes, cleaning teeth, children saying 'please' and 'thank you'. The group acts as a source of encouragement and reinforcement to the parents, as there is a constant stream of comments like 'You are lucky – my child never does that.' The variability in behaviour of children is demonstrated, and gives parents a sense of what behaviours they have been taking for granted. It is stressed that the more positive behaviour is observed and acknowledged to the child, the higher the child's self-esteem will become, and the more positive things she/he is likely to do. Children who see themselves as good behave better than children who perceive themselves as bad and naughty (Patterson et al., 1975). There will also be an increase in the parents' positive attitude towards the children. The homework following this session is for the parents to write down and acknowledge to the children any positive behaviour they observe. Group leaders emphasize the importance of being *specific* when noting the behaviour so that the child knows exactly what the parent is pleased about: for example, the comment 'you have been good this morning' is not specific enough to make the child aware of what she/he has done that has pleased the parent. The aim in the next group is to increase the occurrence of positive behaviour and, therefore, it is important for the parents to be specific.

Positive Reinforcement

At this stage the parents are still viewing their children negatively and only a few of the parents have been able to find any positive things their children have done. The rest of the group offers suggestions to those who have had the greatest difficulty. Even those group members who have managed to note a few positive behaviours in their children end their sentences with a 'but'. Example: 'He was very good at tea time, eating his food without fuss, *but* at bedtime he was an absolute devil.' This sort of example leads into a discussion of how parents deal with bad behaviour and how ineffective they are at preventing their children behaving this way. This enables the leaders to introduce and discuss the concept of reinforcement. We emphasize that children are hungry for attention (reinforcement). Many parents inform us that even if they occupy their children all day they are still naughty. One father admitted his resentment at having to read 20 bedtime stories to his daughter who even then refused to stay in bed and threw a tantrum. He responded angrily and shouted at her and smacked her. Finally, she went to bed, unhappy and sobbing, and he was left feeling guilty. The importance of the intensity of the negative emotional attention which children are given is highlighted by this sort of example. We would like to argue that it is not so much the length of attention children respond to, but to the intensity of the attention, both verbal and nonverbal. 'Good girl', as a reward for positive behaviour when said in a nonemotional way, seems to mean less to children than the intensity of emotion frequently given to misbehaviour. When a child misbehaves, parents act quickly and intensely by shouting, smacking, and grabbing the child. Good behaviour often goes unnoticed, or is rewarded at the end of the day or with a promise of future treats, so little verbal and nonverbal intensity is shown. Parents are, therefore, encouraged to try and match the intensity of positive reinforcement from now on with that of previous negative reinforcement. At this stage the importance of reinforcing the desired behaviour consistently is stressed, although some behaviours will inevitably be missed and so will result in intermittent positive reinforcement.

Parents find it very difficult to reward good behaviour with strong emotional intensity, partly because they feel children should always behave well, and partly because they themselves have rarely been given positive feedback. Therefore they find it difficult to respond positively to their children. They also complain that they feel embarrassed about intensely praising their children, particularly in public. The group leaders remind the parents of their feelings of embarrassment when shouting at a child in public. At least both parties will feel good about themselves if it is praise rather than punishment that is observed. The analogy of discomfort in learning to drive is again discussed to encourage parents to practise praising their children. Such practice will enable them to praise their children with ease so they will not feel stilted and embarrassed about doing so, even in public.

A more detailed discussion follows on the ways positive reinforcement affects behaviour. The parents are encouraged to list types of reinforcers which would work for their child. These are put under three headings: affection and praise, activities, and concrete reinforcers. The group leaders concentrate on warmth, immediacy and intensity of the positive reinforcement. Parents are asked to try to reward positively all the good behaviours they observe in their children the following week.

At about this stage in the group we note a marked change in the parent–child interaction. The children are less miserable and the parents feel more confident and are happier about giving children their time.

It is suggested to parents that instead of reluctantly occupying their children all day in order to stop misbehaviour, they could set aside a specific time each day to be alone with each child (Baruch, 1949). During this time the child should dictate the activity, which gives him/her a sense of being in control and powerful in a safe and limited setting. Parents can make the child feel that it really is the child's time by ignoring the telephone or getting their partners to pretend to interrupt but not being permitted to do so. It also allows the parents to feel in control. They are then actually giving time of their own free will, rather than being dragged into giving attention by a whining, demanding child.

Ambrose and Haworth (personal communication) have suggested that it is important to get parents to focus on existing positive behaviour and to positively reinforce this, before looking at unwanted behaviours, otherwise parents tend to get rather punitive and ignore all attempts on the part of the child to gain attention. We entirely agree. By starting the groups with a focus on positives, the relationship between parent and child has begun to change and be more enjoyable. The substitution of positive reinforcement as an antecedent, in place of negative reinforcement as a consequence, can be more easily comprehended by parents once they have seen the effect of positive reinforcement on their children's behaviour.

Antecedent, Behaviour and Consequences (ABCs)

Parents are taught how and why children learn to behave in certain ways, using learning theory. Examples of behaviour parents would like to understand or change are then discussed within an ABC framework. It is stressed that behaviour never happens in isolation and that the aim of this session is to enable the parents to put their children's behaviour into context, and to work out ways that they could more effectively respond to and modify misbehaviour.

It is pointed out to the parents that if they are to become experts in understanding and solving the children's problems, they first must become keen observers of both their children's and their own behaviour. In this way they will begin to understand why each misbehaviour occurs, and why the child persists in behaving this way. The importance of good behavioural practices is stressed: that is, parents must be specific about the problem behaviour; they must be clear about why and when their child misbehaves, and also how they, or other people, react to the misbehaviour. Common behavioural problems are presented and parents are asked to think about the antecedents and consequences: why do they think the child behaved they way he/she did, did he/she get what he/she wanted, is he/she likely to behave the same way again? It is emphasized that the child will respond to negative reinforcement when positive reinforcement is not forthcoming.

Changing the Antecedents

During the session on antecedents, parents are encouraged to look at the reasons why the children might have behaved they way they did: did they want attention, where was the parent, what was the parent doing, at what time of day does the behaviour usually happen? Other questions about understanding the child's needs and rights are also elicited, such as: did the parent or visitor interrupt the child's activities, is the child feeling frightened or jealous? The child's motives also need to be questioned: for example was he/she trying to get out of doing a task? The aim here is to try and enable parents to understand their children's needs, thereby becoming more skilled at meeting these. Parents are encouraged to think about these sorts of questions, since finding answers to them will enable parents to feel in control. This in turn will help the parents to become more positive about their children and give the children more self-respect.

Having established the circumstances under which behaviours occur, suggestions are made as to how the antecedents could be changed. Ways of preventing the behaviours are discussed.

Attention   Parents are encouraged to give attention at times that recurrently produce problems. Situations parents commonly complain about are when visitors come, or when parents are otherwise occupied, making it difficult to give attention to the children. Ways are suggested to prepare or warn children that visitors are coming or that the parent is going to be occupied. Suggestions are made as to how to engage the child in an activity such as having a 'visitors' bag' of special toys and treats that will only be available when visitors come.

Reflection   We suggest the use of reflection as a way of trying to show the child that parents are trying to understand the way the child is feeling. These feelings are those commonly viewed as 'unacceptable', such as jealousy, anger, hate and possessiveness. The child needs to have these feelings acknowledged but not necessarily condoned. This is done by telling the child that mummy understands how angry he/she feels that mummy has visitors, because he/she wants all mummy's attention. Sometimes mummy wants to talk to her friends as well, but she does understand how cross he/she feels. Reflecting to the child helps the child to understand and accept his/her own feelings, thereby preventing feelings of guilt or shame which erode his/her self-esteem. These techniques are good cognitive practice since they facilitate children's understanding and are accepting of their emotions.

Distraction   We have found distraction techniques can defuse a potentially negative interaction between parents and children. Suggestions are made concerning how parents could distract children's attention from the activity that is producing conflict. Ideas such as looking at books, doing puzzles, playing games etc. are discussed. Attracting children's attention to look for disappearing elephants, cats or Superman through the window, is often a successful way of defusing the situation.

Age appropriateness We encourage the parents to ask themselves whether they are asking too much or too little of their children in terms of parental requests. Some children's motor skills are advanced and therefore they can be expected to do up their shoes; other children's are not. Thus the relevance of children's developmental levels is discussed in the context of how unrealistic expectations can be the antecedent to unwanted behaviour.

Time alone/planned time Parents are reminded of the usefulness of setting aside a special time regularly for parent and child to play together. When the child keeps whining and wanting the parent to play with him/her, the reply could be 'Let mummy/daddy finish this and we'll do that in our time alone together'. This will very often prevent continuing irritation as the child knows he/she will get some undivided attention. But parents must be true to their word and if they have promised to give the child a special time, time should be set aside for this. Children have a great sense of fairness and justice, and these are attributes to be encouraged.

Parents are helped to practise the techniques used to change antecedents to prevent confrontations. Parents have stated how good they felt when they have been able to prevent misbehaviour by anticipating antecedents. Control has in the past usually been perceived as punitive, and parents have been delighted by their ability to control through positive and caring methods.

Changing the Consequences

While going over the homework the group leaders reassert how important it is to stop misbehaviour happening by being expert at changing the antecedent (A). The advantage of good A-spotting is pointed out to the parents. The children's self-esteem is thus maintained since they do not lose face by losing control of themselves as when in a tantrum. Children who feel they are good behave well. Parents also feel good because they are in control and have stopped the behaviour happening. They also do not feel guilty for shouting or smacking. Home is a less noisy place with less tension and anger build-up, and there is also no damage to furniture, doors and so on.

Sometimes it is difficult to change the antecedents, or they have been overlooked and the behaviour has happened whence the consequences (C) have to be looked at. Parents need to learn how to change consequences to make behaviour less likely to happen again.

Parents are reminded to stay cool and calm, because any strong emotion is attention given to the behaviour which parents do not want to recur. Also by staying cool and calm parents will not lose control or have the feelings of remorse and guilt they have felt previously when they have shouted at and smacked the child.

We advise that if the parent has requested something of the child, they repeat the request no more than twice, then ensure the request is carried out. Parents need to make sure that the request to the child is reasonable – for example, that it does not occur in the middle of a child's favourite television programme – and that it is worth making. Parents are encouraged not to get into long discussions over the requests they make to their children. It has been observed that parents will reason with their children for a long time on such trivial matters as to why they must put on their coats or shoes at the end of a session. Children feel more secure with straight simple requests. Children are not good at understanding reasoning, they use it to hold attention and to delay having to carry out the request.

We have found that it is not advisable to suggest time-out to parents. Parents tend to use it too much and for too long. Instead, we have put greater emphasis on the antecedents and how to change these to prevent unwanted behaviour happening. This also leaves both the parent and the child with a sense of dignity.

Cognitive-Behaviour Therapy

The parents who are referred to our groups are desperate because they feel so helpless. We have found that many of the mothers, and to a lesser extent the fathers, who attend, have low self-esteem, and score in the moderately depressed range on Beck's Depression Inventory. Williams (1984) argues that changing incompetent behaviour using behavioural techniques is a necessary precursor of cognitive change. When the parents find that they can begin to take control of their children, and not feel failures as parents, they are in a better/stronger position to see how their thoughts about themselves affect their feelings about themselves and their children and how these are linked to their ability to parent their children effectively. Throughout the curriculum we stress the correlation between thoughts and behaviour for both parents and children, and we encourage parents to think about their own and their children's feelings.

Many of these feelings are brought to the fore when we are analysing or practising the As and Cs, where mothers and fathers complain of the embarrassment of, for example, ignoring a child in a tantrum, or the feelings of hopelessness at being outwitted by a 2-year-old. It brings home to the parents how their negative thoughts often result in ineffective handling of the children, and a sense of hopelessness and depression.

Their own life scripts, which include the ways in which their parents treated them when they were children, have a powerful influence on the confidence with which they cope with their children. There are many conflicting thoughts of never wanting to behave towards their children as their parents did towards them. They are, therefore, reluctant to set limits until they get to a state of desperation, screaming or smacking, repeating the patterns of parenting which they experienced. Their guilt makes them overcompensate with *quantity* rather than *quality* of attention. They feel drained by the amount of time the child has taken, they begin to feel resentful and then angry. They then feel guilty about their anger and a cycle of guilt and overcompensation is set up. Once they have begun to take control of their child, and are beginning to enjoy the child and being a parent, it becomes easier to challenge some of these preconceptions.

During the subsequent sessions, parents are introduced to Beck's cognitive theory of depression (Beck et al., 1979). They are shown, through their own examples, that when people are depressed they interpret events in a negative, personalized and selective way.

In the first of these sessions we look at the parents' thoughts leading to feelings of humiliation and inadequacy, particularly those which have arisen while they have been trying to change the A or C of a problem behaviour. Initially, we look cognitively at situations that have not gone smoothly and have left parents feeling that they have failed. For this purpose we have modified Beck's Dysfunctional Thought Form. The forms have had columns added for behavioural consequences of automatic thoughts and behavioural consequences of alternative thoughts, in order to accentuate how thoughts affect not only feelings but also behaviour. The inevitability of ineffective behaviour and dysphoria resulting from negative thoughts is thus more apparent.

One of these modified forms is here filled in (see Figure 10.1) with an example taken from a situation one of the parents has experienced. Members of the group volunteer the sorts of helpless/automatic thoughts which they would have in that situation. Alternative ways of interpreting the event are then elicited from the group. The session continues making the parents aware of how thoughts determine feelings and behaviour, and that by changing thoughts, feelings about oneself and the way one behaves are altered.

It is emphasized when interpreting situations that there is no truth as such; alternative interpretations are equally valid. However, if an individual is depressed, tired and fed up she/he will evaluate a situation negatively. Group members are helpful and supportive of one another in seeking alternative evaluations. Sharing automatic thoughts and finding that other people, who outwardly appear competent, feel and think the same way, is reassuring. Frequently parents think others are highly critical of them when they are having difficulties with a child. This evaluation is corrected by the other group members who state they often feel sympathetic to parents who have to cope with a difficult child. Instead of being critical, as is presumed, the majority of parents are likely to be sympathetic. Through the cognitive process the parents come to realize the harshness and selectivity of their own self-evaluations, and how negative this makes them feel about themselves.

What happened?	Emotions	Automatic thoughts	Behaviour resulting from automatic thoughts	Rational thoughts/coping thoughts	Behaviour resulting from rational thoughts	How do I feel now?
Be precise about what you are feeling – sad/anxious/angry		Write down the thoughts that came immediately before these feelings		Write down your rational/coping thoughts in response to automatic thoughts	What plan of action will I now make?	
I was shopping and child threw himself on the floor and was screaming	Embarrassed and upset	1 Why does he do this? 2 Why can't I control him? 3 I'm a useless mother 4 Everybody is looking at me and thinking how useless I am 5 I'm never going to to shop again	1 Smacked child 2 Picked him up 3 Left the trolley 4 Left shop 5 Wasted hour. No shopping done	1 Grocery shopping is boring for children 2 I can control him a lot of the time 3 Being a mother is not just about controlling kids 4 Not everybody was staring at me, although it felt like everyone 5 Even if they were, so what. Of course I will shop again. I will just have to think of a plan so that I have less bother when shopping with him	1 When I go shopping I will give him a shopping list to hold 2 Ask him to get things he recognizes such as dog/cat food, baked beans, etc. 3 Play 'I spy' game' – 'I spy a woman with a hat. . .' 4 If he throws himself on the floor I will pick him up and put him in the trolley. *IGNORE* the screams	'A' *I feel in control* 'C'

'A'   Antecedents   Anticipate ways of occupying him
'C'   Consequences   Do not reinforce his bad behaviour with attention

Figure 10.1 *Diary of problem thoughts and feelings*

The homework after this session is for the parents to take an example of a situation which they have found embarrassing or upsetting which has occurred while trying to put into effect either the A or C of a child problem behaviour. The homework is made specific and limited so that parents are not daunted by the modified dysfunctional thought forms.

Hopeless and Depressed Thoughts

When going over the homework with the parents, it is apparent that feelings of hopelessness and depression are prevalent. A repeated theme, especially for mothers in the group, is the loss of self-esteem which occurs with the change of role when they have children. These mothers express the view that, by having children, they stop being individuals and become identified solely as their children's mother. This seems to be true particularly for mothers who do not work outside the home (Brown and Harris, 1978). They find this transition and the way they think society views them demoralizing.

In this session we look at situations where parents feel lonely, miserable, incompetent or depressed. Automatic thoughts are elicited and their inevitable consequences demonstrated. In searching for rational thoughts, we concentrate on separating parental or family tasks from personal attributes. For example, if a husband criticizes his wife for not having done the ironing, it is then interpreted by a depressed and miserable wife in a very personalized, catastrophic way. She would think that not doing the ironing equals 'incompetent housekeeper' equals 'incompetent person', thereby compounding feelings of depression and hopelessness. Parents are helped to see that ironing is only one of many tasks which contribute to efficient housekeeping, and failure to accomplish this task does not reflect on them as people. It is the amplified negative evaluation which causes the dysphoria.

Another area on which we concentrate is parents' difficulty in separating their children's attributes and behaviour from their own. Children are seen as an extension of the parents. Many of the examples centre on how they feel they are judged by others when their children misbehave. This has often resulted in a curtailment of all socializing activities: for example, friends are not invited around any more, children are withdrawn from playgroups, shopping is done alone and so on. Parents are helped through cognitive strategies to see that frequently it is their sensitivities and self-evaluations rather then society's which makes them withdraw.

A number of examples are taken from group members, helpless thoughts are elicited and the group members generate coping thoughts and strategies. For instance, one mother gives her latest disastrous shopping expedition with her 3-year-old daughter as an example (see Figure 10.1). She had collected all her shopping in the trolley and was waiting in the queue to pay when her little daughter started demanding a biscuit. The mother told her daughter that it was too late to get the biscuits since they were stuck in the middle of the queue. The child then suggested that she herself would get them, but the mother did not want the child to go alone to look for them in a vast shop. The little girl then started to throw shopping items out of the trolley and, as the mother tried to stop her, the little girl started to scream. She felt everyone in the shop was looking at her critically. In her desperation the mother picked up the child, left behind all the shopping in the trolley and ran out of the shop.

When asked what action she would take in the future, she said she was never going to shop again and, if she did, no one would ever persuade her to go in that supermarket again, even though it was the closest to her home. When asked what her automatic thoughts had been, she said she thought that she was a useless mother and felt humiliated as she had demonstrated it to everyone in the shop who must also think her useless; she also thought that she was uncaring since she had forgotten to buy biscuits. The group members then shared similar experiences and automatic thoughts. They then offered alternative thoughts, such as biscuits are bad for children, tea time was imminent and biscuits would have taken away her appetite. They also brought up what a good and responsible mother she was in not letting the child loose on her own in a big shop where she could have been abducted. Group members stated that they felt sympathetic to mothers whom they saw in shops trying to cope with difficult children, and that although some of the glances might have been critical, some might have been sympathetic; and anyway does it matter if people are critical? The group then went on to offer strategies as how to plan the next shopping expedition to make it more successful. The inevitable consequences of helpless thoughts resulting in ineffective passive behaviour and unhappiness are highlighted. Similarly, the connection between coping thoughts and coping strategies and feeling a good and able individual who can begin to enjoy his/her children is discussed. The cognitive side of putting into practice effective child management skills covered earlier in the course is reaffirmed. Parents are reassured that children feel more secure and happy when limits are given and kept to and when their parents are in control and happy. The group members are encouraged to use the forms to examine their thoughts in situations where they felt sad or incompetent. Thus, through changing their thoughts, they can remain in control of their emotions and prevent the downward spiral leading to despair and ineffectiveness.

The homework assignment is to get parents to practise using the forms on their own at home. They choose an occasion when a child has made the parent feel miserable and another when an adult has made them feel miserable. The homework is an attempt to help people see that they are like mosaics: that is, they fill a number of different roles, each of which requires different attributes; difficulties with one role make little difference to the overall picture.

Parents have told us at follow-up that they have found the forms useful and have continued to use them whenever problems arise or when they have been ineffective in dealing with their children.

Assertive Behaviour

The goal of this session is to help parents learn to recognize the effectiveness of being assertive. The parents who attend our group tend to behave in either a passive and/or an aggressive way towards their children and partners. Behaving assertively enables an individual to feel in control, which will increase positive self-evaluation. Behaving aggressively or passively means loss of control and will lead to a variety of feelings like anger with oneself and others, shame at being rude, a sense of hopelessness and/or feelings of not being loved.

We use role-playing to demonstrate the differences between passive, aggressive and assertive behaviour and the effects that these different behavioural styles have on oneself and others. It is also pointed out that behaving assertively links in with the As and Cs of the ABCs. For example, if a child is asked to do something, the parent must firmly and unemotionally ensure that it gets done. If the parent behaves in a passive way, the child will not do as requested and the parent will feel miserable because he or she has not been obeyed. This is then equated with lack of love from the child. Since no limits are set, the child will feel out of control. The parent may also feel angry with the child for being so disobedient, and angry with him/herself for not being able to control a young child. There is a high probability of the parent behaving aggressively by shouting, screaming or smacking, thereby giving the negative reinforcing attention that will ensure disobedience again. The negative cycle of exasperation with the child, feelings of guilt and failure as a parent, the inevitable effect on the child's self-image of being horrible and naughty, is set up, and thus the joy of parenthood and childhood is eroded.

The connection between acting assertively and practising good parenting skills, and how that makes parents feel about themselves and their children, is reiterated. Parents are encouraged to help their children to act assertively and not to ask for things in an aggressive or whining way. This will improve the child's sense of dignity and self-esteem.

The homework assignment is to try and get parents to monitor their automatic thoughts when they have behaved passively and to determine what changes in these thoughts would have encouraged them to behave assertively.

Anger and Anger Control

We have found that when group members try to behave assertively they find it very difficult and often fail. They either behave passively, which makes them feel useless and powerless, or behave aggressively, thus alienating the other person and making themselves feel too demanding and, therefore, not likely to be loved by anyone. In both instances they get angry with themselves and others. In going over the homework, occasions are selected when they have not succeeded in being assertive and we use these examples to look at anger and anger control.

Situations which make people feel angry are discussed. These often occur when they have behaved passively. The anger is with themselves for allowing someone to walk over and abuse them. Anger does not happen in isolation, and the myth of the common statement 'I just exploded' is explored. We discuss the need to identify somatic symptoms which are produced by angry automatic thoughts. The physiological symptoms precede the angry behaviour. These are highly individual and various: clenched fists, palpitations, sweating, clenched jaws. The group participants are encouraged to recognize their own physiological symptoms and take them as a warning that they should stop and look at their automatic thoughts as well as the context. It is important that they give themselves time to do this and, therefore, we suggest delaying-tactics like removing themselves from the room (as long as the child is safe), making a cup of coffee, counting to 10 etc., immediately they become aware of their body cues. In this way they can reappraise the situation and take preventative action.

Common situations and automatic thoughts that occur when people get angry are discussed, and the group offer suggestions concerning alternative ways of viewing these situations. For example, when a 3-year-old is disobedient, automatic thoughts might be: 'Horrible child, why does he always disobey me when I most need him to be good?' Alternative coping thoughts might be: 'He is only three. . .he needs to show his independence' (session 1 discussed appropriate developmental levels); 'I had better reflect back his need for independence' (session 5 on antecedents and reflection); 'He may be tired. . .I'll put him to bed' (common sense!); 'He may be jealous of the attention the baby is getting, I'll reflect his feelings of jealousy' (session 5 on antecedents and reflection). Parents are encouraged to look for alternative thoughts; the helpful ones tend to be problem-solving, realistic, and to take others' age and personality into consideration. Another strategy is to try and be empathic and understanding, as it is difficult to feel angry with someone for whom one feels sorry. A frequent complaint by mothers is their fury at their partners who come home from work and sit and read the paper instead of helping. We encourage them to be empathic as well as assertive and state their needs. They are then far more likely to get cooperation from their partners using this approach than if they get angry. Parents role-play these kinds of situations, or ones that are more personally appropriate to them, feeding back their feelings and automatic thoughts while behaving in an angry mode and in a sympathetic and assertive mode.

Cognitive coping strategies are looked at and it is stressed how thinking affects feeling and behaviour (as in depression). Once parents have begun to be more aware of their thoughts when they become angry, it is possible to demonstrate how the automatic/hopeless thoughts in anger tend to be projected on to others. These thoughts are very personalized; for example: 'He wants to show me up', 'He's so selfish he couldn't care about what sort of day I had', 'My friend totally ignored me in the street. . . see if I help her again.' We practise rational/coping thoughts that are not projected and are understanding, such as 'He is only little. . . he just wants my attention.' The importance of not personalizing alternative thoughts is also stressed. The parents are reminded that this is looking at the ABC model from a cognitive perspective. They are also reminded about how good it feels to be emotionally in control.

Parents are asked to practise these strategies when they feel angry, and if they do get into a situation in which they have felt angry and lost control, they should make a plan of how they could have handled it differently using coping thoughts and coping behaviour.

Anger: Other Strategies
The previous session concentrated on the ways in which the person who is feeling angry can cope with his/her feelings of anger. This second session on anger concentrates on how to communicate with the person at whom anger is directed, without eroding or undermining the other's self-confidence. Parents are encouraged to take responsibility for and verbalize their feelings as being their own. For example, they are encouraged to say 'I am getting very angry' *not* 'You make me furious'. It is important to warn children and others that one has a headache or that one is irritable. Thus responsibility for the emotion is taken by the individual who is feeling angry. This will prevent children from taking on responsibility for the adult's anger, and thus prevent the children from feeling bad about themselves. Further, it is emphasized how important it is for children's self-esteem to know that it is *what* they are *doing* which will make their parents angry, rather than they themselves as individuals. We encourage the parents to be specific about the behaviours that are making them angry and not to denounce the child globally – for example: 'I am getting angry because I have a headache and have asked you several times not to fight', rather than 'You naughty, disobedient little boy.' We stress here how it makes a person feel to be globally denounced as bad in contrast to being told a specific behaviour is unacceptable. That is, it is the act and not the child that is being denounced.

We discuss and role-play various strategies, with parents feeding back their feelings of being globally denounced and having to take responsibility for someone else's anger as opposed to using the above strategies.

The cognitive effect of smacking is discussed. Parents are asked to tell us what effect using physical punishment has on themselves. The usual response is short-term release of anger, followed by guilt, which they try and relieve by overcompensating the child with attention. The father who read his daughter 20 bedtime stories demonstrates this. They are then asked about what they think their children feel about being smacked. The response is that the children are usually indignant and angry with their parent, fear him/her, as well as feel badly about themselves. Further we suggest to parents that when an adult hits a child, the adult is in fact teaching the child that it is acceptable to hit someone smaller than oneself and that problems can be solved by violence. Memories of their own childhood smackings are recalled. Commonly it is the humiliation of the smack rather than the provoking reason which is recalled. The difference between obeying for reasons of respect – whether parental-respect or self-respect – rather than for reasons of fear is pointed out, and the desirability of the former is emphasized. Parents are reminded about the effect of smacking as a reinforcer, one of the Cs of the ABCs. They are told that although it may work in the short run, it seldom does in the long run, since smacking is an intense reinforcer of misbehaviour.

The homework assignment is to ask parents to look at the way they have communicated when angry, and to try and put the above skills and strategies into practice.

Revision

There is a final session which is used for revision of the course. We ask parents for feedback and suggestions on the curriculum for use in future courses. The parents are praised for their attendance, enthusiasm and hard work.

Conclusion

Our approach to parent effectiveness training needs to be seen in a historical perspective. Clinicians have experimented with various theoretical frameworks for training parents as therapists. Initially, a single theoretical model was used, but it soon became evident that combined theoretical approaches were necessary and more effective in maintaining improvement and generalization, because parents' problems encompass most areas of their lives and are not just child-related.

In our opinion, the shortcoming of many parental training programmes has been the limited use of cognitive therapy. The cognitive input in these programmes has focused only on anger and impulse control. In addition to assertiveness training and anger control, our training programme includes sessions where the parents are given the opportunity to examine their own emotions and behaviour using Beck's model of cognitive therapy.

An added limitation of training programmes described in the literature is the lack of therapeutic input for the child. In our programme we emphasize and encourage parents' use of reflective techniques with their children. These techniques are also used in play therapy sessions, enabling the children to have their emotions and behaviour acknowledged, thereby enhancing the development of good cognitive practices at an early age.

In conclusion we postulate that it is the inclusion of and importance attached to the cognitive aspects of our parenting programme that have allowed parents and children to feel much more in control. Parents are not only taught behavioural methods of child management, but are also made aware of the cognitive and emotional consequences of effective parenting on both themselves and their children. Teaching parents to monitor and change their automatic thoughts allows them to be more objective and less personal in their evaluations, and therefore more effective as individuals and as parents.

Note

We would like to thank S. Ambrose and J. Haworth-Adams at the Children's Institute International in Los Angeles. They gave time generously and made their material freely available to us for use when we were setting up our first parent training programme.

References

Ambrose, S., Hazzard, A. and Haworth, J. (1980) Cognitive-behavioral parenting groups for abusive families. *Child Abuse and Neglect*, 4: 119–25.

Baruch, D. W. (1949) *New ways in discipline: you and your children today*. New York: McGraw-Hill.

Beck, A. T., Rush, A. J., Shaw, B. F. and Emery, G. (1979) *Cognitive therapy of depression*. New York: Guilford.

Bernal, M. E., Klinnert, M. D. and Schultz, L. A. (1980) Outcome evaluation of behavioral parent training and client-centered parent counseling for children with conduct problems. *Journal of Applied Behavior Analysis*, 13 (4): 677–91.

Brown, G. and Harris, T. (1978) *Social origins of depression: a study of psychiatric disorders in women*. London: Tavistock.

De'Ath, E. (1983) Teaching parenting skills. *Journal of Family Therapy*, 5 (4): 321–35.

Denicola, J. and Sandler, J. (1980) Training abusive parents in child management and self-control skills. *Behavior Therapy*, 11: 263–70.

Dubey, D. R., O'Leary, S. G. and Kaufman, K. F. (1983) Training parents of hyperactive children in child management: a comparative outcome study. *Journal of Abnormal Child Psychology*, 11 (2): 229–46.

Griest, D. L. and Forehand, R. (1982) 'How can I get any parent training done with all these other problems going on?': the role of family variables in child behavior therapy. *Child and Family Behavior Therapy*, 4 (1): 73–80.

Griest, D. L., Forehand, R., Rogers, T., Breiner, G., Furey, W. and Williams, C. A. (1982) Effects of parent enhancement therapy on the treatment outcome and generalization of a parent training programme. *Behaviour Research and Therapy*, 20: 429–36.

Guerney, B. J. (1964) Filial therapy: description and rationale. *Journal of Consulting Psychology*, 28: 304–10.

Hansen, C. (1981) Living in with normal families. *Family Process*, 20: 53–75.

Johnson, C. A. and Katz, R. C. (1973) Using parents as change agents for their children: a review. *Journal of Child Psychology and Psychiatry*, 14: 181–200.

Levitt, E. E. (1971) Research on psychotherapy with children. In A. E. Bergin and S. L. Garfield (eds), *Handbook of psychotherapy and behavior change*. New York: Wiley.

O'Brien, A. and Loudon, P. (1985) Redressing the balance: involving children in family therapy. *Journal of Family Therapy*, 7: 81–98.

Patterson, G. R., Cobb, J. A. and Ray, R. S. (1973) A social engineering technology for retraining the families of aggressive boys. In H. E. Adams and I. P. Unikel (eds), *Issues and trends in behavior therapy*. Springfield, Ill.: Thomas.

Patterson, G. R., Reid, J. B., Jones, R. R. and Conger, R. E. (1975) *A social learning approach to family intervention. Vol. 1: Families with aggressive children*. Oregon: Castalia Publishing Company.

Pevsner, R. (1982) Group parent training versus individual family therapy: an outcome study. *Journal of Behavior Therapy and Experimental Psychiatry*, 13 (2): 119–22.

Williams, J. M. G. (1984) *The psychological treatment of depression: a guide to the theory and practice of cognitive-behaviour therapy*. London: Croom Helm.

Wolfe, D. A., Sandler, J. and Kaufman, K. (1981) A competency-based parent training program for child abusers. *Journal of Consulting and Clinical Psychology*, 49 (5): 633–40.

Index

Index compiled by Peva Keane